The Police in Society

BY THE SAME AUTHOR

The Police
A Radical Future (ed.)
Crime and Society
Participation and Poverty
Parks for People
The Fourth World (ed.)
The Foundations

The Police in Society

Ben Whitaker

Eyre Methuen · London

First published 1979 by
Eyre Methuen Ltd
11 New Fetter Lane, London EC4P 4EE

Printed in Great Britain by
Cox & Wyman Ltd, Fakenham, Norfolk
ISBN 0 413 34200 X

CONTENTS

Acknowledgement

I am grateful to all those police officers, and others at the Home Office, NCCL, and elsewhere, who have 'assisted me in my inquiries'. As when I wrote my earlier book on the police fifteen years ago, so many people are not allowed to be, or have asked not to be, named that it is invidious to mention any individually; nevertheless I thank them all sincerely for their patience and help which made this book possible. I am also grateful to Marie Healey for typing the Bibliography, to Graham Marsden, Richard Wells, my wife Janet and to her father Alan Stewart for kindly commenting on the draft, and to the patience of my children during all the evenings this book prevented my being with them.

Dedicated to Frank Williamson
and all others like him.

ONE

Eye of the Storm: The Public's Police

'As force is always on the side of the governed, the governors have nothing to support them but opinion.'
Hume

'Certainly an equal distribution of property is just, but since we are unable to enforce justice, we have made it just to obey force; unable to strengthen justice, we have justified strength so that justice and strength go together and there is peace, which is the overriding good.'
Pascal

The public and the police enjoy an ambivalent relationship with each other. They reciprocate equivocal attitudes, mixed with fear and respect, like some echo of the wariness people feel towards their image in a mirror. The sight of an approaching uniformed man stirs unease inside almost everybody, awakening ambiguous intuitions of submission and disquiet, reassurance conflicting with guilt, deference coupled with hostility. Some people's temperaments naturally identify with authority and are ever ready to kiss the rod, as a release from the cares of personal responsibility. A Madrid crowd in 1823 greeted the fall of the Liberals with shouts of 'Death to Liberty; hurrah for despotism and chains'; in 1977 many Spanish policemen suffered a similar bewilderment at the return of the burdens of democracy. Other people are disconcerted to discover the rebellious reactions that an encounter with a police officer triggers within them: many romanticize even violent crime, though almost all of us submit to being protected from ourselves by the police. None the less a crowd can be relied upon to cheer when authority's helmet blows off (a policeman seems disconcertingly disarmed without his headgear). Policemen are one of the subjects we most often like to joke about, in order to distance our nervousness. At the same time the job exercises a fascination for us: programmes featuring the law today take up ever more of television time.

The police provide a continual public welfare service, yet one that is instinctively suspect to the left; at the same time they form the only civilian bureaucracy that the average conservative supports emotionally and wishes to see expanded. But few people readily welcome authority – unless they themselves exercise it – for others' power diminishes one's own. Often the police are protecting people who are scarcely more honest than their criminal enemies: in one recent case a man reported he had had £3,000 stolen from his home, whereas the police knew that the true sum was £10,000, undeclared for tax reasons. A survey of 1,700 American citizens found that 91 per cent admitted they had committed at least one crime for which they might have received a prison sentence. The public's equivocal attitude towards law officers reflects contradictions inherent in the paternal task of policing itself. It attempts a superhuman role: part priest, part scapegoat. The actions of policemen and a policed society towards each other result not only from their perception of the other's behaviour and conduct; inextricably they are shaped by the fact that a police officer can never detach himself from being part of the community he is meant to be policing. 'The police force,' Sir Robert Mark suggests, 'is the best reflection of a society. If society is violent, so are the police; if society is corrupt, so are the police; but if the society is tolerant, literate and humane, police will act accordingly.' In July 1942 the Paris police rounded up thousands of Jews; yet by August 1944 the same force were defending their prefecture as a bastion of the Resistance against the Germans. 'Never show the public you're a human being,' counselled one London officer. But a policeman's humanity is both his strength and weakness, since he often cannot help sharing the political or racial views of his flock, as well as feeling the same temptations which cause them to break laws. The officers who succumb are discussed later, in Chapter 7.

Society's and the police's attempts to understand each other are complicated by the fact that there is never one 'public', but many, and all with differing values and views about crime and the role of the police. A policeman said that he and his fellow officers were 'Rorschach in uniform'. In the same way, it is rash – as often riskily attempted in this book – to generalize about 'the police'. Each category is formed of disparate individual men and women. The police themselves divide into 'bosses' and 'other ranks' just as much as other sections of British society. Policemen appear differently to outsiders according to the context of their role; just as, internally, their view of themselves varies as to whether they see themselves as part of a force or a service; whether they regard the law as a means or an end; or which priorities in the final resort they hold uppermost. Outwardly the same officer can appear variously as a saviour to a victim of crime; an agent of retribution to a deviant (though the tie between them can be close, as Dostoevsky and others knew); and the cutting edge of malevolent bureaucracy, the personification of officious fate to the man in the street. The British police may be the least unpopular in the world, but anybody who wears a uniform thereby runs a particular risk of being physically attacked: more than 700 policemen in Britain are assaulted each month, and the number of Metropolitan officers injured on duty rose from 2,999 in 1975 to 4,030 in 1977. Superintendent Hunt points out that conflicts in an advanced society today are often between different interest-groups rather than between any clear-cut right and wrong, and therefore whatever action or inaction the police decide on is bound to alienate some section of the public. Such interest-groups are becoming increasingly well organized as well as proliferating, and not all of them believe in changing laws rather than breaking them. On top of this, the police are likely to be a prime target for those who wish to overthrow society as it is at present constituted, by weakening its defenders and trying to goad them in order to discredit them – as a strategy to provoke public reaction. The police cannot escape being in the firing-line (sometimes literally so) of those who use violence against what they conceive to be the repressive violence of the state. How the Special Branch, the CIA or the FBI can be publicly accountable and at the same time effective in counter-intelligence work is an increasing dilemma for democracies.

Peter Evans of *The Times* points out that public support for the police is at its lowest when the gap between public and government is widest. But at any one time, different areas, classes and age-groups have varying expectations of police officers, and consequent varying relationships with them. Research shows that the younger and the lower down the social scale people are, the less likely they are in general to like or help the police. Whites in the US have been found to be more than twice as likely to have positive feelings towards the police as blacks are. About half the British constabulary is currently under thirty-two years old – whereas the average age of cops in New York is climbing towards thirty-eight – but the majority of people arrested in both Britain and the United States are under twenty-one, and include more young people of fifteen and sixteen years old than any other age group. (This is not proof that young people commit that proportion of crime, for the police believe that the inexperience of junior criminals leads to a much higher rate of arrest.) But even though the police's task is to maintain order rather than blindly to enforce all laws, the degree of support the police receive also hinges to a marked extent upon which law they are enforcing. One man's moral duty to protest may be another's riot by a hoodlum: views about poaching, undergraduates' high spirits, squatting or knocking-off goods at work generally depend on the onlooker's place in society. By contrast, the damage caused by major economic crimes, by huge frauds, massive pollution or unsafe work practices frequently goes unrecorded though it amounts to a far greater total than the petty larcenies which fill the bulk of the criminal statistics. The average prison sentence for a six- or seven-figure fraud is generally less than for many minor burglaries. Recently it was found that tax evasion was annually costing France at least 29,000 million francs, whereas hold-ups and armed attacks netted only 37 million francs a year. Although the police themselves cannot be agents of social change, the public's attitude to crime is nevertheless greatly affected by the extent to which the society in which it occurs is felt to be equitable or just. The police perform a thankless and painful social function in showing where laws pinch. The official view of crime changes too: for example, swearing was technically a criminal offence in England up to 1966. One study calculated that 76 per cent of the prisoners in the United States in 1931 had been convicted of offences which had not been illegal sixteen years earlier.

A trusted policeman can be the chief human regulator of our adult conduct: no public agency daily affects the life of more people. He plays the part of a permanent father figure, but without the personal ties which sometimes can endear our parents to us. But he can also share much of society's bewilderment as the yardsticks of acceptable conduct shift away from traditional frameworks of right and wrong. Together with the community losing many of its certainties, authority has forfeited much of its self-confidence. Is a police officer's function to be a passive buffer between state and public? Or is he to be viewed as an activator of that most constant but unwelcome of human traits: the instinct to interfere with, and to try to improve, others' behaviour? The role of the police is discussed in detail in the next chapter. Its dilemma stems from the paradox that today, on the one hand, we prize efficiency and demand results, while at the same time we are suspicious of strong authority and champion the human rights of individuals more than ever before. We ask the police, as the agents of the coercion which in the last resort may be necessary even in a peacetime democratic society, to fulfil for us many responsibilities that we acknowledge are essential even though unpleasant. But we also use officers' uniforms as the most readily identifiable targets for our resentment at this – or at our own failure to carry out such work ourselves. The uneasy and illogical result is that the police can only attempt to perform the duties society gives them by a mixture of stratagems and bluff to supplement the strictly circumscribed powers they are legally permitted. Reciprocally, the police understandably rankle at the fickle public's failure to cooperate with them, and at times cannot restrain their angry frustration at the morality of silver-tongued lawyers, legalistic judges or gullible juries who contrive to free guilty criminals whom the police have caught with so much trouble. Habitually treated shabbily in the Honours List, many police officers feel they are the continual victims of unfair demands and carping – blamed when criminals are not brought to justice, and frequently criticized for the way they handle a defendant when they do make an arrest. In addition, they cannot escape having to bear the brunt of resentment against acts of government from which they can never dissociate themselves. As one London officer said, 'These days we're always in the wrong. Too many members of the public regard us as the symbol of government, and hold us responsible for everything that's wrong with society. We can't cope with that.'

Who is policed?

The subject of this book is the police's exposed position in the crossfire between the needs of the community and the rights of the individual. One view of this interprets society as divided between those policed for, and those policed against. A new radical school of criminology has recently challenged previous positivist ideas of morality and the view of criminals as a distinct species (whether born or made), and has instead described crimes in terms of power and the socio-political boundaries between society and the individual. 'Our job has become much more complicated since crime has been explained away,' one English inspector observed, only half ironically. Others comment on the continual modern tendency to minimize personal responsibility and always to blame someone else: parents, society, shops for displaying goods so accessibly and temptingly. Was Sir William Erle right to hold that law is for the protection of the weak more than the strong? Or was Anatole France nearer the mark with his thrust that 'the law, in its majestic equality, forbids the rich as well as the poor to sleep under bridges, to beg in the streets, and to steal bread'? Certainly a number of policemen are critical of the system of which they form a keystone. Inspector Reg Gale, a recent chairman of the Police Federation for England and Wales, believes that the present operation of the law favours the rich: it was part of Britain's 'feudal social system', he said, that the police pay more attention to complaints from 'squire officialdom' than from poor people; that they are more likely to stop youths on scooters than the middle class in their cars; and that poorer people, with less education, run the most risk of breaking laws through ignorance. But when at some demonstrations middle-class students claiming to represent the working class revile police officers, it does not seem to occur to them that almost all police officers are working class. The courteous manner in which four wealthy men were charged with conspiracy to murder in August 1978, meeting the police by arrangement, contrasts with the peremptory way lesser people are traditionally arrested and remanded in custody for much more trivial offences. When in 1977 an Old Etonian convicted of committing two violent bank robberies was given a lenient suspended sentence (by a judge who happened also to be an Old Etonian), many policemen themselves expressed cynical disgust. They also remark that a middle-class psychopathic offender often manages to be dealt with by a doctor, where his working-class equivalent finds himself before a court. Recently, an eighteen-year-old public schoolboy who had gone to Harrow was awarded a conditional discharge after setting fire to his school and causing £92,000 worth of destruction, whereas a fourteen-year-old working-class boy was given a life sentence for causing £20,000 worth of fire damage to his school in York. Even allowing for disparities between the two cases, the difference in punishment remains striking. A spokesman at the Lord Chancellor's Office in 1976 said that although a serious conviction would debar a person from becoming a magistrate, a man who pinched a policeman's helmet in Cambridge when he was at Oxford would not be disqualified'. Yet the same action might very well result in a boy from the East End being sent to a detention centre, with a conviction for assaulting the police, seriously handicapping him throughout his life. Youths from richer families sometimes escape prosecution altogether if they or their parents pay for the damage they have caused. Sir Robert Mark is fond of quoting Roger Woddis's poem 'Ethics for Everyman':

> Throwing a bomb is bad
> Dropping a bomb is good;

Terror, no need to add,
Depends on who's wearing the hood . . .
Daily the Church declares
Betting-shops are a curse;
Gambling with stocks and shares
Enlarges the national purse . . .
Social Morality
Has a duality –
One for each side of the tracks.

Many 'white collar' offences, such as using a firm's telephone or postage, never feature in criminal statistics. The eighteenth-century anarchist William Godwin went further: 'Government was intended to suppress injustice, but its effect has been to embody and perpetuate it. . . . Law is in almost every country the favourer of the rich against the poor.' In the eyes of the left throughout history, the police have been a part of the working class who have been duped into forging their own class's fetters. Yet the paradox is that it is principally the poor and less privileged whose persons and possessions are most vulnerable to crime.

The police, however, must be the trusted protectors and servants of pluralistic societies, never agents of the power structure. They are, it is true, only one element in law enforcement; their best efforts can be stymied by the court system or by a venial or subservient judiciary. But as long as legal advantage can be purchased, as long as unconventional or poorly-dressed people sometimes receive different legal treatment, the law and its enforcement officers will appear oppressors as well as protectors. The economic historian R. H. Tawney observed, 'It is still confidently asserted by the privileged classes that when the state holds its hand what remains as a result of that inaction is liberty. In reality, as far as the mass of mankind is concerned, what commonly remains is not liberty but tyranny.' The majority of policemen, like lawyers and doctors, seem instinctively to acquire a conservative cast of mind from their professional task of attempting to maintain the *status quo*. Mark is probably the only police leader who would have had the courage to say, as he did at the height of the furore about violent picketing, that many social changes now regarded as inevitable have been achieved by violence; or to remind hardliners to compare the number of casualties from terrorist bombs with that of the regular carnage on the roads. The majority of policemen, coming from a working-class background, often have different views about crime from judges and lawyers who are overwhelmingly middle-class. Policemen, for example, tend to feel more indignant about sex offences, where many judges and magistrates show a greater concern about property offences. The imperfect laws themselves – laid down by legislators and administered by judges no longer young – often lag behind current views. Prejudice, emotion or political expediency affect new laws or movements to repeal old ones. Imprisonment, for example, is at present quite often imposed on people who defraud the Social Security, but only rarely on richer people who practise much larger tax evasion, which is both much more damaging and less easily explained by any plea of need. Some laws are in danger of being, as Francis Bacon described, like cobwebs: 'where small flies were caught, and the great break through.' At times of rapid social change and economic crisis, when class divisions exacerbate industrial and racial bitterness, there is always a latent danger that 'law and order' will be invoked by privileged people against even peaceful challenges to authority. Authoritarians of the left as well as the right have sought to enlist the police against their critics in the name of national unity or historical determinism. In the US, as well as the USSR, an increasing number of criminal prisoners are interpreting their situation in terms of political or social victimization. The one certainty is that growing awareness of, and refusal to accept, contradictions and inequalities in national or international society is liable to make the police's role of trying to preserve stability even harder. They incur frequent hostility when attempting to enforce laws relating to political demonstrations or trade disputes. They are the hostages of governments' failure to respond to change. People who feel society is unfair are not likely to help the police. Sometimes law is not up to date with changes in public opinion or standards; at other times the reverse may be the situation; but either way it is the police who are likely to bear the brunt.

The police therefore form a microcosm of many of the

dilemmas endemic in human society. Bertrand Russell recounts with amusement in his autobiography how, when he was organizing the Committee of One Hundred's civil disobedience campaign, he had to call in the police to remove an actress and two friends who had sat down in his own home to get publicity. History records many instances of the police surviving revolutions: the police do not lean on the state for support, so much as the state depends on them. How a community should police itself is one of the more interesting and intractable problems to be solved by democracy. When the ordinary constable meets the man in the street, contact is finally and definitely being joined between government and people. At a demonstration against the police in London, Commander Randall commented: 'What other police force in the world would spend the first hours protecting this lot and the next two marching with them while they shout abuse at us?' Jill Tweedie points out that civil rights are less often a question of clear absolutes as of priorities which can conflict with each other. One man's freedom of speech or demonstration can prejudice another person's right to live free from insult or harassment; society's right to safety from crime may depend upon it forfeiting its right to privacy and freedom from phone-tapping or closed-circuit television cameras. Additionally, the unease of the police's position derives from the fact that they are expected to impose authority on, at the same time as being accountable to, the public. At first sight, it is curious that we pay some of our number to set limits on our freedom. 'The sole end for which mankind are warranted, individually or collectively,' in J. S. Mill's well-known view, 'in interfering with the liberty of action of any of their number is self-protection. That the only purpose for which power can be rightfully exercised over any member of a civilized community, against his will, is to prevent harm to others.' In primitive societies, where violations of behaviour could breed vendettas, social classes or families undertook a police function. But as society grew more diverse and complex, the ordinary citizen became less inclined or willing to police his neighbour and increasingly devolved his responsibilities on to full-time scapegoats labelled peace-officers. But it is the accountability of its police which principally distinguishes a democratic from a totalitarian state.

The absence in the United Kingdom of any written constitution or court charged with reviewing administrative decisions makes the discretionary powers of the police, such as when to prosecute and whether to allow public meetings, of more than usually crucial importance.

The modern function and performance of the police therefore call for clear as well as cool consideration. To appreciate the value of the police in society, it is only necessary to recollect that more people have been killed by shooting inside the United States in the present century than the sum total of those who died in all the wars in which the United States has ever been engaged; or that in Western Europe, a greater number of people are estimated to have been slain in road accidents since 1900 than in all the wars fought in recorded history. All too often, however, public interest in policemen has either focused on superficial scapegoats or looked at them through a rosy glow of complacent historical sentiment. Both the most recent British Royal Commissions on the Police of 1929 and 1960 were set up in response to a clamour triggered off by ephemeral and relatively trivial incidents. The membership of the last one, asked to resolve economic and sociological issues, contained no economist or sociologist. But policemen – like deviants also – must be studied not as a group but as individuals; not in isolation, but in the context of their contemporary community. A witness before the 1929 Royal Commission said: 'To represent the English police as the one unaltered element of the national life is to talk without meaning. When the times change, all men change with them. So many of both the friends and the critics of the police talk as if police constables were not men.'

The balance between liberty and safety

Policing a democracy is never easy or uncontroversial, but today the attempt is criticized more than ever before. At the same time, an increasing number of thinking policemen are beginning publicly to question the legal system in which they have to operate. The law – and even the order – which the police primarily exist to implement is not an abstract framework of immutable rules. Laws, and the fashion in which they are applied, reflect both compromises in opinion and the changing values of the society which creates and annuls them. The social value which the English place on freedom from arbitrary arrest, and from police intrusion into their homes, gives rise to a defence of the freedom from even having to go into the witness-box which outweighs mere logical justification. Those who hold power in society delegate to the police the task of enforcing the law by means which, if they are to be effective, often necessarily infringe the very principles that the law protects. Contradictorily, the public asks for law to be enforced, but not too efficiently. Hence arise the crucial questions of police discretion – which has grown in scope and incidence with the rise in the number of laws and the impossibility of enforcing them all – and of the limits of power allowed to the police, considered in more detail in Chapter 4. The paradoxical position over whether to permit in court evidence that has been illegally obtained is a classic illustration of the British habit of ambivalence. Evidence which has been found by unlawful means is not allowed to be presented at all in a federal court in the United States. The argument is clear: in the American view of the balance between liberty and law enforcement, based on the constitution, it is not considered right to admit as evidence anything that was discovered by, say, an illegal search, even if it is crucial to prove a murder charge. The rejection of such evidence is one method of punishing the police for their illegality: the fact that society is also thereby punished, by having someone who may be a danger loosed again, is not considered relevant. On the other hand, evidence retains a certain value whatever its origins; in England the social good of law enforcement, predominantly judge-made, tilts the scales partly the other way: tangible – though not verbal – evidence obtained by unlawful means may or may not, at the judge's discretion, be admitted in a court trial.

Behind the increase in police activity and controversy in modern times lies a profound shift in society's use of the criminal law and thus of the police. This is the case not only because the majority of the public and offenders today encounter the policeman as a traffic regulator – a situation never envisaged by those who originally created a professional police force: it is also because we have come to rely on both a vast increase in legislation and a persistently growing number of 'public welfare offences' to enforce public standards for the running of highly populated and industrialized nations. Unlike traditional crimes for which a guilty intention (*mens rea*) is required, many of the more recently-created offences are committable on a basis of 'strict liability': witting intent of guilt is not necessary for a person to be convicted of breaching them. A moment's inadvertance by an assistant, which a shopkeeper has no means of knowing about let alone preventing, subjects the latter to criminal provisions such as under the Food and Drugs Act. Some public welfare offences such as derelictions of safety, which are often discounted, have much more serious anti-social consequences than for example larceny. (How many employers have ever been jailed in Britain for breaking safety regulations – sometimes thereby causing deaths – as is done elsewhere in western Europe?) Yet this new corpus of administrative, rather than penal, law has resulted in basic changes in the public's attitude towards the law in general and also towards the police and their work. Apart from the consideration that laws which are incomprehensible to potential offenders can negative public identification with law-enforcement, criminals are no longer so unusual a minority or so ostracized as a separate species by the majority. At the beginning of this century, 250 crimes were recorded for each 100,000 of the British population; by 1967 the number of crimes had risen to more than 3,000; ten years later it was 4,000. The fact that many of the latter were comparatively petty only served to erode the stigma of criminality. The amateur pilferers, who are estimated to steal £1,300 million a year in Britain (compared with the £80 million which are the proceeds of burglary or robbery), rarely think of themselves as being criminals. Today the Sunday trading, drinking, cannabis, censorship, gambling, prostitution, customs, currency and motoring laws are frequently disregarded; and there is an amorphous new mass of controls, about such matters as prices, incomes and fuel-saving, about which few people are sure whether they are law or exhortation. At present even the most law-abiding can feel guilty when they see a policeman, because they are uneasily conscious they may have committed an offence they did not know was a crime.

The police similarly have less and less certainty about their role. They see familiar landmarks in society undermined or disappear. In addition to the problem of trying to uphold set moral standards in a community which appears increasingly unsure of what these now are, mobile and amorphous modern societies are obviously much harder to police than traditionally homogeneous or hierarchical ones. The tradition of pessimism is long established among all ranks of policemen. 'The task of the police today is almost impossible,' is the view of Inspector General Rosolio, the head of Israel's national police. His view was echoed by a Liverpool sergeant, who said, 'Society pushes its problems into the dustbin and requires the policeman to sit on the lid'. But the creed that crime was rooted in the various social evils of the past has been shaken by statistics which show that two-thirds of this century's increase has taken place in the most recent decade and a half. All criminal statistics have to be approached with cautious scepticism, because of the 'iceberg' and other distorting factors discussed in Chapter 3. But indictable offences in England and Wales today number over two and a half million a year, compared with 78,000 at the start of this century, and represent a four-fold increase per head of the population over the last twenty years alone. On current projections, one British male in three will be convicted of an indictable offence in his lifetime. Nor are some future indicators encouraging: hard-core unemployment, political violence, and the consumption of alcohol – undoubtedly a major contributory factor in crime – are rising; and 29 per cent of the people arrested for indictable offences in London in 1975 were aged between ten and sixteen, compared with 15 per cent the previous year. Violent crime by youths under eighteen rose 154 per cent in the US between 1960 and 1974. In West Germany, the most numerous category of offenders are aged sixteen to eighteen, but experts predict that this will shortly be overtaken by young offenders aged fourteen. Despite the introduction of parole and suspended sentences, there are on present projections likely to be over 50,000 people in prison in the United Kingdom by 1979, compared with 11,000 in 1939. Between 1973 and the end of 1977 there were 367 terrorist incidents in England, Wales and Scotland involving 205 time bombs, 79 incendiary devices, 63 letter bombs and 20 shootings. Over half of these occurred in Metropolitan

London, but loss of life from any criminal incident remains a minute figure compared with the total population of Britain – the statistical chance of being attacked in the street is some twenty times less than being injured by traffic – but offences involving personal violence have gone up by a factor of no less than sixteen in the last twenty-five years. Professor R. L. Carter of Nottingham University estimates that the cost of crimes against property, including spending on prevention and control, has now reached as much as 2 per cent of the national income. In 1978 32 per cent of London motorists were breaking the law at parking meters, compared with 26 per cent who did so in 1970 and 10 per cent in 1966. The following-up of traffic tickets is now so far in arrears that many car owners are not traced within the statutory six months – with the result that, as in a Swiftian satire, only the honest pay any penalty while the dishonest escape scot free. It is costing the police at least £20 to enforce the payment of each £6 penalty ticket, and this often takes more than a year to achieve. A properly reformed system with computerized records should instead be able to ensure that all tickets were paid before a car's licence was able to be renewed. This situation is echoed across the Channel. Only 10 per cent of Paris motorists trouble to pay their fines when they should, and the level of ignored fines successfully recovered by the police has fallen from 53 per cent in 1970 to 34 per cent in 1976. More than 1,000 million francs' (£119 million) worth of fines are outstanding in France as a whole; recorded crime has doubled in the past decade. (The fact that there is now a robbery there every three minutes may not be unconnected with the characteristic suggested by the advice sometimes given in France: 'Never shout "Stop Thief"; instead, shout "Fire". If you shout "Stop Thief", sometimes your neighbours will be afraid of becoming involved or getting hurt, whereas if you shout "Fire", they will come to help you for fear that the fire might spread to their homes.') The USA's estimate of an annual cost of crime of $25 billion may not be very meaningful, but the much more real psychological cost in fear and insecurity cannot be denied or quantified. More than four out of every ten American males are now likely to be arrested for a non-traffic offence in their lifetime. Among the suspected causes of the recent growth in crime in both Europe and America are higher proportions of younger people in the population, coupled with lack of legitimate employment opportunities for them. With some economic forecasters predicting permanent unemployment of at least five million people in Britain in the next decade, this longer-term outlook for the police is not optimistic. Schoolchildren and unemployed people were responsible for seven out of ten crimes detected by Northumbria police in 1977. Some youths are imitating their more successful criminal elders. But in 1976 and 1977 the figures for serious crime in the US stabilized, most probably due to a decline in the number of males aged between fifteen and twenty-four. Approximately half the annual six million arrests of adults for non-traffic offences there are for charges of drunkenness, disorder, vagrancy, gambling and minor sexual deviancy. If such conduct were to be decriminalized, a massive reduction of pressure on the police (as well as the courts and correctional service) would enable them to concentrate on protecting people and property.

Figure 1

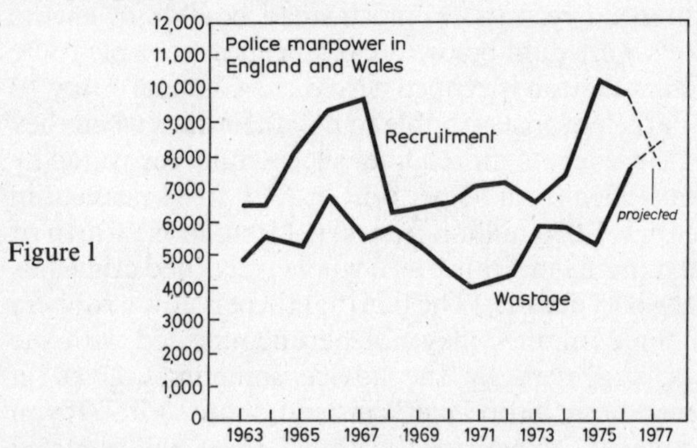

France, with over 167,000 men in its various police forces, has virtually half again as many as Britain to police a similar sized population. In Metropolitan London (which covers an area with a radius of fifteen miles from Charing Cross), despite a declining population, the annual total of arrests for indictable offences more than doubled in the eight years up to 1975; by contrast, the strength of the police themselves rose by only some 10 per cent, and in 1977 the number of Metropolitan policemen in fact went down by 191 officers. A private security company is actually being paid to provide guards for Tintagel House, the administrative headquarters of the Metropolitan force itself and for the detention centre at Harmondsworth, as well as to escort people to and from prison. Policemen have been interested to read recent advertisements stating 'Security guards are required for Metropolitan police offices at New Scotland Yard, Putney and Lambeth. No qualifications or previous experience necessary.' Sixteen different British government departments are in all currently spending over £1.5 million a year on contracts with profit-making private security companies, at a time when the police themselves are suffering from shortage of finance – apart from the additional consideration that none of these private officers are trained or publicly accountable even to the limited extent that the police service is. But at the same time, to the detriment of their delicate relations with immigrant communities, police officers are being expected to make inquiries about matters such as the adequacy of accommodation for immigrants' dependants – assessments much better left to professional social workers. It is of equally doubtful logic to use trained police officers for many traffic-control duties which could be performed by traffic wardens. Ways in which to improve police effectiveness are suggested in Chapter 3. Far and away the greatest deterrent to crime is the likelihood of detection and conviction; but in London the percentage of indictable offences cleared up declined from the already low base of 30 in 1973 to 26 in 1975, and a mere 21 in 1977. The percentage went down nationally in 1976 and yet further in 1977; and even these low figures are bolstered by a large number of offences volunteered to be taken into consideration by the minority of offenders who are caught. The incentive to commit crime is as a result growing exponentially.

The same problems are echoed in other countries. New York City and Detroit, despite having the worst crime problems in the US, are being forced by financial crises to lay off many hundred patrolmen. Detectives have ceased investigating burglaries which involve losses of less than $10,000 in Manhattan. A decade after Lyndon Johnson pledged himself to spend his remaining days as President using 'every single resource of the federal government to banish crime from the

USA, the crime rate reported there has increased by 90 per cent. The new phenomenon of computer crime has expanded into a $500 million industry: cases are often short-sightedly hidden by companies that fear loss of public confidence. The average proceeds of a computer bank fraud is now $430,000, compared with an average $10,000 for armed bank robbery. In many American cities, a growing number of patrol officers have themselves moved to live outside the inner city area; mostly white, they increasingly lose contact and sympathy with problems of urban centres predominantly populated by blacks and other minorities. Even though the concealed iceberg of unreported offences disguises from public concern the full reality of the situation, fear of crime has damaged many cities' communal feeling and social fabric. Barred windows, identification checks at the entrances of schools and apartment buildings, and withdrawal into 'defensible space' have in the worst areas blighted social contact and sown suspicion and apprehension, so that the open society in city areas is in danger of ending by putting itself in prison. Uniquely, in Japan crimes have declined by one third in the past twenty years. But in a number of other parts of the world, the police are now increasingly uneasy, squeezed between diminution of effectiveness and a crisis of identity and authority. Hold-ups in France have increased by 3,000 per cent in the last fifteen years. In North Rhine–Westphalia, which has 17.2 million inhabitants and is the most populous of the West German states, juveniles now commit 40 per cent of all crimes, despite a sharply declining birth rate: local experts explain 'they suffer from boredom and a lack of challenge in the national stress on materialism: they turn to crime as a type of sport, and as a challenge to authority.' In Paris, where the number of break-ins has more than tripled since 1964, there are now fewer policemen than five years ago. Although Paris's inhabitants have to pay, in proportion to population, over forty times as much as other French cities such as Marseilles or Lyons towards the cost of the police, at night time there are only 600 uniformed police to protect 2.3 million Parisians. A senior French officer said ruefully, 'Here the police have become the whipping-boy of the left, while the right will only talk to them at the back door.' The Paris police in particular feel, not without justification, that they are disliked by virtually everybody. M. Gérard Monate, the head of the police union, states, 'We want to get out of our ghetto', and recently the Parisian police handed out tracts in the streets asking to be liked by the public and protesting at the intimidatory role into which the authorities forced them. Malaise about the effectiveness and status of the police is widespread both inside and outside many different forces. In Australia, two-thirds of people who had been the victims of crimes but had not reported them, when questioned, gave as their reason that they did not believe the police could do anything. In Italy, a police captain was fêted when he was court-martialled for protesting that his fellow officers were 'sick of making violence a way of life'; while 105 Cologne detectives in 1977 placed a collective advertisement in a newspaper saying that they wished to work in another job. China in 1978 conceded it had a serious crime problem.

The Pakistan police recently went on strike, demanding more respect from the public. Even in Moscow – where failings are not easily admitted – General Kozlov, the head of the militia-police, concedes that the change from foot to motorized patrolling has resulted in loss of contact with citizens: 'Some people complain that the militia is no longer visible. Muscovites were used to having militiamen on the street, complete with whistle, for all to see. Now it is said they remain hidden in their cars and cannot be seen.'

Police in a democracy

The subject of 'law'n'order' is bedevilled by emotive hyperbole more perhaps than any other social issue. Comparing 1960 and 1976, the number of indictable offences increased by 168 per cent in England and Wales, by 370 per cent in Northern Ireland, and in Scotland (excluding motoring offences) by 128 per cent. But in virtually every country throughout the world, the modern growth of crime – like society itself – is increasingly concentrated in urban areas. It finds its roots in factors such as the rapid changes and anonymity of most city life, coupled with the erosion of social and moral constants, especially in communities which have a disproportionate share of poor housing and other handicaps. Antagonistic attitudes between different classes and races, which can neutralize guilt feelings about criminality, are there liable to be most bitter. In 1972, one person in every three living in the central urban cities of the United States was the direct victim of some form of crime. Comparing 1968 and 1977, indictable offences in London increased by 60 per cent, violence against the person by 120 per cent and robbery by 175 per cent. The most aggravated problems of policing today are concentrated and self-reinforcing in metropolitan areas where at the same time criminality is at its most sophisticated, social control at its most tenuous, and the chances of detection at their lowest. In 1960 the average number of indictable crimes per police officer was 10.1 for England and Wales as a whole, and 10.9 for Metropolitan London. By 1973 the corresponding figures were 13.5 and 17.1, increases of 34 per cent and 57 per cent respectively. In addition, the police during the same period saw the number of cars in Britain double and driving prosecutions go up by 82 per cent; while convictions for drunkenness have increased by 100 per cent in the last two decades, and cases of drunken driving have more than doubled in the last six years.

One product of the increasing strain on the public police lately has been an almost mushroom growth of private detective agencies and security forces. Some idea of the complexity of contemporary city policing can be gathered from the diversity of the branches of London's New Scotland Yard:

TABLE 1: BRANCHES OF THE FOUR MAIN POLICE DEPARTMENTS OF NEW SCOTLAND YARD, LONDON

A: Administration

Branch	Function
A1 (1)/CIB (1)	Complaints against police (non-criminal)
A2 (1)	Duties in division
(2)	Dog section
(3)	Crime prevention
(4)	Security of police buildings
A3 (1)/CIB (3)	Discipline
(2)	Administrative directions
(3)	Supervision of specialist police duties
A4 (1)	Firearms and explosives
(2)	Liquor licensing; gaming

(3)	Obscene publications
A5	Mounted branch
A6	Metropolitan Special Constabulary
A7	Community Relations:
	(i) Race Relations
	(ii) Young people
	(iii) Sociological research
	(iv) Missing persons
A8 (1)	Operations, public order
(2)	Special patrol group (a mobile reserve of six units)
A9	Communications
A10/CIB (2)	Complaints against the police
B: Traffic	
B1	Secretariat
B2	Traffic management application and special events
B3	Public Carriage Office
B4	Traffic process and Civil proceedings
B5	Traffic and accident research; Accident prevention unit
B6	Communications
B7	Traffic wardens
B8	Traffic division
B9	Central ticket office
B10	Police transport, maintenance, etc.
B11	Transport, prison vans, etc.
B12	Fingerprint branch; police photographic and scenes-of-crime work
B13	Criminal record office
C: Crime	
C1	The central office of the CID (previously known as the Detective office): Murder squad (3 teams on 24-hour stand-by duty); Reserve squad; Government liaison; Serious crime branch (formed to combat organized crime and specialized criminal gangs); Dangerous drugs squad;

	Forged currency squad; Extradition and illegal immigration squad; Art and antiques squad; Post Office inquiries; Bomb squad
C2	Case papers and correspondence
C5	CID personnel, discipline and policy; liaison with Police national computer unit at Hendon; crime legislation; intelligence statistical unit
C6	Fraud squad; organized car thefts; cheque and credit frauds; public service bribery and corruption
C7	Special equipment unit, including explosives officers
C8	Flying squad
C9	Metropolitan and provincial crime branch
C10	Stolen motor vehicle investigation branch
C11	Criminal intelligence branch; central drugs and illegal immigration intelligence unit; Interpol section
C12	Regional crime squad for No. 9 (South-Eastern) District
C13	Special crime and anti-terrorist branch; hijacking; extradition; industrial espionage; Post Office offences; charities and lotteries

Special Branch
Forensic science laboratory
D: Personnel and Training

D1	Recruiting and careers section
D2	Personnel records
D3	Police welfare
D4	Accommodation
D5	Promotions
D6	Training secretariat
D7	Cadet training
D8	Training school
D9	Detective training school
D10	Driver training school

D11	Firearms training; special marksmen; police war duties
D12	Publication of Orders, etc.
D13/14	Catering

For this calling, almost unique in the difficulty and diversity of its demands, men of not higher than average ability are given wholly inadequate preparation. The occupation, in the words Sir Robert Mark used in 1975 to a class at Bramshill, is 'the anvil on which society beats out the problems and abrasions of social inequality, racial prejudice, weak laws and ineffectual legislation.' For more than a century, he said, the police had been an artisan service trained to uphold a social system but not to think too much about it while doing so; but now the nature of police work in a questioning society requires that policemen themselves should exercise a similar curiosity about their role. 'When most people were humble, ignorant and poor,' he said in his Dimbleby lecture, 'it was comparatively easy to do our job without effective criticism. Authority as such was respected.' Policing was far simpler before most people were aware of their rights. Now a transformation has occurred, increasingly since the two world wars, because of the democratization of the civil liberties of the individual. The jury in the *Lady Chatterley's Lover* case decided that freedom from censorship is the right of wives and servants too. But most earlier ideologists in this field tended to practise the eighteenth- and nineteenth-century Whig habit of lauding concepts of English freedom and policing rooted in Saxon times, while not hesitating to disregard the contemporary rights of their own employees and women. As Barry Cox pointed out in *Civil Liberties in Britain*, some of Britain's liberties are indeed ancient, but only in the twentieth century have they been taken up on any scale by ordinary people. Freedom of expression, for example, was easy to pay homage to when the majority of people were not able to read. In a debate at Oxford in 1977, a student (the son of a judge) regretted that the spread of literacy made censorship necessary in order that undesirable books should not fall into the hands of the working classes. Hypocrisy has never been far removed from laws which seek to prescribe morality. Prior to recent reforms in several countries, if a person were wealthy enough he or she could always obtain an abortion, divorce or pornography, just as their predecessors used to be able to buy a commission in the armed forces or a seat in Parliament. Workers' street-betting was denounced as evil by judges who enjoyed turf-accounts; prostitution was outlawed by MPs known to have mistresses. Some recent changes in attitudes and, belatedly, in laws have merely extended opportunities to other people besides the rich, who have always if they wished been able to enjoy 'permissiveness' or other rights as much as their freedoms of choice in education or medical treatment.

Today, it is the CID whose outlook in particular suffers because they are in contact mainly with anti-police sections of the population, and they are deeply pessimistic about the public's attitude towards them – although some of the least inhibited self-criticism also comes in private from police officers themselves. A considerable number of policemen maintain the view that they are a misunderstood minority who are performing the dirty work of the majority of the population without much pay or appreciation; but perhaps the most impressive sight epitomizing a free society was when London policemen recently protected a march of demonstrators supporting the IRA – who had murdered more than fifty of their United Kingdom colleagues in the previous five years. However, by 1978 the Metropolitan police were forced to admit that they could no longer protect some other political processions from violence. Maurice Duverger, a Paris journalist, believes that today 'the vast upheaval in values which industrial democracies are experiencing is likely to invest police forces with an influence similar to that which they usually wield in undeveloped and emerging nations'. Perceptively he points out, 'if democrats blindly assume that the police are their enemies, then they will in fact become their enemies' – as is a danger perhaps in Paris and certainly in many Latin American countries. In fact an undemocratic government has a vested interest in encouraging the unpopularity of the police: the more the force is attacked and becomes unacceptable to the public, the more it must cling to the government as its one source of support. 'This is the biggest threat hanging over democracy. No state has so far succeeded in existing without a police force, and none is likely to do so for a long time to come.' Even the IRA enforces its own brutal vigilante measures against criminals in the republican areas of Northern Ireland which the RUC is not strong enough to police.

The task inevitably therefore is to improve the quality of policemen: since we cannot dispense with them, to make them as humanitarian, effective and responsive to society's needs as possible. In fact, some democratic police forces enjoy more common ground with the public than they suppose. In 1975 Dr William Belson, of the London School of Economics, published an independent survey of the public's view of the Metropolitan force. (Significantly, Scotland Yard commented, 'Had we done it ourselves it would have been very doubtful if anyone would have believed us.') Although there were familiar contradictions – 97 per cent of adults said that given the chance they would be helpful to the police, but 54 per cent said they would not inform the police if they knew their neighbour was driving a stolen car – the survey found that 90 per cent of people were satisfied and 60 per cent were indeed very satisfied with the police's work. Dr Belson believes that one reason why the police continually underestimate their actual support in the community is because of their contact with the attitudes of those people who take up a major proportion of police time: complainants, criminals and young delinquents. Nobody on the other hand troubles to congratulate the police when a house is never burgled or traffic flows smoothly. In a 1976 'sympathy scale' survey in Britain, the police headed every other section of the community in the opinion of both left-wing and right-wing thinkers.

This unduly defensive attitude on the part of policemen has unfortunate results. One cause of mistakes and rudeness can be a lack of self-confidence. 'People always take any good we do for granted, and concentrate on the slightest bad,' is a common police complaint about the public. Hypersensitivity to criticism makes necessary changes harder to achieve, and some policemen who resent the lack of public understanding reciprocate by returning hostility for the antagonism towards themselves they sense or imagine. The greatest danger is that the police could come to feel themselves a besieged minority.

The best amongst their number, like Sir Robert Mark, recognize that they must change with society; but too many of them instead are still expecting society to move back to their own ideas.

The public cannot escape from its need for police to avert the social disaster of private feuds, or the communal slide into chaos. One insight into life when policing breaks down could recently be seen in Kirkby on Merseyside, the original site for the *Z cars* television series. Chief superintendent Chappel reported that an exceptional combination of social problems together with an inner-city tradition of anti-authoritarianism caused many inhabitants to come to accept crime as the norm. Fear of reprisals became widespread; 'probably the most frightening aspect, however, is the general apathy which prevails in the town, so that conditions of gross vandalism are accepted as normal and in many cases little or no immediate attempt is made to repair, replace or clean damaged property.' The dangers of vigilante justice were shown by one recent case in New York when a twenty-year-old girl was so incensed when her television set was stolen that she hired six armed men to track the burglars down; working on the descriptions of neighbours, the men went to a house and shot dead two women and a man and wounded four others. The police reported that not one of the people shot by the gunmen had in fact been a suspect in the case. But nevertheless the police do depend on the public – however much some 'practical coppers' are inclined to think their work would be easier without any of them. Since the load of their work increasingly makes the police operate reactively rather than proactively, their effectiveness is more and more dependent upon the willingness of members of the public – especially social workers, teachers and employers – to summon them or give information. This in turn depends on how much the police are trusted and the amount of confidence there is in their attitude and approach to social and personal problems. A community has always been liable to close its ranks against policemen who become too autocratic. Members of the public have a discretion in dealing with the police, as much as vice versa.

Where this symbiosis breaks down, the consequences are disastrous, often tragic. In one classic case in 1964, when a young woman called Catherine Genovese was slowly murdered in a street in middle-class New York, it was afterwards found that there were thirty-eight witnesses who could have saved her life, but not one of whom went to her assistance or even telephoned the police, despite the fact that she screamed for help for thirty-five minutes. They gave as their reasons to A. M. Rosenthal, an editor of the *New York Times*, 'I didn't want to get involved,' and 'I was tired. I went back to bed.' Recently, there have been similarly damning indictments of contemporary urban society in London. During the rush-hour on a weekday evening in 1976, three armed men carried out a robbery of £4,700 in the pedestrian underpass connecting St Pancras and Kings Cross stations (two of the capital's largest main-line railway termini) at a time when it was crowded with commuters. They were clearly seen by at least fifty eyewitnesses, but when the police arrived within five minutes of the robbery, every one of these witnesses had disappeared. Three weeks earlier a young policeman had been kicked unconscious in the same underpass, but no witness ever came forward despite the fact that several people had watched the incident. In the summer of the same year, a retarded, amiable fifteen-year-old boy called Enrico Sidoli had been set upon and drowned by a gang of youths in a crowded public swimming-pool at Parliament Hill, an area of north-west London which prides itself upon a reputation for moral crusades. Although the police knew the identity of the culprits, they could not persuade any of the score or more of witnesses to come forward and give evidence: all their inquiries were met with a silent wall against 'grassing', and a local social worker replied, 'We don't help the police' – even about murder. In the same year a clergyman in the Lambeth part of south London was attacked by a gang and left unconscious with two ribs broken, yet did not report the assault to the police because he was afraid it would have alienated him from many of his parishioners who regard the police as 'a repressive force'. In another incident in Florida in 1973, a crowd of 300 people actually attacked policemen and firemen who were attempting to rescue a woman suffering from depression who was threatening to jump from a 150-foot-high water-tower. Throwing stones at the rescue squad, the crowd shouted to the woman to jump; later, cheated of her death, they smashed the windscreen of the police car which was trying to take her to hospital. 'I can't understand what is wrong with society,' said Fred Willis, the head of the local Dania police force. 'Here we are trying to save a life, and we've got 300 people screaming for blood.'

These cases may be one extreme; on other occasions, when policemen are killed, a wave of sympathy for members of the force overtakes the population. But instances of the converse situation that can result from a breakdown in the police–public relationship can be deeply disquieting. In Paris in June 1971, during a period of particular public controversy about police practices, a body of disciplined plain-clothed men widely suspected of being police officers systematically made a coordinated series of attacks on cafés and smashed the windows of shops in the Boul' Mich. Unprecedentedly, no uniformed policeman was to be seen on duty anywhere in the area; for two hours subsequently calls to police stations for assistance met a blank wall. Ten years earlier, over sixty Algerian demonstrators are now known to have been killed by the French police in barracks and police stations. The ultimate outcome can be witnessed in Brazil and some neighbouring countries, where the police out of frustration have formed their own illegal 'Death Squads' which have eliminated several hundred people whom the police suspected of being offenders or even merely disliked.

Order in a community primarily rests on the self-restraint individuals exercise quite independently of any police force. The ideal for a society to achieve is to be as self-policing as possible; but meanwhile there is little future for either the police or the public if they mistrust or isolate each other.

TWO

The Role of the Police: Force or Service?

'The most vulnerable part of that elaborate confidence trick which is government.'
Anthony Sampson

'This boy,' says the constable, 'although he's repeatedly told to, won't move on' . . .
'But where?' cries the boy . . .
'My instructions don't go to that,' replies the constable. 'My instructions are that this boy is to move on.'
Dickens, *Bleak House*

Before examining the effectiveness of the police and any ways it might be improved, we should attempt to map their modern function.

It is interesting to speculate how a community might be if – like the Shakers in America – it did not have any police at all. The term itself derives from *polis* – the Greek word for a city-state which also gave the English language 'policy' and 'politics'. A constable on the other hand was originally a stable-groom – a 'count of the stable'. Only in comparatively recent times has policing been linked mainly to law and order; in earlier history it was synonymous with all non-ecclesiastical administration. The Greek *politeia*, like the Roman *politia*, meant the art of governing the city-state for its comprehensive good, including the power to regulate in the public interest security, order, supplies, morality and welfare. Caesar Augustus organized the police of Rome from the ranks of his bodyguard. A Roman prefect had under him fourteen magistrates, each responsible for a district and assisted by *vigiles* (who patrolled the streets), *lictores* (enforcement officers), and *stationarii* (residents of a city block); but this system ended with the Roman Empire. Britain traditionally has been reluctant to admit the necessity for any professional policemen, perhaps from a historical antipathy to *gens d'armes* as descendants of standing armies. Many people still like to describe a police officer as only being a professional citizen: a person paid to perform, as a duty, acts which he or she might have done voluntarily. Historically this was his role, deriving from the ancient principle of common law that the inhabitants of each area had a duty to suppress any disorder within it; if they failed they were accountable to pay a fine or compensation for the damage – a liability still borne by local British police authorities for riot damage in their area. In England from the time of King Alfred, groupings of ten families, known as tythings, and of ten tythings known as hundreds, were held responsible for keeping local peace and order. They were required to guarantee that none of their number would break the law, and that if anyone did they would arrest him by means of hue and cry or else be obliged to pay a collective fine. (Professor Paul Rothstein has recently suggested that the US federal government today should compensate all victims of crime, because a compact exists between government and its citizens that, in return for its protection, they need not resort to private vigilante armies.) When the Normans invaded England, they adopted the Saxon system and converted it into frankpledge, the conquerors' form of requiring the conquered to be of good behaviour – of which today's court order of binding over is the modern survival. The unpaid magistrates and amateur Special Constables of Britain, together with the office of sheriff in Scotland and the US, are other historical survivals. An even more direct Anglo-French link survives in the semi-feudal Channel Islands, where Jersey's forty-two unpaid centeniers are still elected every three years by the parish in which they live. But frankpledge, although persevered with for two centuries, was never really effective, any more that its successor, watch and ward, which was instituted by the Statute of Westminster in 1285. Citizens increasingly began to depute their protective obligations to paid watchmen or beadles, while justices of the peace relied on common informers for detective results. Those men – commonly from the new mercantile classes – who were nominated by rota to act for a year as the unpaid and unloved parish constables, used to contract out of their duty of law-enforcement by paying substitute deputies (popularly known as 'Charlies') who were untrained, not infrequently corrupt and seem often to have been as useless as Shakespeare's constable Elbow. Henry Fielding described them as 'chosen out of those poor decrepit people who are from their want of bodily strength rendered incapable of getting a living by work. These men, armed only with a pole which some are scarcely able to lift, are to secure the persons and houses of His Majesty's subjects from the attacks of young, bold, stout, desperate and well-armed villains.' In 1978 Spain was so alarmed by the spread of crime that it decided to reintroduce the old system of *serenos* (night-watchmen) which had previously been discarded. But in England in 1742 Horace Walpole was observing that the greatest criminals in town were in fact the officers of justice. The system cracked apart totally under the strains of the Industrial Revolution. Although it had demonstrated its futility by several hundred deaths in the Gordon Riots of 1780, Charles James Fox still declared he would 'much rather be governed by a mob than by a standing army'; but after Peterloo in 1819 many Members of Parliament decided with Peel that a proper police force would be preferable to either mob or militia. The report of the massacre in *The Times* recounted that 'nearly a hundred of the King's unarmed subjects have been sabred by a body of cavalry . . . in the presence of those magistrates whose sworn duty it is to protect and preserve the life of the meanest Englishman.' Seven years earlier Britain had had to keep a standing army of over 12,000 soldiers to contain industrial unrest in the north of England – more troops than Wellington had to fight the war in Europe; and the Duke himself at times feared that his infantry might be tempted to show solidarity with their protesting fellow countrymen.

Peel's Metropolitan London Police began almost 150 years ago on 29 September 1829. Why had it not been founded earlier? Seven different Parliamentary committees between 1770 and 1829 had jibbed at the idea of professional policing: the one of 1818 denounced Bentham's proposal for a Ministry of Police as 'of necessity odious and repulsive' and liable to make 'all classes of society spies on each other'. Tories resented the idea of a professional police force because of its threat to the powers of local magistrates; Whigs because they feared its consequential increase in the powers of the Crown. Pitt's earlier attempt in 1785 to found a Metropolitan police force had been killed by the antagonism of the City of London, which had the effect of postponing the plan for forty-four years; but in 1829 Peel's Act was passed without opposition in return for the City being excluded from its ambit – hence the anomaly of its separate force today. A few City men still patronizingly address policemen as 'Robert'. It is fitting that in 1977 it was Glasgow which provided London with its new Commissioner, for it was that Scottish city which had the first organized professional force in Britain. The Local Improvement Act enabled Glasgow to raise her own force in 1800, Edinburgh followed five years later – both more than a score of years before London. Dublin indeed had a force even earlier, in 1786, though in a more militarized form. In 1835 the Municipal Corporations Act required new authorities in Britain to establish police forces – Manchester, Bristol and Birmingham did so speedily – and four years later counties were enabled, but not required, to follow the boroughs' example. By 1848 there were 182 police forces in Britain; eleven years later, there were 239.

New York emulated Peel after fifteen years: in 1844 its legislature passed a law creating a day and night police which was the start of the modern United States force. Its armed character derived from the historical tradition of frontier violence and was inevitable in a society whose members are constitutionally still allowed to be armed. Chicago and Baltimore (1851), Cincinnati and New Orleans (1852), Philadelphia and Boston (1854) followed. The FBI – originally the Bureau of Investigation – was not formed until 1908, initially to deal with labour troubles. (Three years earlier the

Automobile Association had been started in Britain principally to protect motorists from police speed-traps.)

From the Tudor times of Walsingham, to the schemes of Titus Oates and again in the campaign in the next century against the Luddites, widespread spies had been used by the government as a substitute for a police force, and had come to be considered even more distasteful and un-English than visible police officers. Thomas Nashe, who died in 1600, had pronounced that 'A man were better to be a hangman than an intelligencer ... a sneaking eaves-dropper, a scraping hedge-creeper, and a piperly pickthanke.' By the time of eighteenth-century Prussia and the France of Vidocq and Fouquier-Tinville, centralized policing had a black reputation for its autocracy and reliance on networks of undercover agents and secret informers. Vidocq's Sûreté, which he created in 1812 and headed until 1827, was largely manned by former criminals working undercover; Vidocq built up his own encyclopedic knowledge of criminals and their methods from the years he himself spent in prison. At one moment in Tsarist Russia both the head of the Social Revolutionary terrorist organization, Azev, and the leader of the Bolshevik group in the Duma, Malinovsky, were in fact police agents. A few years earlier, the police themselves had organized the first effective trade unions in Russia.

France's gendarmerie were originally formed from para-military *gens d'armes* appointed and armed to maintain the authority of the French kings, and later the public safety of the revolution. For British people, as the historian of the police Tom Critchley says, it was crucial to the success of their new police force that it was not imposed by rulers, as elsewhere on the continent of Europe, but was adopted by a Parliament persuaded that in a mild and unarmed form its inexpensive benefits out-balanced its possible dangers. Its first leaders were at pains, with pragmatic political genius, to endeavour to persuade people that its officers were the employees of society, not its masters. Their uniform was designed to belie any idea of militarism. But initially, public opinion was widely antagonistic to the Peelers or Bobbies – they were suspected, *inter alia*, of being soldiers disguised in top hats to put Wellington on the throne. When in 1833 one of the first policemen was stabbed to death during a mass meeting of the National Union of the Working Classes in Clerkenwell, a coroner's jury returned a verdict of 'justifiable homicide'.

However, the first thousand policemen, carrying not whistles but rattles, gradually won public confidence by their tactful moderation. The outcome resulted in one of the keystones in the whole development of the state's public services. The character of the New Police was modelled on the Irish Constabulary (where Peel had tried out his ideas), and was shaped by Colonel Charles Rowan and a thirty-three-year-old barrister, Richard Mayne, both Irishmen who were its Commissioners for the first twenty-one years. They subjected the earliest Metropolitan policemen to military-style discipline; but their instructions to them were influenced by the reforming magistrate Sir Patrick Colquhoun who realized that a preventive uniformed branch was as necessary as the 'Criminal Investigation Department' which was to derive from the 'Runners' and 'thief-takers' developed by Henry and John Fielding, the brothers who were successive chief magistrates of Bow Street in London. Colquhoun had in 1797 argued that 'Police is an improved state of Society', and his ideas had led to the successful creation the next year of the Marine Police Establishment, as an experimental force for the River Thames docks. Rowan's and Mayne's original words are still used today in teaching police recruits their role, even if the pressure of crime has now eroded the priority they advocated: 'The primary object of an efficient police is the prevention of crime; the next that of detection and punishment of offenders if crime is committed. . . . It should be understood at the outset that the object to be attained is the prevention of crime. To this great end every effort of the police is directed. The security of person and property, the preservation of the public tranquillity, and all other objects of a police establishment will thus be better effected than by the detection and punishment of the offender after he has succeeded in committing the crime. Every member of the Force must remember that his duty is to protect and help members of the public no less than to apprehend guilty persons. Consequently, while prompt to prevent crime and to arrest criminals, he must look upon himself as a servant and guardian of the general public and treat all law-abiding citizens, irrespective of their social position, with unfailing patience and courtesy.' (In 1978 a Merseyside officer was actually prosecuted for not helping a civilian who was being assaulted.)

It is interesting to note to how great an extent society held together in much the same way before as after Peel's police came into existence. This was organized in the shadow of the unrest which followed the French Revolution and the end of the Napoleonic Wars, and the social disturbances caused by the industrial revolution. Unemployed soldiers were roaming the countryside in lawless bands. The Late Tom Bowden pointed out that 'As the buffer between elites and masses the police developed everywhere as a response to internal crisis.' But the founders of the British police were motivated more by a wish to safeguard property than by any real fear of revolution. 'I want,' wrote Peel, 'to teach people that liberty does not consist in having your house robbed by organized gangs of thieves.' But Britain has always remained a very anti-authoritarian society. In 1869 the Commissioners reported that the CID, set up twenty-seven years earlier, was still 'viewed with the greatest suspicion and jealousy by the majority of Englishmen and is, in fact, entirely foreign to the habits and feelings of the nation.' A large part of the success of the new force was probably due to the fact that it coincided with a period of social reform, compared to the preceding era of repression. In turn, the growth of policing allowed a reduction in the law's Draconian canon of capital offences. It was also an achievement to have separated, despite opposition from magistrates, the executive and judicial branches of the law.

Ironically it was almost exclusively working-class men who were employed in this new force designed to protect the property of the governing classes. Peel had directed that only men 'who had not the rank, habits or station of gentlemen' should be enrolled. This may have had some effect on radicals like Francis Place, who not only cooperated with but welcomed the police as likely to avert any repetition of Peterloo at a demonstration – as also did O'Connor in 1848 and John Burns in 1889. In how many other countries would strikers fifty years ago have played a game of football with the police, as happened in Plymouth during the General Strike in 1926? Or, as at the end of the huge demonstration against the United States' involvement in Vietnam, which took place in London's Grosvenor Square on 27 October 1968, would the demonstrators (to the despair of their militant leaders) join with the police in singing 'Auld Lang Syne'? At another recent left-wing rally in London held to denounce the police's part in the violence at Red Lion Square, the relay of the speeches condemning 'the Fascists in blue uniforms' was powered from an accompanying police van's battery, at the suggestion of a friendly police officer when the organizers' own amplification equipment failed. Is this consensus attitude a symptom of repressive tolerance, or does it – as Camus felt – merely show that the British are politically effete? Professor Michael Banton of Bristol University has pointed out that the police can scarcely evade political involvement: if some strikers break the picketing law, the police are thought to be acting politically whether they intervene or whether they stand aside; and conversely the political effects are one of the factors senior officers have to consider when deciding whether to enforce the law up to the hilt. When they can find the time, reflective police officers sometimes debate whether their real function is to enforce laws – defined by the jurist Blackstone as rules of action prescribed or dictated by some superior which an inferior is bound to obey – or whether they are in fact being used to support the interests of the dominant political, social and economic groupings in society. To the simplistic left, the police's political function is to keep those groups without power from sharing in it. Some radical criminologists are often more critical of agents of power and control for creating crime than of those who are labelled criminals. This attitude ignores the fact that the police's role is to execute any political changes which Parliament decrees, although the considerable discretion, both explicit and assumed, that the police exercise makes 'enforcing' laws inevitably shade into the arena of 'making' them. (Whence in fact do the police derive their authority to ignore some offences while prosecuting others, and how can this power be made democratically accountable?) A somewhat more detailed left-wing critique interprets the founding of the British police as a move by the propertied class to protect its privileges, while seeing that to do so by means of its own members would exacerbate too much resentment – and hence the Machiavellian decision to set up a police system manned by working-class men who would protect their oppressors' property while drawing unpopularity for doing this on themselves. 'In reality the primary function of the law and police is to maintain existing class relations and to contain working-class power,' argues the left-wing barrister Ian McDonald. 'When the Metropolitan Police was set up in 1829, working-class power and organization had reached a level where it could no longer be confronted by a police force which was undisguisedly part of the ruling class.' Certainly, the use of British police throughout the nineteenth century against the struggle for working men's union and political rights – troops were called upon to help the police twenty-four times in the thirty years prior to 1908 – left a legacy of suspicion against the force that is far from extinct today. (Though ironically the police, lacking any union themselves – two strikes in 1872 and 1890 having been followed by wholesale sackings – were worse paid than most of their working-class critics.) A number of policemen in West Germany are today publicly questioning why they receive so much more training to deal with petty offences than with more substantial white-collar crime. But, against the left-wing attack on the police, it is worth remembering that in many ways the poor need their protection more than the rich do. Poor people can afford to be robbed or burgled much less than rich ones, and unlike the latter are unlikely to be able to turn to private security firms. The bulk of law in general acts as a brake on the abuse of power: much of medieval common law was developed by extending the protection of central justice to those who feared oppression from those stronger than themselves. The reality – and the origin of many of the problems of the police – is that laws simultaneously provide both the necessary framework of order to protect people's rights, and also are an expression of class rule.

Ireland's police history provides an interesting comparison with that of Britain. The Constabulary there had been united under a single Inspector-General in 1836. Besides centralized control, the Royal Irish Constabulary was distinguished by an officer cadre with quasi-military training and discipline.

Similar types of forces, rather than the London model, were set up in India and in British colonies elsewhere. But characteristically when Eire at independence established its own Garda Siochana, this was given an unarmed character like in England. (In an Irish fashion, the Republic's Garda adopted blue uniforms and the British rank structure, whereas the North on partition took green uniforms and Irish ranks until 1970.) In Northern Ireland, the 6,000-strong Royal Ulster Constabulary formed in 1922 was intended to be one-third Roman Catholic: unfortunately, it is scarcely 9 per cent so today, and the mainly part-time reserves have virtually none at all. More than half the members of the regular force have been injured in the last five years. But fuller support for the police in Northern Ireland depends on a matter outside the police's remit: a political settlement in the province. Like its predecessor the Royal Irish Constabulary, the RUC was at first additionally given responsibility for security duties of a military nature; in 1969 the Hunt Committee (of which Robert Mark was a member) recommended these should be taken away – and that it should be disarmed as soon as possible, because 'policing in a free society depends on a wide measure of public approval and consent. This has never been obtained in the long term by military or para-military means. We believe that any police force, military in appearance and equipment, is less acceptable to minority and moderate opinion than if it is clearly civilian in character, particularly now that better education and improved communications have spread awareness of the rights of civilians.'

Each police officer in England and Wales swears an oath: 'I do solemnly and sincerely declare and affirm that I will well and truly serve our Sovereign Lady the Queen in the office of Constable without favour or affection, malice or ill-will; and that I will, to the best of my power cause the peace to be kept and preserved and prevent all offences against the persons and property of Her Majesty's subjects; and that while I continue to hold the said office I will to the best of my skill and knowledge discharge all the duties thereof, faithfully according to law.' His general duties are not laid down in any statute. The twentieth-century shift in the uses of criminal law, and consequently in the strains upon the police, show how perceptive Mayne and Rowan were when they recognized that for any real power the force would have to depend not on extra laws but on the toleration, if not the cooperation, of the public. The restrained and deliberately unthreatening character they imprinted on the Metropolitan force at its inception was a deliberate strategy bidding for consensus at a time of very real class conflict. How vital the relationship with the public would be they appreciated from the outset: the first policemen were instructed they must cultivate it by 'combining modesty and firmness, and dignity of manner and address, with good humour and kindly friendliness, and by showing infinite patience under provocation. . . . He [the constable] will be civil and obliging to all people of every rank and class. He must be particularly cautious not to interfere idly or unnecessarily in order to make a display of his authority; when required to act, he will do so with decision and boldness; on all occasions he may expect to receive the fullest support in the proper exercise of his authority. He must remember that there is no qualification so indispensable to a police officer as a perfect command of temper, never suffering himself to be moved in the slightest degree by any language or threats that may be used, if he do his duty in a quiet and determined manner, such conduct will probably excite the well-disposed of the bystanders to assist him, if he requires them. . . . In the novelty of the present establishment, particular care is to be taken that the constables of the police do not form false notions of their duties and powers.'

The same lesson is now being emphasized in America. Edward Davis, until recently the Chief of the Los Angeles police, says: 'The ability of the police to perform their duties is dependent upon public approval of police existence, actions, behaviour and the ability of the police to secure and maintain public respect.' But the police's success brought developments which had never been anticipated by their founders: society incessantly has transferred fresh new responsibilities on to their shoulders. In the same way as in Tudor times the supervision of apprentices and vagrants had been given to constables – whose office in fact antedated Parliament itself – modern governments have designated policemen as their agents for implementing measures dealing with everything from aliens and London taxis to diseased animals and certificates for firearms. They have to service parading dignitaries and dissident demonstrators; cats marooned in trees as readily as premature babies; drug-addicts as well as lost or drunken drivers. The demand for the police, like that for the health service, is virtually insatiable. No legislator or judge has ever declared that the police must give first-aid, act as a local lost property office, understand the three-card trick, tackle rabid dogs, or rescue the drowning, the flooded, the snowed in, the burning, or the trapped; but they do not hesitate to do so. Although they do not deal with tax evasion, and occasionally they are able to offload a duty such as street betting, changes in opinion about the laws on pornography and cannabis can undermine their role, and the car has made every driver a potential criminal. They subsumed a duty to control road traffic, which takes over 11 per cent of police time, with their general responsibility for protecting life and property. In France the police's functions include in addition issuing passports and driving licences, dealing with the *constatation* (verification) of adultery, the safety of buildings, and even the collection of social, political and economic data for the government.

The police's role thus continues to develop, almost always increasing their work-load, as the society in which they live changes. A successful crime prevention campaign rarely reflects in the statistics; but today there is less and less time for any preventive role or for fraternizing with the public. None the less the idea in Britain that a constable is only a citizen conscientiously doing his natural duty dies hard. Private citizens retain the right to arrest policemen as much as each other. They can themselves institute prosecutions in England and Wales, though not in Scotland. But they must by law respond to a call for assistance from a police officer; in 1976 a Londoner was fined for not doing so. A policeman has few statutory powers and legal rights that the ordinary citizen does not also possess (and until 1964 none outside his own and adjoining police areas). A Bristol detective-sergeant, who was recently prosecuted for parking his car when on duty on double yellow lines outside a police station, and who pleaded that police officers on duty should be exempt in the same way that drivers of ambulances, fire engines and Post Office vehicles are, had his plea rejected and was fined. In 1978 the magistrates at Portsmouth even convicted a constable for causing obstruction while he parked his car to deal with a crime. When a police driver is pursuing criminals, he may exceed the speed limit, but he is liable for an accident in the same way as a private citizen and can be prosecuted for dangerous driving. Most people will agree with this perspective, because, as one senior officer said, 'It is not right to jeopardize lives even when chasing bank-robbers.' A fear of despotism still echoes in British ears in the pejorative associations of the tautologous phrase 'police state'. Our policemen themselves have always been very anxious to keep civilian roots. They like to wear civilian clothes whenever possible – part of the reason for the permanent waiting-list of men wanting to transfer to the CID, despite its slower promotion and enormously greater overtime than in the uniform branch. CID life in general is less oppressively supervised, and gives greater scope for initiative of all sorts. But a considerable majority of all officers and their families prefer to live among the public rather than to be corralled in their homes with other policemen. A wish for recruits to have civilian experience is also one reason why many senior officers advocate a higher age of entry, and prefer the proportion of cadets (who are trained as police from school-leaving age) to be kept to a minority. The Police Federation told the 1962 Royal Commission that there 'could be nothing more disastrous for relationships between police and public' than to make the police a profession. As their work becomes increasingly technical, specialization and training must inevitably increase, but the police are no exception to that nostalgia for the amateur and for historical tradition which still pervades every bone of Britain's anatomy.

Special Constables

The truer descendant of the original policing citizen in Britain today is the part-time Special Constable, who is an unpaid volunteer. By a 1673 Act of Charles II, any citizen could, formerly, be summoned to be sworn in as a Special Constable, and could be heavily fined if he refused; this law was still in force just before the Second World War when the Hartlepool Magistrates tried to enrol an unwilling transport driver, amid protests of 'Press Gang'. Specials today are given a sketchy training for two hours a week for twenty-three weeks, followed by thirty-two hours duty with a regular officer and then duty on their own for an average throughout the country of ninety minutes a week. In uniform, they have the same powers as regular police officers, but receive no pay except a small allowance for expenses. Their ranks range up to chief commandant, but they are not subject to a disciplinary code. They ride as observers in patrol cars but are not allowed to act as police officers, or to do plain-clothes work. Besides being used in war-time as replacements for regulars who joined up, Specials in the past were often employed to control industrial disputes, from the era of the Chartists down to the time when 226,300 Special Constables were enrolled by a worried government during the General Strike. This stamped them with an unfortunate particular political and class connotation: members of Hurlingham Polo Club are still remembered, dressed in their kit of boots, spurs and topees and swinging their riding crops, as they cantered off to fresh sport against the strikers. Their total number fell from 60,000 to 21,269 between the Second World War and 1978, and is now barely a quarter of their authorized complement. The regulars' Police Federation has always shown a barely concealed jealousy of the Specials, accusing officialdom of using them as blacklegs to 'paper over recruiting cracks' in an economical way; other regular officers allege that 'Most of the time they are a burden to us', or 'Without them, our conditions would have improved years ago.' A recent Home Office working party responded to the Federation's attitude by proposing that Specials should not do more than four hours duty on average each week, and that this should be principally used to train them for emergencies. In Scotland their use is in fact banned altogether except for emergencies. An inspector at Mansfield in the Midlands explained another factor in the Specials' relationship with the regulars: 'The fact that they are volunteers worries regulars in a moral way also. The best sort of policeman in my view does his job without passion – because of what needs to be done, not because he enjoys it. There's therefore suspicion about the emotional balance of a man who wants to do the same for fun.' But the Metropolitan London area is so undermanned that many regulars there welcome Specials because they provide relief on Sundays – particularly valued as the only day on which an officer can be united with all his family – and there their number has risen from 1,645 to 2,017. They are not used at demonstrations, but provide the relief manpower to release regular officers to police such events. In rural areas they give assistance with election duties and with crowds at football matches, shows and fairs; but some officers would like to see them used more widely on traffic and other routine work, allowing the regulars to concentrate on their special functions of crime prevention and detection. Perhaps Specials' most valuable present function could be to act as a badly needed link between the police and the public, not so much by acting as local eyes and ears as by interpreting the one body to the other: this role would be strengthened if the membership of the Specials more broadly represented the general population.

Should the police be armed?

Frank Norman, the expert about Soho, gave as his opinion of police work: 'I reckon it is just about the last job I would ever take even if I was starving to death.' Over twenty British policemen are injured on duty every day. The frequency of recorded assaults on the police has trebled since the Second World War. But it is still difficult to find a police officer in Britain who wants to be armed, although virtually every other national force in the world except for Norway and Sweden now is. Being unarmed is seen as a crucial benefit to the British police's relations with their public. Sir Robert Mark believes 'the real art of policing a free society or a democracy is to win by appearing to lose, or at least to win by not appearing to win.' Most British police officers are convinced that as soon as they were armed, they would overnight lose much of the public's cooperation and would themselves be more likely to attract the wrong type of recruits. Although they are trained in unarmed combat, and male officers carry a 'stick' for extra confidence in a special pocket down their right-hand trouser-leg, neither is much used. No. 10 Downing Street is still guarded by an unarmed officer. For forty years after the seige of Sidney Street in 1911, no British policeman fired a shot in anger. There has been no mounted or baton-charge, of the kind used against the hunger-marchers, since the Second World War. For special assignments, any policeman can be issued with a firearm on request; although the number of such occasions has recently increased, many officers continue to be against carrying arms regularly lest more criminals in turn reciprocate. A special group of armed policemen to counter armed raids is currently being seriously considered by the Irish government, whose Garda (apart from its Special Branch) have been unarmed since the force was established. But the proposal is opposed by the junior officers' association on the grounds that arming the police would only escalate the level of violence.

In Australia's six states, which range from arming their police on the American pattern in New South Wales to doing so only very exceptionally in Tasmania, police vulnerability to armed attacks appears to be directly related to the frequency with which they themselves carry firearms. Fifty-seven police officers have been killed in the United Kingdom in the last sixty-six years, compared with 132 on duty in the USA in the twelve months of 1974 alone. (New York police regulations stipulate that male and female officers must carry a revolver at all times, including when off duty, in a shoulder-holster under their jackets – in contrast with the position in the Philippines, where policemen caught carrying firearms off duty are liable to death by firing squad.)

There have been cases of New York officers in plain clothes shooting each other, each believing their colleague to be a criminal. One of the unfortunate effects of armed intervention by untrained policemen was seen at the Detroit riot of 1967: one half of the city was handed over to police and the National Guard, who shot off several thousand rounds of ammunition and killed thirty people; while in the other half US army paratroopers used only 200 rounds, killing one person, and had their sector calm in a matter of hours. In firearms training in the United States policemen are taught to aim to kill, whereas in Sweden they are penalized for so doing. Only about 10 per cent of British police officers are at present qualified as marksmen. A specially trained armed squad of uniformed Metropolitan policemen, the Diplomatic Protection Group, has recently been formed to protect foreign embassies and consulates from terrorist attacks. Only a fifth of London's 131 missions are able to be given a permanent guard. Another and separate unit of the Bomb Squad, wearing plain clothes and driving unmarked cars, also carry pistols and sub-machine guns. On average there are some 215 armed policemen on the streets of London at any one time. But for the increasing number of other criminal incidents which now involve arms and hostages, there is an unanswerable case for the development of more non-lethal weapons for the police which would temporarily incapacitate dangerous criminals.

Against serious violence, however, the police are keenly insistent on keeping their role as clearly distinct as possible from that of the military. They are adamant that it should be troops, and not themselves, who should be used for strike-breaking when a state of emergency is declared. The use of the army for policing has always been unpopular in Britain since Cromwell's time and has not been attempted on a regular basis since the First World War. At present the British 22 Special Air Service Regiment has anti-terrorist units, wearing plain clothes and using Range Rovers and Rover 3500 cars, on permanent three-minute standby; but 'if troops appeared in any industrial trouble where they had not been requested by us, I would order their arrest,' said one senior officer. Another, a chief constable, commented: 'Did the heavy involvement of the military in Northern Ireland produce the present situation or did it prevent something worse? We have seen in other parts of the world that the involvement of the military can lead to a crystallization of affairs with a stalemate, no progress one way or the other. Paradoxically sometimes a weak police force causes society to come to terms with its problems and take political action which it would be discouraged from doing if the security services were strong.' Ironically, however, the police's fierce insistence on excluding the military will inevitably, under increasing terrorist pressure, end by making more and more of their own members play an armed para-military role.

Not every civilian realizes that the British police are divided in two, between the uniform branch and the plain-clothed Criminal Investigation Department. In some areas there is more competition than cooperation between the two branches: the CID, feeling greater independence and prestige in their atavistic male role of hunter, look down upon the 'wooden-tops' or 'woollies' who have to plod their beats in uniform. But in the same way as the vast majority of the public never in their lives knowingly encounter any CID men – who account for only 13 per cent of the total strength – most police officers in the whole of their careers never see a case of murder or armed robbery outside a TV programme. Although urban forces have tended to be swamped by the twin problems of traffic and the protection of premises, a police officer in a rural district is still more concerned with human matters such as poachers and poultry thieves, or dealing with outbreaks of fire or animal disease: when foot-and-mouth disease starts, a twenty-four-hour guard on the farm gate is necessary. Rural policing has its own very different tempo: ample time for stopping and talking to try to gain the confidence and information of the community, resulting in a consequently greater rapport with the local public – and a correspondingly less close solidarity with other policemen – than is known in urban forces. Country officers who are traditionally reluctant to make arrests are known to the city colleagues as 'the Gurkhas' – 'because they take no prisoners'. One village constable said that eighteen families regularly bring him their income-tax forms to fill in, besides looking on him as their doctor, marriage counsellor, mediator, trouble-shooter, peacemaker and general adviser. But as the Panda car replaces the bicycle, rural areas are now losing their neighbourhood policeman just at the time that it has become the policy of most urban areas to reinstate him.

Some police duties, for instance acting as a father figure to women and children, may be personally satisfying; others such as being present at the eviction of tenants may be distasteful; but a policeman is not allowed to have – or at least show – any public feelings. Although his oath as a constable is to serve the Crown and not the local authority, he is often also asked to execute the ratepayers' wishes – by, for instance, running hirsute beatniks out of a seaside resort, or urging gipsies and tramps to move on to neighbouring districts. The days when a chief constable employed a policeman as his batman or for digging in his garden are gone, but in at least one borough the washing of councillors' cars by policemen continued until recently. Few members of the public are aware that they can still hire a policeman for a private function: in the Metropolitan area, for example, the tariff runs from a PC who costs £3.13 an hour in uniform (morning or evening dress are £1.50 extra) up to a Deputy Assistant Commissioner at a cost of £8.08 an hour. Police horses come at £1.15 and police dogs at 95p per day. The police send a bill for protecting football matches, but do not do so for even provocative marches and demonstrations – rightly, because the latter are a civil right whereas the former are commercial events.

Social conflict in their role

It is obviously essential for the police to be free from any suspicion of partiality – social, political, racial, or any other – even though they are part of a national society where prejudice and class influences are deep-seated if not endemic. In 1971 the Police Federation itself in fact protested against a proposal in the government's new Immigration Bill which required immigrants to register at police stations, arguing that such a measure would damage police relations with members of immigrant minorities. The role of the police is inevitably more difficult in heterogeneous societies, especially those with differing cultural norms. By their own Disciplinary Code police officers are prohibited from taking any active part in politics: they were not even allowed to vote in Parliamentary elections before 1887, or in local ones until 1893. Fortunately, outside a few local disputes such as at Nottingham in 1959, the police have never really become a party political issue in this country, despite habitual references to 'law'n'order' in election campaigns. We do not suffer from what is called the 'numbers game' in the US, whereby a traffic violator will ask the cop for his number and at the same time allude to his friendship with the Mayor. 'I know that my man is going to make a good police chief,' one Mayor of Indianapolis proclaimed, 'because he has been my tailor for twenty years.' Policemen themselves are fully aware how important it is for them not even to be suspected of bias. They are indignant when a titled landowner or a magistrate or MP is not prosecuted for a driving offence within his own area. They are probably less socially influenced than some lay magistrates, who in a recent study were shown to be relatively more severe when, for instance, sentencing a working-class man in a middle-class district.

Nevertheless, different social classes make use of the police in varying ways: working-class people – although often still generically more hostile – are likely to take their personal problems to a respected individual policeman in a way a middle-class person would not. The situation in the past, when a police officer was expected to be deferential, if not obsequious, to landowners while stern but paternal to their workers, has been radically altered – especially by the motoring laws, which have unkindly included many of the former in the largest criminal class of all. Nevertheless they are still likely to be addressed, 'Excuse me, sir,' whereas a motorcyclist will hear, 'Hey, you' – though when a policeman says to a car driver, 'Good evening, sir,' he may craftily be inviting a reply in order to smell his breath for alcohol. It is still true that if you want to find out which British social class you are in, you should ask a policeman something. (One serving inspector comments: 'Accent and vocabulary are the criteria, in that order, with appearance now trailing third: but even if you have an Oxbridge accent and a PhD, if you happen to be black you will still be spoken to as if you were an ESN child.') In the Social Survey for the Royal Commission in 1960, 24.1 per cent of the public said they thought that the 'upper classes, rich or influential people' were inclined to receive preferential treatment, although only 5.6 per cent said they had personal knowledge of such cases. But on the other hand one PC said that he never prosecuted anybody as meticulously as the woman driver who began, 'My son works in the Home Office ...', and at least one chief constable gave strict orders that 'any offender attempting to swing the "I was dining with the chief constable last night" line is to be jumped on.' In the 1936–7 riots, the police were accused – not always fairly – of being more lenient to the Fascists than to their opponents. Much of the resentment of the police in some districts, such as those parts of east and south London and south Wales where they are still booed on the cinema screen, dates from the time of the hunger marches. Except in areas of racial tension, it is now diminishing: old songs like 'We'll kill all the coppers who come down our way' have disappeared, and today there are few streets down which policemen can only safely venture in pairs.

But many mothers still teach their children to fear a policeman by using him as a traditional threat for misbehaviour, and middle-class people support the police more readily than working men do. Poorer people tend to mistrust policemen for 'always watching' and being the agents of 'Them'. One policeman said, 'My own experience of political demonstrators confirms that this attitude still exists and is fully used by unscrupulous public elements to arouse strong feelings. The inability of the police to express political opinions adds to the impression that they're on the side of the establishment.' In parts of Liverpool and some housing estates in north-west England, the police live like an occupying army – occasionally almost in siege conditions with their windows being broken twice a year. In these areas the policeman can be an isolated figure, attempting to enforce and advocate middle-class values of restraint and behaviour such as the channelling of aggression into social ambition. Many policemen themselves originate from lower social and economic groups, but soon acquire the middle-class standards of obedience, orderliness and punctuality which are built into the police Disciplinary Code.

The surest sign of a democracy is that its police not only allow, but protect, public demonstrations, pickets, and processions opposing the government. At the head of marches in Britain calling for the resignation of the government there proceeds a senior police officer, fending off those who disagree with the marchers. Nevertheless, vehement if at times simplistic views about demonstrators are often vented in the privacy of police stations. At the beginning of this century, the British police were criticized for failing to protect with sufficient enthusiasm the civil liberties of certain unpopular minorities, such as pacifists during the Boer War, and the early Salvation Army against its hooligan enemies the Skeleton Army (which was suspected of having been financed by publicans). British police technique at demonstrations in the Home Country has always relied as much as possible on moral authority rather than on physical force which – except in the short-run – is counter-persuasive. Their tactics at some meetings today are little changed from those Tom Critchley describes being used against Chartist disturbances 138 years ago when the

Metropolitan force was only ten years old: 'They kept well in the background, holding adequate reserves out of sight of the crowd and making no attempt to interfere. However, one or two men in plain clothes would be sent to mingle with the audience with instructions to report to a senior officer at once if there were evidence that disorder might develop.' On other occasions, as in Lewisham and Manchester in 1978, a massive police presence was deployed. In 1977 there were 585 demonstrations and marches in London mostly at weekends. At over sixty events more than 500 officers were called for duty, and at twenty-four of these over 1,000 officers were employed to deal with up to 20,000 demonstrators. In October of that year, the chief constable of Greater Manchester assembled 6,000 police officers to control one event. But almost inevitably, an individual police officer has to think fast on his feet: in 1864 a court held that a sub-inspector had acted rightly in taking an orange lily away from a woman who was attracting a hostile crowd by wearing it in an Irish street (Humphries *v.* Connor 17 Ir. C.L. Rep. 1. 115). The group dynamics of marches and demonstrations can produce their own psychological effects; if policemen talk to demonstrators on a march this helps to establish personal relations and defuse feelings of confrontation. In coping with disorder most British policemen have learnt that human control by close contact is infinitely preferable to a situation where helmeted men crouch behind water-cannon, so depersonalized as to encourage reciprocal aggression. Traffic policemen are not used, because their gauntlets, high boots and metal helmets might appear 'fascist'. John Alderson, the chief constable of Devon and Cornwall, advises, 'At all costs avoid a gap, which can become a kind of battleground between the two parties.' The riot at the Notting Hill carnival in 1976 brought calls for better protection for the police than dustbin-lids, yet their unarmoured vulnerability is regarded by many officers – despite the danger – as a crucial human touch that helps their relations with the public. Paradoxically, it probably makes a big contribution to the fact that most British demonstrators behave restrainedly. Many demonstrations today in fact take the form of traditional rituals, with the real contest between the demonstrators and the police being for the sympathy of the public, principally via the media of press and television. Sir Robert Mark's pragmatic view is that restraint is the best police tactic at demonstrations, since the use of force attracts coverage by the media, and any subsequent recourse to the courts can be an ordeal for the police as much as for the demonstrator: 'Our generally resigned and apprehensive approach to those events is hardly surprising once it is realized that an excess of fervour can produce controversy, complaints, unreason and lies in circumstances in which it is usually impossible to expose the truth.' But occasionally there have been lapses when policemen, sometimes goaded by abuse, have smashed reporters' cameras as well as demonstrators' heads. One very senior officer said, 'Probably our major function on these occasions is to control the police.' However, John Alderson also warns:

> There have been some disturbing signs recently that the very virtue of the police in ensuring freedom of protest for all has rebounded on them. They are placed in a virtually impossible position by escorting extreme right-wing and orderly processions with offensive racial characteristics through hostile and violent crowds of coloured minorities and their activist supporters. The police are thus made to appear identified with racist groups and accordingly lose the confidence of some of the coloured people who at the best of times have somewhat uneasy relationships with them. It is one of the great challenges for the police at the present time to develop their own counters to this dilemma and to build up amongst minority groups confidence in their impartiality.

Police strikes

In 1977 some London detectives, in protest at restrictions on their overtime, threatened to 'work to rule' by refusing to use their own cars or their home telephones for police work. But it is not easy to believe today that bitter police strikes happened in English history (in the same way as it is hard to remember that this country was once a Republic, that its service officers mutinied at the Curragh, or even the Abdication crisis). But in 1872 and 1890 part of the police went on strike for more pay;

in 1918 about 6,000, and in 1919 2,400, men came out in support of a request for recognition of their union. The 1918 strike successfully obtained a pay rise, but the repeat effort the next year ended in disaster when the government decided on exemplary firmness and sent three warships from Scapa Flow to the Mersey area where the strike was concentrated. The strike was broken and every participant in it was dismissed. It is now a criminal offence under section 53 of the Police Act 1964 to cause disaffection among the police, rendering criminally liable, 'any person who causes or attempts to cause or does any act calculated to induce any member of the police force to withhold his services or to commit breaches of discipline . . .'.

Section 47 of the same Act stipulates that 'a member of a police force shall not be a member of any trade union or of any association having for its objects, or one of its objects, to control or influence the pay, pensions or conditions of service of any police force'. But the Police Federation – to which all officers up to the rank of chief inspector automatically belong – is today in most ways equivalent to a trade union, except that it cannot affiliate with other unions, or call its members out on strike. Many policemen at present are in favour of the latter power, but not of their affiliating to the TUC for fear of being politically compromised. In March 1977 the Joint Central Committee of the Police Federation for England and Wales decided 'to seek the repeal of all prohibitions placed by the Police Act on the Federation's freedom of action, and the enactment of legislation to grant to the Federation similar status and protection as that afforded to Trade Unions under the Trade Unions and Labour Relations Act 1974'. One of the arguments used by the Federation against employing civilians in police stations is that the latter are liable to be immobilized by outside strike calls. But recently the International Union of Police Federations has complained to the UN Human Rights Commission that restrictions on their powers are contrary to the Universal Declaration of Human Rights. In 1926 the police refused to join the General Strike, although their situation was not an easy one and their feelings must have been mixed during some incidents. Afterwards *The Times* collected a public subscription of £242,000 in gratitude – a 'gargantuan tip' in the words of one chief inspector – but some policemen disliked it because it came from the upper classes and impugned their impartiality, and they wrote to the *Police Review* suggesting it should be distributed to people who were in real need of it.

There was no looting in London during the 1918 police strike – the occasion which Lloyd George said was 'the nearest the country ever came to bolshevism' – or any extra crime in Finland when it had its first similar stoppage in 1976. During a recent strike in Quebec, there were fewer road deaths than usual despite the fact there was not a single traffic policeman on duty: motorists, fearing a free-for-all, drove more carefully during this limited period. But during the strikes in Liverpool in 1919 and Montreal in 1969 shops were pillaged, and robberies increased tenfold when the Germans removed all the Danish police in 1944. The police in many countries are the only non-military body prohibited from striking by law. The Edmund Davies Committee in Britain in 1978 recommended that a right to strike is incompatible with a police service. The separate local police forces in Britain have mutual reinforcement arrangements, but, in the event of a local police strike, it is doubtful whether neighbouring officers could be persuaded to move in as blacklegs. The government would be driven to calling in the army in its MACP (military assistance to a civil power) role. But as the sociologist Robert Reiner of Bristol University says, 'It is arguable that strikes by others such as doctors, nurses, firemen and ambulancemen might cause equal or greater danger to life or property. The unique horror with which police strikes are viewed seems to be due as much to the symbolic significance of indiscipline in a body whose function it is to control others, as to the public danger involved.' In any event, it would hardly seem necessary for the police to strike. If they merely enforced every statute, they could bring society to a standstill. In London, for example, taxis can technically be booked if they have not got a bale of hay on their roofs; anybody wheeling a pram on the footway, or beating their door mat after 8 a.m., is breaking the law. If the police worked to rule by enforcing all the traffic laws up to the hilt, or if all officers simultaneously reported sick (succumbing to what is known as 'blue flu') or went so far as to hand in their resignations in unison, they could scarcely fail to wield similar negotiating strength.

What are the police for?

Overall, as a result of Parliament having made him an all-purpose public servant, the average policeman today is called upon to play not one role but a wide variety. A limited number of former duties have been passed to public health or NSPCC inspectors, or to traffic wardens. But only a tiny minority of police work – the past Commissioner estimated about 3 per cent – is directly concerned with crime. A police officer needs something of the experience of an arbitrator, a social worker, a lawyer and a doctor, without being trained as any of them. Balzac said being a policeman was the noblest profession of all because such a man simultaneously plays the role of soldier, priest and artist. A number of social services that policemen perform, such as delivering messages about deaths and injuries, although not strictly necessary to their primary task, are invaluable in cementing contact and trust with the public. But a good policeman knows his limitations and when to contact a specialist social worker (many policemen, for instance, take potential suicides to their local Samaritan branch). Because they are often the first public servants to come into contact with social misfits and failures, it is highly important that police officers should be trained to be able to give advice and to diagnose cases correctly. In most areas, the police station – in contrast to specialist social services – is one place open twenty-four hours every day of the year where people can go for help. The 'Kobans' (neighbourhood urban police posts) of Japan, commended in Chapter 8, provide library and moneylending services as well as information and first-aid. Any nation's police service has the organization and communication network to respond to emergencies of virtually any size. It provides one of the first comprehensive and free public welfare services: 'free' in the sense that if you are helped you do not get a bill for having your burglary investigated or cat rescued (though it is surprising that no right-wing economist has suggested this). At Camborne the Devon and Cornwall policemen introduced PAT, a telephone service which members of the public can use at any time of the day or night to seek advice or discuss difficulties. Superintendent Rowland points out, 'It must not be forgotten that unlike British Rail or the Post Office, who can cancel trains or mail collections on the grounds of staff shortage, the police must respond to all calls for assistance if the life of the community is to continue, and yet at all times must have spare capacity to deal with any subsequent contingency.' The percentage of people in Britain who report having been helped by the police ranges from 73 in a rural area to 63 in a middle-class urban area, and from 48 in a stable working-class urban community to 40 in a run-down urban area which is racially mixed. In the United States, 34 per cent of all calls to the police are for assistance in non-criminal matters. (In parts of Georgia, contraceptives are free on demand at police stations: Richard Neville has suggested that policemen should carry them and also boxes of matches for members of the public.)

A good policeman will settle a wide variety of social difficulties through his personal authority and relations with the community. In areas where he is known and can count on an unspoken consensus, he can deploy his unarmed authority with confidence that his bluff is unlikely to be called. Although the informal controls of small-knit communities fade as society becomes more metropolitan and mobile, a policeman's advice often still carries weight and is respected in disputes even when he has no legal *locus standi.* But coping with humanity from birth to death can cause problems of identification. Too close a relationship with the locality can invite suspicion of partiality and thus endanger his other role of law officer. Michael Banton points to the dilemma: 'If a policeman is too involved, he forfeits respect. If he is too detached, people resent his implied claim to moral superiority.' His service functions – inspecting, licensing, counselling – can create ambiguities about his law-enforcement work. The argument among the police themselves about whether they should be "gang-smashers or hand-holders" echoes their other debate as to whether their role should primarily be initiatory, or reactive like a fire-brigade's. CID members in particular regard their job as being the only real police work, and some of them think juvenile liaison officers and even neighbourhood beat officers have "gone over to the other side".' Suspicion between them and social workers is even more marked. Detectives criticize the latter for naivety, for withholding criminal information, for identifying too much with their clients rather than with the victims of their clients, for often being 'politicized students', and in general for failing to be agents of social control. In turn, social workers criticize the police for being more interested in the short-term aim of a prosecution than in long-term goals such as keeping a family together; for intolerance of non-conformity; and for trying to impose middle-class habits on others. But in police stations in Chicago, a duty social worker regularly sits alongside the desk sergeant. In 1978 Sir Colin Woods suggested that the answer to the disturbing crime figures in Britain could lie in stopping crime before it starts by increased aid for and cooperation with social agencies. Better liaison and more discussion between the two callings would help both to understand their respective tasks better, though some areas of ambivalence towards each other – such as over the question of the confidentiality of the knowledge or criminal hearsay that social workers learn from their clients – will always remain hard to resolve.

A number of mainly young officers have come to believe that since much crime has its roots in lack of social or racial integration, the police's role of crime prevention should be expressed by practical work that actively promotes better social conditions and implements reconstruction. Despite the risk that such work by them would be suspected of being a cover for informers or even the start of a police-state, and despite opposition from some social workers, some successful projects have been developed on Merseyside and, most especially, in Lanark, Greenock and other parts of Scotland. Each Scottish force has a Community Involvement Department, set up largely as a result of the recommendation of David Gray, Scotland's Chief Inspector of Constabulary, who said: 'In my own very long experience as a policeman I have found that one good policeman who is known and respected by the people on his beat can achieve more than two or three who walk aloof, alone and unknown. The latter may produce more offence reports; the former will help produce a more peaceful neighbourhood.' The Scottish experiment avoided the American mistake of delegating community work solely to specialists, which has the result that other officers opt out. In Glasgow the chief constable successfully involved all the uniformed beat officers in the work of juvenile liaison. In its tough ghetto area of Blackhill the police gained goodwill by being able to save from vandalism the only bus-stop and public telephone for the 9,000 inhabitants by operating a new police station in a former shop to protect them. But understandably, the greatest efforts have been made with young people. More than 700 Metropolitan policemen voluntarily give regular help to youth organizations. The Royal Ulster Constabulary is the biggest discothèque organizer in the United Kingdom: more than 30,000 young people a month in Northern Ireland attend Blue Lamp discos run by rank-and-file police officers. The ultimate implications of such moves may go further. As John Tusa, the journalist, points out: 'They are that the police should be in some way agents of change in society. If social injustice breeds crime, if it is part of the police's task to identify that injustice and draw it to the attention of government, then the police can hardly be indifferent if government does not act on their advice.'

Before the Second World War, many policemen saw themselves as playing a 'cuff-on-the-ear' role against petty criminals. A sergeant in Wiltshire recounted how he regularly used to control gangs of unruly youths by 'setting upon them in the dark when there were not more than two of them together and giving them a good thumping'. But when in 1957 a police constable at Thurso gave 'a moderate cuff on the face' to a provocative fifteen-year-old boy, the full panoply of a Tribunal was later set up by both Houses of Parliament which heard evidence for six days and published a long official report (under the motto '*Nemo me impune lacessit*'). This report on the Waters case publicly discouraged such methods on the part of the police, although they continue to be used against poachers and are more tolerated in northern, and particularly in the tougher parts of north-eastern, England.

In theory, the concern of the police stops short of the verdict and sentence: 94 per cent of policemen who were questioned by me in 1963 said that they thought they should not be concerned with the punishment of crime, although 18 per cent in answer to another question replied that they thought that lay magistrates were too lenient. But in 1927 the Glasgow police did publicly protest against the acquittal and reprieve of Oscar Slater, a man who had spent nineteen years in prison for a murder of which he was innocent. This however is a wholly different matter from the squads of policemen in Latin America who on their own initiative have in recent years killed over 2,000 petty criminals, though sometimes British policemen express particular outrage at certain crimes – especially those committed by sex-offenders, who also fall outside the pale of the prison community. Several chief constables regularly urge heavier sentences for various categories of offence, and in 1975 Sir Robert Mark publicly alleged when he was Commissioner that violent demonstrators were receiving such lenient penalties from the courts that there was an argument for abandoning almost all prosecutions of them. In the past the police, like the majority of the general public, have been more interested in the methods of crime than its causes. One quite senior serving officer seriously said that he thought that the Howard League for Penal Reform was responsible for the recent rise in offences. But an increasing number of policemen are now growing aware of the complexity of the problems of criminology. When London University started a three-year course in the subject, 800 police officers applied for the 100 places, and over 1,000 applied to join a similar course in Manchester. The National Association of Probation Officers told the 1960 Royal Commission that, since attendance centres had been introduced,

> Where the police have been asked to take part in the organization or running of such centres, this has in many cases been used as an opportunity for preventive and constructive work, and for understanding by the police of the inherent possibilities of some apparently criminal young people. The end of a period of attendance has frequently been followed by continued interest by the police in the welfare of the young person, usually by a request to a probation officer to keep in touch with the lad or his family.

Quite apart from the psychological, family and social effects of imprisonment, the average weekly cost of keeping a person in custody is now £100, compared with about £4 for superintending someone on probation.

One of the best-known developments in the social work of the police is the juvenile liaison officer scheme, launched by Liverpool in 1949 and subsequently copied by other forces, particularly since the establishment of juvenile bureaux following the Children and Young Persons Act 1969. Under the Liverpool plan, selected volunteer police officers do full-time duty supervising cautioned juveniles in liaison with their parents, school or youth club authorities, together with the probation service. Three basic conditions are required for supervision: (1) the child must admit the offence, which cannot be a grave one; (2) he must not have been in trouble previously (magistrates permit a previous caution to be cited in court); and (3) his parents must give their consent. The juvenile liaison officer investigates his background and attempts to 'foster in the mind of the child ideas which will lead to responsible citizenship', and also, where necessary, to bring home to the parents their responsibilities. The method he uses is a 'mixture of cajoling and threats'. When he suspects that a child requires more specialized treatment, he hands the case over to the appropriate authority, i.e. school medical officer, child guidance clinic, or the psychiatric department of children's hospitals. If the juvenile liaison officer discovers another social agency is actively interested, he is required to withdraw from the case. And if the juvenile cannot be released from custody because his parents refuse to accept him, he often will have to be charged.

By 1970, 44,486 formal cautions were being given annually to young persons under seventeen. Oral cautions in England are delivered by a senior officer at a police station, and the offender's parents are required to attend. Factors taken into account in deciding to caution rather than prosecute an offender include the crime's gravity, his or her age and previous character, whether his parents agree and will be likely to control their child in the future, and whether any victim of the offence desires a prosecution. One criticism of the procedure is the disparity in different areas' use of it. In 1976, for example, Kent's rate of cautioning was half that of Wiltshire's; South Wales's rate was less than a third of that in Dyfed and Powys. Some researchers, such as Dr Anne Campbell of Oxford University's department of experimental psychology, believe that the police show discriminatory gallantry towards girl offenders, and are much more reluctant to prosecute them than if they are boys and especially boys who are not deferential towards the police. Serving officers admit that they have no formal training as cautioners, usually lack skills when trying to identify children in need, and that their background reports are sketchy in the extreme. 'Contrary to the published view, cautions usually take place hurriedly and in the form of a blistering, irrespective of the personality of the child,' were the words of one experienced officer. Support for liaison schemes among the police has grown from a wish to keep young people (the peak age for theft is fourteen) out of court: partly in order to avoid giving a child a criminal label at an early age, and partly because of universal dislike of the inordinate delays of the juvenile courts which have replaced the earlier cuff-on-the-ear methods. The Juvenile Bureau is not regarded as a specialist department, and officers generally work there for an average of four years before reverting to normal duties. The supervision scheme is in reality only a more constructive extension of the power of discretion which the police have always possessed, discussed in detail in Chapter 4; but it has met with criticism because 42 per cent of the 818 children supervised in Liverpool in 1960, for example, had not yet committed any offence, but had been suggested by parents, teachers, or other policemen as 'potential delinquents'. It was objected that this practice was depriving the courts of their role, and that policemen – however wide an experience they may have of adult human nature – had not received the professional training of children's or probation officers. However J. A. Mack in a survey estimated that of the juveniles who have been supervised – four out of five of whom are boys – roughly 90 per cent are not known to have offended within the following three years.

Neighbourhood policing

The most recent innovation has been the organization of the system of neighbourhood (otherwise known as area, unit, resident, or home) beat police officers. Pioneered by Orlando Wilson in Chicago, it was first systematically introduced in Britain by Sussex in 1961 and Hertfordshire in 1962; while the Lancashire force started team policing at Accrington in 1966. Its basic principle is that the neighbourhood constable lives on or near his beat, and is relied upon to make his own plans for policing his area. He is expected to have as much personal contact as possible with its inhabitants, in the way a rural policeman does in his village's area. One particular role is collecting detailed local knowledge for the wider police organization: the information gathered is collated and put to use by a sergeant at headquarters. Each two adjoining beats are served by a patrol car and a detective who is always on call from the beat officer's personal radio. The scheme is a return to some territorial basis of organizing policing, after the continual pull towards functional specialization, and a response to the strains placed on police work by the fact that Britain's built-up area has increased by more than one-third since 1939. A feeling of control over his territory is very important to a police officer whatever his rank. In addition, uniform officers plodding the old-style beat had continually complained of being bored: relating to a neighbourhood is an attempt to make police work more human and interesting although some men are better than others at working alone. But it has an important further value in crime prevention and is helping the police to gain insight into the social causes of crime in each particular local community. Sir Derrick Capper points out that the whole system depends on the neighbourhood officer being able to be continuously present and not being called away for other duties: unfortunately when extra men need to be drafted – as they invariably are, because of sickness or injury, or for football matches or demonstrations – neighbourhood constables are the first to be withdrawn. About 800 inhabitants are the maximum for a meaningful neighbourhood beat; however, such a scheme is at present largely only academic in the Metropolitan area due to its shortage of men. Most Londoners are still unaware who their neighbourhood officer is, or even if they have one; and it is difficult for every neighbourhood officer to live in his area if, like almost all married policemen, he wants to own his own house. But at Milton Keynes new town, the police have asked to have their houses built in each neighbourhood, instead of being segregated as at Kirkby. Months of patient work by a neighbourhood officer in gaining his local community's trust, however, can be undone overnight by an insensitive visit from the Flying Squad or Special Patrol Group. (The latter were formed in 1965 as a highly mobile squad available to tackle outbreaks of anything from pickpocketing to terrorism. They are the nearest Britain has to riot police.) Geoffrey Dear, the assistant chief constable of Nottinghamshire, explains: 'They might apparently solve one problem, but in its wake create another of aggravated relationships between minority groups and the police in general. It is then in this atmosphere that the permanent beat officer is expected to continue his work – often finding that his task, which was always difficult and delicate, has now been made almost impossible.' Graham Howes of Trinity Hall, Cambridge, however, comments that paradoxically more community solidarity may in fact be generated by the sudden presence of the Special Patrol Group than by the painstaking efforts of the neighbourhood officer.

James Anderton, the articulate chief constable of Greater Manchester, lays great – almost a populist – stress on 'community contact'. A number of American forces – such as Jacksonville (Florida), Dover (New Jersey), and Blythe (California) – have gone further and done away with police uniforms, which they believe alienate the public. Sheriff Bernard Clark says, 'Military style uniforms impede an officer in his work. A more casual dress lets people see that a policeman is just a normal human being. Instead of tensing up, they relax and talk more freely.' A different approach, with more disturbing implications, was announced by superintendent James Rochford in Chicago in 1975. Under the plan, civilian 'beat representatives', 'block captains' and 'crime prevention teams' were recruited for each of the city's 1,200 beats. They would be asked to collect information for the police – but the dangers of this reporting, including for example other people's political views, need no stressing, particularly in the context of the United States where police chiefs are politically appointed. The state of Indiana ran into similar controversy over a recent plan to hire civilians to report on conversations about potentially criminal or dangerous acts. Fort Wayne, one city in the state, hired twelve young people to attend gatherings and report on what was said.

The closest unpaid civilian allies of the police in cities usually tend to be taxi-drivers and newsvendors (especially in London, where Scotland Yard licenses them). But inside or outside the neighbourhood beat system, the individual police constable will always continue to carry enormous personal responsibility. No superior officer can tell him 'arrest that man'; he alone is responsible and answerable for his actions. Dr Maureen Cain of Brunel University points out that policing is an occupation, like nursing, which is hierarchically organized yet where the distinctive technical professional skills are exercised by those at the bottom level. Which laws each policeman will select to enforce will depend on factors ranging from his own views and the example of his superior colleagues to his reaction to current pressure from the public and press. The differing concepts policemen have of their role stem in part from their varied backgrounds: the older amongst them tend to have a more short formal education and, quite often, military experience. A constable continually needs to be very tactful about people's privacy; it is a nice matter of discretion and judgement for him how far he should always respect the public's confidences. However detached and impartial he may aim to be, he can never be a mechanical bureaucrat: each problem he faces, being human, is liable to be a unique one. Policemen tend to encounter their fellow human beings when they are at their most threatening, at their most vulnerable, at their most frightened or at their most ashamed. But whereas his success will often depend on instinctive reactions, he himself alone must always be prepared to defend what he does in court later. The psychological rewards however can include both those of altruism and of its near relation the exercise of power.

In turn, different sections of the public view a policeman in varying ways. Many upper- and middle-class people wish him to enforce the law legalistically, if not strictly; while poorer people often feel it is more important that the police should regulate behaviour and settle issues without making arrests. Sociologically most police have more in common with the second approach, and recognize that laws anyway are incapable of total enforcement. The socialist journalist Paul Foot comments: 'Ordinary policemen are placed in a dilemma. They think they are just enforcing the law, and are politically neutral. In fact, they find themselves enforcing *some* laws, while other laws are broken without any police activity at all. Thousands of police are ordered to protect a few scabs at Grunwicks, yet every day the law on safety in factories or working conditions in offices is wilfully broken. No police are ordered in to stop the killing and maiming of hundreds of women are drawn.' Lieutenant Thomas Adams of the US more you look at the laws which police are ordered by their officers to enforce, the more you see that they are the laws which protect property, and not the laws which protect ordinary people, from whose ranks most policemen and women are drawn. Lieutenant Thomas Adams of the US describes the police's job as being 'to enforce that *intent* of the law in deference to the letter of the law'. How laws are applied can be just as important as the laws themselves. Collectively and as individuals, the police mediate between the law and the public, often exercising a crucial and little researched function in redefining justice in their own terms.

How is the role of the police likely to develop in the future? Their primary function – which shows no sign of withering away – will remain: in the American phrase, 'the maintenance of public order and the protection of persons and property from the hazards of public accidents and the commission of unlawful acts'. There will always be a need for the 'preventive medicine' of the mere sight of policemen and patrol cars. The deterrent effect of this has been learnt in several countries: the stationing of a *gendarme* at a blind corner has been shown to reduce accidents, and the Paris force in 1959, when many police were in Algeria, successfully deployed even cut-out dummies at dangerous cross roads. In Kyoto in Japan, a uniformed traffic policeman made entirely of plastic has had a salutary effect on drivers, and robots dressed in police uniform have been used for directing traffic in Japan. The degree of need for policemen varies from nation to nation. Lenin is reputed to have observed that before storming a railway-station, the order-loving Germans would first buy a platform-ticket. After the German occupying army had deported the Danish police force in 1944, larceny and fraud, but interestingly not murder or sexual crimes, increased sharply amongst the Danes. The value in Britain of the presence of the man on the beat was shown in an experiment by the Metropolitan police, when one of their twenty-two divisions was brought up to its pre-war strength on the beat by borrowing 102 men: during the experimental period, indictable crimes in this one division fell (those of housebreaking by 32 per cent) compared with the other divisions whose crimes showed an increase of 9.2 per cent.

All laws should regularly be re-examined to see if they are still necessary and new laws in particular should be scrutinized to consider their effect on the police. The service has always been reluctant to become involved in domestic disputes, yet the Domestic Violence and Matrimonial Proceedings Act 1977 now requires them to; and the New York police have now agreed to perform a similar role for the first time. The ancient distinction between civil and criminal law has become blurred by new laws against squatters.

But the more interesting and constructive a role the police can be given, the less wastage they will suffer and the higher will be the quality of recruits who are attracted to the service. Community involvement gives the police a chance to improve their image and to achieve a new status for themselves in future society. Some social workers and probation officers are understandably jealous of their territory, but both are at present badly overworked: probation officers, whose maximum case-load should be forty to fifty, are frequently each having to deal with double that number of cases. Many policemen, because of the respect in which they are generally held and because of their ability to share in the interests and language of a variety of people, have been highly successful in such work. The real need would seem to be for more training of at least some, and preferably all, police officers – as is recognised in many continental and American forces. To those who regret the 'blurring of an image' it can be answered that it does nothing but good for a policeman to be seen as someone other than a bogeyman. It is particularly desirable that parents in delinquent parts of the community should be persuaded to view the police as allies rather than enemies. An increasing number of police officers, particularly policewomen, are today developing, along with the general rise in education, deeper and wider views of their function. A considered development of the role of police work should be welcomed if it increases its satisfaction and value in human terms, instead of making it the repository of the unwanted jobs of society: such a move will encourage the cooperation of the public at the same time as it improves the interest and morale of the force.

Policemen have in fact always been unofficial social workers in their dealings with a wide spectrum of problems: what is necessary is that this should now be properly recognized and that they should be better trained for these tasks. The police station could become a key social centre in each community (and certainly should not, as in the Maidstone area, have its telephone number ex-directory). The police form a fulcrum: the point where the community interacts with the individual, whether intervening to control or to protect him. In future, the training of policemen should reflect the fact that, because much of their work is concerned with all those people who for various reasons are not integrated into society, the police provide in many ways the most universally relevant – and relied upon – social service of all.

THREE

The Price of Effectiveness

'Injustice is relatively easy to bear; what stings is justice.'
H. L. Mencken

'The citizen is free to do whatever he likes, but under police supervision.'
I. Guyot

In judging police work, effectiveness should be distinguished from efficiency. An illustration of the difference between the two was given by the police superintendent at Whitby who during the 1864 election enrolled as temporary Special Constables a band of roughs who were likely to cause disorder and so kept them quietly at the station-house throughout polling day.

The most usual indices of police effectiveness – although they are not the only measures of good policing – are the 'number of indictable offences known to the police' as a measure of their preventive success (see Figure 2), and the 'percentage cleared up' as a guide to their detective skill – though this includes only those cases able to be proved in a law-court. Yet the Whitby superintendent's coup would have featured in no such statistic. And these figures, like all crime data, must be treated with considerable reserve. It is impossible to catalogue how many other offences lie, like the bulk of an iceberg, unknown to the police, because of for example victims' or employers'

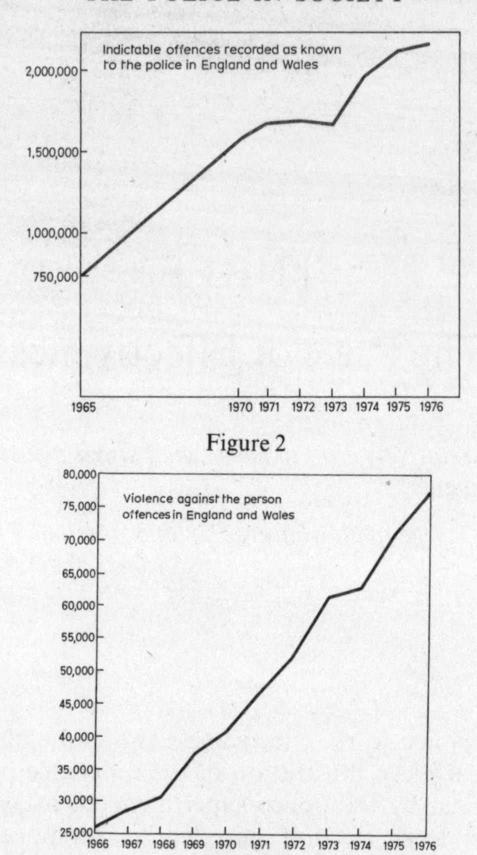

Figure 2

Figure 3

discretion. There were 40,000 meter thefts in a recent year which gas and electricity boards did not report to the police. One large firm in twelve months dealt with 371 cases of staff larceny without reporting a single one of them to the police, though the total cost of such internal pilfering (called 'shrinkage' in the trade) in Britain is estimated to be over £2 million a day – several times more than the haul of all burglaries and robberies. Losses from shoplifting in England and Wales amounted to more than £3.5 million in 1977 – over £1.1 million more than in 1976. In the United States, $8,000 million worth of goods are estimated to be shoplifted annually, with the rate increasing by over 25 per cent every year, despite

600,000 arrests for shoplifting in 1976. A police official in West Germany estimated that the 200,000 shoplifters caught there in 1976 probably represented only about 1 per cent of the real number of such offenders. People may fail to report a crime because they do not recognize it as being one, or because they wish to avoid publicity or the trouble of being a witness in court; or out of either fear or embarrassment, particularly in sex cases, or from antagonism towards the police or uncertainty about how to report it; or because they believe there is little point in doing so, or do not wish to incriminate the offender – who in many other cases may be the same person as the sole witness. Particularly in certain areas, people traditionally prefer to settle scores concerning crimes in their own way without involving outsiders such as the police. A male or female victim in such a group loses face if he or she runs to the common enemy: many fights only become known to the police when their casualties are found in hospital; and before the breaking of the power of London strong-arm protection gangs, most of their victims used to discharge themselves anonymously as soon as they were bandaged. A study by the Vera Institute in the United States found that the offender was previously known to the victim in not just the majority of killings, but in 83 per cent of rape cases, 69 per cent of assaults and even 39 per cent of burglaries. The proportions of blackmail, shoplifting, fraud, illegal abortions, homosexual offences and incest that are recorded and solved are likely to be particularly unrealistic. Such 'self-detecting' offences, like handling stolen goods or drug violations, only tend to be reported when an alleged offender is caught, and therefore are characterized by a deceptively high clear-up rate. The latter figures are boosted as well by the number of cases which arrested criminals ask to be 'taken into consideration'. Bill Hewitt, a perspicacious former chief inspector in the City of London force, explains:

> This clears up an awful lot of crimes spuriously; a man who can't get a much heavier sentence than what's coming to him anyway can be persuaded to 'admit' a whole list of crimes the police can't solve and which he may really know nothing about, sometimes in return for the suppression of some part

of his story that would harm him in court. This is a kind of plea-bargaining that never gets mentioned.

A low level of offences known to the police, far from indicating police effectiveness, may point to the very reverse. Some decreases in reported crime could be because members of the public find it harder to approach policemen who are in cars than formerly when they were walking a beat. In the United States, one sample survey in 1966 found that 35 per cent of robberies, 54 per cent of assaults, 63 per cent of petty larcenies, 74 per cent of financial frauds and 90 per cent of consumer frauds were never notified to the police. It is estimated that for every case of wife-beating that is recorded, eight go unreported. In other confidential questioning, more than 90 per cent of the public themselves confessed to having done some lawbreaking, at least half of whom admitted offences punishable by imprisonment; but of these only one out of ten had been detected, and no more than 3 per cent of their crimes were known to the police. Such large estimates, coming as they do from both victims and instigators, of unreported crime must suggest – at least in part – some lack of confidence in the police. Suspects being questioned over racial attacks in London's East End in 1978 surprised the police by confessing to several hundred assaults which were unknown to the police; senior officers were seriously concerned by the resultant threat that Asians there might form their own self-protection force. The reason most often given by unreporting victims or witnesses is a belief that 'the police can't do anything': if many of the public think this, criminals are hardly likely to view matters any differently.

Most policemen are almost completely untrained to deal with or even unearth 'white collar' crime, of which the community's tolerance creates, as Clive Davies of Liverpool University says, a particular problem for law-enforcement. The police themselves frequently choose not to record many petty offences, such as cycle thefts or vandalism, that they know about; they are also often reluctant to make an arrest in cases of domestic fights. Incidents of violence in families tend to be very under-reported and under-recorded. The litter laws are barely enforced at all; prosecutions for serving drink to minors are virtually unknown; and any motorist who keeps within a speed limit must expect to be frequently overtaken. The Home Office in 1972 issued a directive that thefts under £5 should no longer be recorded in the crime statistics. Sir Leon Radzinowicz, for twelve years Director of the Institute of Criminology at Cambridge, estimates that overall no more than 15 per cent of committed crime is known and punished. Dr Howard Jones gauges that the total 'dark number' of unrecorded crimes may be four times that of those known to the police; but of these, only two-fifths are cleared up, so a criminal's chance of success at present is better than eleven to one. The most recent survey in three areas of London by the criminologist Hazel Genn of Wolfson College, Oxford, suggests that there is probably more than ten times as much crime committed as is recorded in police statistics. For offences against the person and miscellaneous thefts, the proportion recorded was found to be only 3 per cent, and even for burglaries and thefts in dwelling houses, the figure was only 24 per cent. Any theorizing about criminals tends to ignore the blindingly obvious fallacy that it is only the unsuccessful ones who are ever 'known to' the police or the media or criminologists. Their more effective and presumably often more dangerous colleagues are moving freely amongst us. The unpalatable consequence is that all of society's penal, reformative and rehabilitative resources are devoted to less than a tenth of offenders. And this perspective applies only to more serious crimes. John Alderson, chief constable of Devon and Cornwall, points out that 'even this is a gross underestimation if minor criminal offences involving for example motoring, honesty, and sex are involved. Criminality is now just a question of degree. The law has made criminals of us all, though there is as much hypocrisy about crime today as there was about sex in Victorian times.' In the converse direction, criminal statistics may be exaggerated by 'thefts' of articles which are only mislaid – sometimes in order to claim the insurance (though, if this is done fraudulently, each of these occasions would be a crime and so not affect the total). A number of offences are committed or cleared up in a different year from when they come to light. Others have only recently come to be regarded as crimes, either by the law itself, or by members of the public whose educational and socio-cultural standards have risen. Violent behaviour formerly used both to be accepted in institutions and homes and publicly taken for granted much more than it is today. Similarly, assaults or cases of vandalism which used never to be reported in slum communities may now feature in the statistics when their inhabitants move to new housing estates. Insurance has always cast an erratic light upon the reporting of property offences; in recent years the compensation offered to victims by the British Criminal Injuries Board has provided additional incentive for the reporting of crimes involving personal injuries. An apparent crisis in crime may therefore arise principally from the public's increased readiness to report – a trend which may partly in fact represent a bench-mark of greater, not less, confidence in the police.

Another wide variable is due to the fact that different police forces vary considerably in their policies and methods of classification, as well as in the amount of regard they pay to statistics. Some may wish to emphasize the seriousness of their crime situation in order to wring an increased budget or strength from their local authority; others may be tempted to minimize the unsolved proportion by 'scrubbing' minor or insoluble offences, or the ones they feel belong to a neighbouring force. Official ambivalence about crime figures was demonstrated in 1973, when Home Office ministers simultaneously expressed satisfaction both that the number of cannabis cases were up, and that those for LSD offences were down.

However, even when every allowance is made for all these distorting factors, it would be wilful to deny the seriousness of the current crime figures. Between 1900 and 1919 the average number of crimes recorded annually in England and Wales was 100,000; by 1939 it was 300,000; after the Second World War, in 1947, it was just under 500,000; but by 1971 with a static population it was 1.7 million and seven years later with a declining total population it was still rising sharply with a total of over 2.6 million – more than treble the 1960 figure. Looking only at the most disturbing cases – those indictable offences which involve force – the known cases of violence against the person (murder, manslaughter, infanticide, woundings and assaults), which are often sentenced much too lightly in comparison with offences involving property, have risen from 4,900 in 1949 to 37,400 by 1969, and to double that number in 1976. (It is however reassuring to the opponents of capital punishment that murders have risen less rapidly than other offences since the abolition of the death penalty, and in 1977 fell to the lowest number for four years.) In the twenty years following 1949 violent offences involving property rose from 92,000 to 427,000; robbery alone increased from 990 to 6,041 cases. By 1976, there were some twenty indictable crimes per police officer in England and Wales; in 1960 the ratio had been approximately six to one. 544,000 people were found guilty of, or cautioned for, indictable offences in England and Wales in 1977. Northern Ireland's special problems are well known: fewer than a quarter of murders there and scarcely a fifth of all serious crimes are cleared up.

TABLE 2: PERCENTAGES CLEARED UP OF INDICTABLE OFFENCES KNOWN TO THE POLICE IN THE METROPOLITAN LONDON AREA 1972–7.

Offence group (Home Office classification)	*1972*	*1973*	*1974*	*1975*	*1976*	*1977*
Violence against the person	71%	72%	67%	62%	59%	55%
Sexual offences	70	70	70	65	60	57
Burglary	20	18	17	15	14	12
Robbery	33	34	29	26	20	16
Theft and handling stolen goods	26	26	25	23	22	21
Fraud and forgery	69	67	65	66	58	59
Criminal damage	28	30	27	25	22	13
Other offences	95	94	91	88	84	85
All crimes known	30	30	28	26	23	21

The population of Greater London itself diminished by almost half a million people during the same period.

Nor is the problem confined to London, as Table 3 shows. In 1977 serious crimes in England and Wales outside London increased by a further 16 per cent over the previous year's total, embracing virtually every category except – to the chagrin of the anti-permissive brigade – that of sexual offences which declined by a further 5 per cent, on top of a fall of 6 per cent in 1976. In Scotland, crime overall rose by 14 per cent in 1977, while the strength of the police force decreased. The chief constable of the West Midlands, Philip Knights, warned in 1978 that some lesser crimes would not be investigated unless more police were recruited, and that the region's police were 'in very real danger of being overwhelmed'. Vandalism is now costing Britain, in the Home Office's estimate, £100 million a year; in Merseyside it rose by almost two-thirds during 1977. The statistical incentives for a criminal career have become more attractive at the same time as unemployment spreads: in 1977 out of over £198 million stolen in Britain, the police recovered less than £32 million, and in recent years less than 15 per cent of the planned robberies of goods in transit have been cleared up. By the start of 1978, less than one London burglary in ten was being solved. Sir David McNee that year complained that of 230 people arrested for major crimes, 52 were already out on bail on other charges. Other social problems faced by the police cause equal concern. The annual cost of road accidents in Britain is now estimated by the government to be running at well over £970 million – compared with £102 million lost in burglaries; while France estimates that her road accidents annually cost some 35,000 million francs (£4,142 million), of which 14,000 million francs are directly attributable to accidents caused by drinking.

Patterns of crime change: now that more payments are made by cheque because cash in transit had become so vulnerable, thieves have switched their tactics and have recently made cheques, credit cards and even computers primary targets. Brighter thieves have learnt that it is simpler to change the decimal point on a computerized accounting system than to blow open a bank. Other computer offences (for some of which the police can only bring a charge of stealing electricity) include moon-lighting on computers, the manipulation of electronic financial accounts, altering or destroying stored data, and the theft of electronic information. But some long-term indicators are even more disturbing: increasing numbers both of women and of young people – perhaps inspired by the example of their parents' perks and pilfering – are involved in the practice of crime. The 1977 number of young people between the ages of ten and sixteen (inclusive) found guilty or cautioned for indictable offences (195,000) was up by 11 per cent on the total for 1976. In 1954 fewer than 165 crimes of violence were recorded as committed by under-fourteens; the 1977 figure is now over 1,600. Whereas in 1965, 37,234 women were found guilty of or cautioned for indictable crimes in England and Wales, ten years later the annual figure had become 86,304. This pattern is echoed in almost all 'developed' nations, where detected female crime is overall rising three to five times as fast as that of males.

If the work of the police falls below a certain level of success – as has already happened in some countries – the result is first to sap and then seriously to endanger public confidence in them. It is important for British people to keep their own crime figures in a correct perspective. Each year there are some 1,800 murders in the single city of New York compared to the annual average of 94 cases of murder and 220 of manslaughter in the whole of England and Wales, and the 200 killings a year in Northern Ireland even at the worst time of the Emergency. Easily the greatest cause of violent death in Northern Ireland still continues to be road traffic (the road accident rate there is double that of the United Kingdom as a whole). Too great a preoccupation with crime statistics can distort the wider aims of policing. Even so, the current direction indicates problems which any society is crass to ignore. Every country seems to be having more crime as it becomes more affluent – and most particularly where the affluence is unevenly distributed. Contrary to expectations as to what would happen when education and living standards improved, crime has become many countries' best growth industry. The United States would do well to reflect on why it annually has 9.7 murders per 100,000 of population, compared with Israel's 1.4: whether its policies, for example regarding private guns or heroin addicts, contribute to it having a homicide rate 49 times greater than West Germany's, Britain's and Japan's put together. Detroit's

TABLE 3(i): ENGLAND AND WALES – INDICTABLE OFFENCES KNOWN TO POLICE 1960–76 (OFFENCES CLEARED UP ARE SHOWN IN BRACKETS) (Figures in Thousands)

	1960	*1961*	*1962*	*1963*	*1964*	*1965*	*1966*	*1967*	*1968*	*1969*	*1970*	*1971*	*1972*	*1973*	*1974*	*1975*	*1976*
Violence against the person	15.8 (13.9)	17.6 (15.5)	17.9 (16.0)	20.1 (17.6)	23.5 (19.8)	25.5 (21.7)	26.7 (22.4)	29.0 (24.5)	31.9 (26.0)	37.8 (30.8)	41.1 (33.8)	47.0 (38.4)	52.4 (42.4)	61.3 (50.2)	63.8 (57.1)	71.0 (57.6)	77.7 (61.4)
Sexual Offences	19.9 (16.1)	20.4 (16.7)	20.0 (16.0)	20.5 (16.4)	19.9 (15.5)	20.2 (15.3)	21.3 (16.5)	22.5 (17.4)	23.4 (17.9)	23.5 (17.9)	24.2 (18.4)	23.6 (18.1)	23.5 (18.2)	25.7 (20.0)	24.7 (19.2)	23.7 (18.6)	22.2 (17.2)
*Burglary, *Robbery, *Theft and handling stolen goods, *Fraud and forgery (combined)	750.7 (307.6)	820.0 (339.0)	917.4 (375.3)	1,008.6 (404.9)	1,110.6 (406.3)	1,179.4 (427.2)	1,247.2 (464.9)	1,243.1 (475.3)	1,328.9 (518.1)								
*Burglary										420.8 (141.1)	431.5 (155.9)	451.5 (165.2)	438.7 (160.6)	393.2 (147.0)	483.8 (164.3)	521.9 (175.6)	515.4 (173.4)
*Robbery										6.0 (2.4)	6.3 (2.6)	7.5 (3.1)	8.9 (3.8)	7.3 (3.4)	8.7 (3.4)	11.3 (4.5)	11.6 (3.8)
*Theft and handling stolen goods										911.5 (363.8)	952.7 (408.3)	1,003.6 (430.9)	1,009.5 (438.1)	998.8 (432.7)	1,189.9 (501.0)	1,267.7 (525.1)	1,285.7 (521.6)
*Fraud and forgery										78.8 (63.3)	89.5 (73.8)	99.8 (83.0)	108.4 (89.6)	110.7 (91.2)	117.2 (96.7)	123.1 (103.7)	119.9 (97.6)
Malicious or criminal damage (value exceeding £20)	4.8 (3.0)	5.6 (3.2)	6.3 (3.6)	6.9 (3.9)	7.9 (3.6)	8.5 (3.8)	10.1 (4.2)	10.7 (4.5)	12.2 (4.8)	14.7 (5.6)	17.9 (7.0)	27.0 (9.2)	41.9 (15.6)	52.8 (20.5)	67.1 (25.4)	78.5 (28.7)	93.0 (32.2)
Other indictable offences	6.2 (6.1)	4.2 (4.0)	1.1 (0.9)	1.1 (0.9)	1.3 (1.0)	1.6 (1.4)	1.6 (1.4)	2.9 (1.7)	2.1 (1.8)	5.5 (5.0)	5.4 (5.0)	5.6 (5.1)	6.9 (6.4)	7.8 (7.3)	8.2 (7.5)	8.4 (7.8)	10.1 (9.4)
Total	797.5 (346.7)	867.2 (378.4)	962.7 (411.9)	1,057.2 (443.7)	1,163.1 (446.2)	1,235.2 (469.3)	1,306.9 (509.5)	1,307.3 (523.4)	1,398.6 (568.7)	1,498.7 (629.9)	1,568.4 (704.7)	1,665.7 (753.1)	1,690.2 (774.1)	1,657.7 (772.1)	1,963.4 (868.6)	2,105.6 (921.6)	2,135.0 (916.5)

* A combined figure is given until 1969 as the Theft Act 1968 redefined offences of larceny.

(ii): SCOTLAND – CRIMES AND MISCELLANEOUS OFFENCES KNOWN TO POLICE 1960–76 (THE NUMBER OF CRIMES AND MISCELLANEOUS OFFENCES CLEARED UP AS A PERCENTAGE OF THOSE KNOWN ARE SHOWN IN BRACKETS)

	1960	*1961*	*1962*	*1963*	*1964*	*1965*	*1966*	*1967*	*1968*	*1969*	*1970*	*1971*	*1972*	*1973*	*1974*	*1975*	*1976*
Crimes against the person	4,298 (84.7)	4,216 (90.4)	4,508 (85.9)	4,604 (86.9)	5,517 (87.1)	6,345 (86.9)	6,539 (86.4)	7,229 (83.7)	7,385 (83.6)	6,986 (83.1)	6,840 (82.6)	7,904 (83.3)	8,107 (84.4)	8,480 (84.8)	8,081 (80.2)	8,482 (75.8)	8,582 (74.2)
Crimes against property with violence	45,813 (24.9)	49,882 (26.9)	54,847 (27.0)	61,517 (27.2)	60,869 (25.0)	64,232 (23.4)	67,452 (24.2)	69,254 (24.2)	66,091 (24.9)	68,124 (25.1)	72,693 (25.8)	79,947 (26.1)	76,790 (25.9)	66,006 (26.6)	77,499 (27.2)	100,880 (22.9)	113,748 (18.4)
Crimes against property without violence	50,012 (43.5)	52,181 (45.2)	55,324 (46.0)	58,688 (45.5)	63,535 (43.0)	65,155 (41.8)	68,772 (43.1)	71,414 (42.7)	72,552 (42.7)	74,057 (43.6)	79,738 (44,4)	83,314 (43.9)	82,593 (43.9)	80,986 (44.3)	92,623 (45.7)	107,242 (42.3)	118,816 (39.7)
Malicious injuries to property	530 (60.4)	574 (57.1)	821 (47.5)	731 (57.5)	1,013 (46.2)	1,496 (36.4)	1,867 (35.5)	1,971 (34.3)	2,407 (31.0)	2,811 (31.9)	3,590 (31.5)	4,202 (28.7)	5,209 (27.9)	6,737 (30.9)	8,532 (29.6)	10,240 (28.0)	16,708 (20.6)
Forgery and crimes against currency	536 (96.3)	624 (95.0)	692 (100.0)	1,159 (90.9)	804 (97.8)	1,016 (91.9)	1,097 (93.5)	1,044 (90.5)	1,151 (79.9)	1,307 (86.8)	1,342 (83.5)	1,706 (80.0)	1,754 (77.4)	1,613 (72.7)	1,478 (80.9)	1,606 (83.9)	2,140 (76.3)
Other crimes not included above	1,428 (59.0)	1,443 (53.4)	1,632 (52.6)	1,700 (54.6)	1,916 (55.2)	1,897 (58.7)	2,022 (59.8)	2,301 (60.9)	2,625 (70.8)	2,685 (67.8)	3,020 (76.3)	3,650 (75.6)	3,931 (79.5)	4,193 (78.7)	4,020 (77.5)	4,032 (81.4)	4,621 (82.0)
Crimes total	102,617 (37.5)	108,920 (39.0)	117,824 (39.1)	128,399 (38.8)	133,654 (37.2)	140,141 (36.0)	147,749 (36.9)	153,213 (36.6)	152,242 (37.5)	155,970 (37.8)	167,223 (38.5)	180,723 (38.4)	178,384 (38.7)	168,015 (40.0)	192,233 (39.9)	232,482 (35.5)	264,613 (31.5)
Motor vehicle offences	84,259 (98.9)	88,066 (99.6)	89,906 (99.3)	89,671 (99.6)	101,087 (99.0)	105,300 (100.0)	117,331 (99.9)	123,242 (90.0)	119,219 (99.4)	125,610 (99.3)	129,938 (99.5)	140,655 (99.1)	145,383 (98.4)	160,077 (96.1)	165,596 (97.3)	156,165 (100.0)	148,537 (99.8)
Miscellaneous offences – excluding MVO	95,779 (91.8)	100,231 (90.8)	108,693 (90.4)	112,316 (90.8)	117,617 (88.9)	118,960 (89.3)	124,180 (89.9)	125,975 (87.9)	124,932 (86.8)	128,518 (85.7)	133,875 (87.0)	145,649 (83.0)	157,460 (81.5)	177,607 (80.5)	180,962 (80.1)	186,189 (76.0)	188,114 (74.4)
Crimes and offences Total	282,655 (74.2)	297,217 (74.4)	316,423 (73.8)	330,386 (73.0)	352,358 (72.2)	364,401 (71.9)	389,260 (72.8)	402,430 (71.8)	396,393 (71.7)	410,098 (71.7)	431,036 (71.9)	467,027 (70.6)	481,227 (70.7)	505,699 (72.0)	538,791 (71.1)	576,836 (66.7)	601,266 (61.8)

(iii): NORTHERN IRELAND – INDICTABLE OFFENCES KNOWN TO THE POLICE 1960–76 (OFFENCES CLEARED UP ARE SHOWN IN BRACKETS)

	1960	*1961*	*1962*	*1963*	*1964*	*1965*	*1966*	*1967*	*1968*	*1969*	*1970*	*1971*	*1972*	*1973*	*1974*	*1975*	*1976*
Offences against the person	162 (151)	110 (89)	175 (168)	245 (225)	247 (196)	210 (193)	264 (224)	249 (215)	389 (309)	1,092 (268)	534 (275)	1,479 (425)	2,797 (298)	2,129 (444)	2,220 (358)	2,036 (306)	2,178 (561)
Sexual offences	181 (165)	222 (206)	158 (157)	181 (172)	197 (191)	236 (223)	198 (191)	247 (242)	290 (281)	223 (213)	203 (189)	159 (146)	149 (136)	170 (142)	228 (216)	238 (168)	269 (214)
Burglary	2,786 (1,580)	3.010 (1,592)	3,201 (1,746)	3,435 (2,033)	3,198 (1,836)	3,915 (2,143)	4,861 (2,424)	4,918 (2,335)	5,455 (2,503)	7,509 (2,728)	11,405 (3,314)	10,481 (2,724)	9,439 (1,616)	9,888 (2,114)	11,436 (2,470)	14,149 (2,110)	15,833 (2,526)
Robbery	35 (18)	39 (15)	48 (48)	27 (10)	23 (13)	43 (20)	37 (19)	45 (26)	50 (25)	89 (40)	109 (29)	640 (45)	2,310 (155)	1,886 (231)	2,092 (223)	1,962 (272)	2,052 (285)
Theft (including handling)	4,461 (2,482)	5,589 (2,837)	5,672 (3,444)	5,930 (3,324)	5,677 (3,059)	6,572 (3,537)	8,135 (3,885)	8,413 (4,115)	8,704 (5,312)	8,363 (4,534)	9,913 (5,166)	9,701 (4,954)	9,188 (3,571)	9,209 (3,862)	9,269 (4,138)	13,209 (3,543)	12,884 (3,768)
Fraud and forgery	476 (431)	491 (398)	611 (532)	517 (518)	534 (483)	1,237 (1,185)	635 (603)	983 (976)	410 (396)	356 (347)	368 (338)	564 (446)	445 (331)	368 (282)	849 (814)	930 (426)	1,379 (499)
Criminal damage	285 (203)	329 (227)	318 (257)	325 (264)	429 (322)	460 (369)	426 (266)	421 (316)	824 (506)	2,535 (487)	2,034 (534)	7,401 (724)	10,709 (768)	7,190 (902)	5,971 (726)	3,744 (389)	4,164 (800)
Other indictable offences	74 (73)	60 (59)	103 (103)	199 (199)	123 (121)	173 (173)	119 (119)	128 (127)	172 (172)	136 (115)	226 (224)	403 (358)	847 (650)	1,217 (873)	1,249 (731)	971 (557)	1,020 (714)
Total	8,460 (5,103)	9,850 (5,423)	10,286 (6,435)	10,859 (6,745)	10,428 (6,221)	12,846 (7,843)	14,673 (7,732)	15,404 (8,352)	16,294 (9,504)	20,303 (8,732)	24,810 (10,069)	30,828 (9,822)	35,884 (7,525)	32,057 (8,850)	33,314 (9,676)	37,239 (7,771)	39,779 (9,367)

murder rate is over 48 killings per 100,000 population; statistically, according to the Massachusetts Institute of Technology, one out of every eleven children born in the city of Atlanta will be murdered if he or she stays there; and one in every six males in Harlem will be murdered by the age of sixty-five. Crime is also rising in almost every part of Europe: in the Republic of Eire, serious crimes rose by 15 per cent and offences against the person by 20 per cent in 1977. The police's detection rate has dropped to a third of all offences; only £1 million of £8 million taken in robberies in that year has been recovered. In France, the total of serious offences increased from 581,618 to 1,763,372 in the decade up to 1973. Armed robberies in Paris increased by 52 per cent in 1977 alone. Italy, where the police have the additional burden of an archaic legal system, saw in 1975–6 1,479,000 out of 1,945,000 crimes go unpunished (the number of burglaries in Turin, for example, rose from 4,702 in 1953 to 77,642 in 1974, while the population only increased by a factor of two), while the escalation of kidnappings – both political and as a commercial private enterprise – is public knowledge.

Following the pattern of multinational corporations, crime itself is increasingly becoming more international; as Jim Crane, recently an Assistant Commissioner in Scotland Yard's Fraud Squad, describes, 'One project can embrace two or, quite commonly, four or five countries. You may have a fraud conceived in New York, with a second stage in Panama, a third in Bermuda and a fourth in Switzerland or Britain, with the victims in another country.'

The Fraud Squad overstretched

Fraud detection presents a special problem for the police, even were they not overworked in other directions. As a former Commissioner, Sir Harold Scott, said, 'The investigation of fraud, especially company fraud, is a highly specialized business calling for a knowledge of company law and accountancy that the average CID officer does not possess.' Several prosecutions have not been launched until after detailed exposures have been made by newspapers despite the libel risk. At present the London Fraud Squad of less than ninety men does not include professional accountants and is attempting to unravel far more cases than it can cope with: although its members often work a sixteen-hour day for several weeks running, a case such as the Rolls Razor one can take five years to complete and others have taken twice as long. It is a sensitive, as well as an extremely complex, field: public knowledge that the Fraud Squad are investigating almost inevitably spells ruin for a company or an individual, and competitors have been known to arrange 'stings' or to bait the Fraud Squad's interest in order to discredit a rival. Members of the Squad, who are paid the same as other CID men and a derisory fraction of the earnings of most of those they investigate, are only seconded to it and can have no career structure in the Squad. Chief superintendent Hudson, who moved from the Fraud to the Murder Squad, explains that the problem is that 'the Fraud Squad is a relatively small unit, so chances of promotion are restricted. We can't stand in a man's way if he finds his opportunity for promotion in another branch slipping away.' Consequently new men have continually to be recruited from the regular force, and volunteers are not always forthcoming. After about four years many members, just at the time when they are gaining experience in threading their way more easily through balance sheets and prospectuses, revert to wholly different types of police work elsewhere. This state of affairs is indefensible, and an encouragement to the less reputable entrepreneurs in the City. The Fraud Squad's complement should be increased to 300 – one tenth of whom should be qualified accountants (whatever their height) – so that it can provide a proper career to retain men specializing in its critical task.

Another even greater priority for reinforcement is Northern Ireland, whose total police service is at least 2,000 men (34 per cent) below its real needs. On top of the problems caused by the real danger and devastation, the police cannot afford to ignore any of the 6,000 bomb warnings which annually turn out to be hoaxes in Belfast. More than a third of the RUC's entire strength is tied up in guarding different leaders of the community from assassination. The recent attempts by the IRA to spread its campaign to England shows how vulnerable is any protection that inadequate police reserves can offer against violence: at present there are no more than 7,000 officers on duty at any one time in London, but to provide an effective round-the-clock guard even for MPs and their families alone would require 5,000 officers.

The burden on the urban CID

The most serious continual overwork falls on the shoulders of inner urban officers. Sir Colin Woods, the self-effacing but able Chief Inspector of Constabulary, points out that the more successful detectives are in making arrests, the more they are subsequently tied up in court and consequently have less chance of solving new crime. Sir Robert Mark's view is that some fines imposed for violence are so derisory that they do not justify the police's time in court: 'the withdrawal of police officers from the street for futile court appearances has the cumulative effect of facilitating burglary and petty crime without discouraging hooliganism and violence'.

The quality and patterns of professional crime have changed drastically with the increase in the numbers of cars and lorries, and major thefts are becoming more and more the work of organized teams who make full use of motorways and aircraft. Some of the cash flowing into the underworld is funnelled into financing even more ambitious crimes. Criminal leaders are now known to look after the welfare of families of men who are caught, to rehearse an operation with several dummy-runs, and to plan a jailbreak in order to obtain a specialist for a particular job. Modern criminals blend into society much more easily than their predecessors. Many of the old, close communities based on social areas have broken up: the big men the police seek are now much more likely to be living in respectable suburbia than in a Dickensian slum. Today's captains of the crime industry frequently come from social locations previously little known to the police, and well outside the CID's customary net of informers: 'company director' is an increasingly popular description for defendants to give in court.

Another of the difficulties the CID currently face is the large number of offences now being committed by skilled amateurs who inconsiderately omit to conform to traditional patterns or feature in any criminal record file. Commander John Nesbitt of Northumbria emphasizes the additional effects of 'a dramatic increase in under age drinking', and states that 'the majority of assaults on the police are by people who are under the influence'. In some places the basic beat system of policing has itself broken down, despite cadets increasingly being pressed into regular work: as an economy, the number of cadets in 1978 were only half what they were in 1974. The last Royal Commission on the police visited one town with a population of 110,000 where it had been possible to send only three policemen – all of them probationers – out on beat-duty the previous day. In 1975 there were times when none of the six stations of London's E Division could spare any man to put on the beat. But the root of overwork in the police lies in the city CIDs, where some men are working more than seventy hours a week and cannot do more without risk of breaking down under the strain. Some Flying Squad officers work 120 hours of overtime a month. If detectives observed a strict forty-hour week, the strength of the Metropolitan CID would need to be doubled. The burden on individual officers varies widely according to the locality: each CID officer at Sydenham station on the outskirts of London, for instance, has an annual average case-load of 723, while the mean for those at West Drayton is only 161. The Dixon Committee reported that the most any one detective can handle properly is 150 cases a year; J. Edgar Hoover described a case-load of 20 per FBI agent as 'too high' to a Congressional sub-committee. Whereas Barlow's or Kojak's teams on television often seem to have a fortnight to concentrate on a single crime, in Leeds detectives had to investigate some 100 cases during such a period. But a case-load total alone is not necessarily a significant guide: one child murder not long ago required visits to 39,000 homes and necessitated 14,000 written statements and 21,000 telephone calls to be taken by the police over a period of seventy-eight weeks. Even a single traffic case can consume sixteen hours in paperwork.

If the current trend of crime is to be reversed, the number of CID officers in the most hard-pressed urban areas needs to be increased by at least one third. On each occasion that an experienced detective retires or is moved, invaluable information is inevitably lost, and detectives complain that at present they have not the time to cultivate the new contacts necessary to gather intelligence. Any crime prevention role has had to be shelved; the sole possibility is 'fire brigade policing' – trying to find the men to deal with one emergency before the next one breaks. At a time when the numbers of offences, traffic and new duties are all increasing inexorably, some city police forces continue to be seriously below strength, and the authorized establishments underestimate real needs. Overall the Metropolitan London force at the beginning of 1978 was 4,389 officers below its nominal authorized establishment of 26,628, a figure that has not been changed for some time and which many experts believe should, but for the economic situation, realistically be much nearer 32,500. Sir David McNee went on record in his evidence to the Edmund Davies committee that the figure should be 'at least 31,000'. (New York City, which is less than half the size of London in area, has 32,000 officers.) One serious consequence of the present pressure on the police is the likelihood of success in petty crime acting as an encouragement to greater ambition. 'The belief is gaining hold in some quarters that crime pays,' stated the Inspectors of Constabulary in 1960, and the number of offenders who ask courts to take into consideration a list of undetected crimes running into three figures shows that this belief is making converts. One man arrested in London in October 1976 admitted to the police that he was responsible for burglaries or attempted burglaries at some 600 houses since his release from prison only eight months previously. Whether as a cause or effect of the crime statistics, more graduates must be becoming criminals than policemen each year.

Another result is that police forces have increasingly been compelled to allot priorities in investigation, and now concentrate on selected 'target' criminals. In the Catford area, the investigation of individual burglaries has had to be discontinued entirely, and a number of London police stations are unable to be manned in the night-time. Understandably, offences against a person are given attention first, both for their importance and because they are more likely to be solved: 62 per cent of all assaults (including homicide) in London in 1975 were cleared up, compared with only 15 per cent of burglaries and 12 per cent of autocrime (thefts of or from cars or bicycles). Murder cases receive absolute precedence: in England and

Wales outside London in 1975, the 375 reported cases of homicide – which includes manslaughter and infanticide as well as murder – actually had a 100 per cent clear-up rate, and the 370 cases of attempted murder a 99 per cent one; but urban CID officers will candidly admit they have little or no time to give such matters as vandalism or attempting to trace stolen car radios. Larceny of vehicles in London is now so frequent that lists of over 1,000 become dead letters. The inevitable selection of offences and areas for priority causes resentment amongst articulate householders and car-owners, who feel a need for the police only when they personally lose something, and then discover that their loss receives lowest priority of all. Nor does everyone agree which offences are the most serious. Mr James Anderton, the Methodist lay preacher chief constable of Greater Manchester, ordered his men to make an intensive drive against allegedly pornographic booksellers. (Not all Mancunians thought that the police's claim to be seriously undermanned had been helped by this new policy.) Drunk drivers are objectively a more important priority than burglars, since they threaten lives, not merely property; but drunken driving is still socially accepted, and in one recent case eighteen doctors successively refused the police's request to come to examine a driver suspected of being intoxicated. Police officers in Nottingham estimate that 70 per cent of drivers who are drunk when arrested are able to sober up before a doctor can be found who can be persuaded to test them. A steadily increasing number of British car-drivers are coming to laugh at their fixed penalty tickets as much as foreign diplomats have always done, because the police are no longer able to trace or prosecute them (21 per cent succeeded in evading any penalty in 1969, compared with under 10 per cent three years earlier). Some companies regularly send a cheque for accrued tickets as a matter-of-course tax-deduction. A different but persistent irritant is created by burglar alarms, 98 per cent of whose 158,000 annual calls in London are false, but each of which demands emergency police time and attention. They create what the Commissioner describes as 'an extremely serious problem' for the police – as well as for the alarms' unfortunate neighbours – by at times completely blocking the 999 system so that genuine emergency calls cannot get through.

Officers, in the end, have to cope with things as they are, not as they would like them to be. What are the remedies for the tightening pressure on the police? The first is to spare them unnecessary or peripheral duties wherever possible, so that they can concentrate on essential work. Apart from the 'decriminalization' of certain activities proposed in the next chapter, the police should be relieved of all their current responsibilities for such matters as licensing dogs, charitable street-collections or taxi cabs. A review of court procedures affecting the police should be executed urgently; as an immediate start, police officers should no longer be required to waste their professionally-trained time acting as ushers in magistrates' courts. (Trial delays also are getting worse: nearly one in five defendants in 1977 had to wait over twenty weeks for trial – almost twice as many as in 1975.) Some idea of the annually increasing new burdens that at present are cumulatively being loaded on to the police is conveyed by the following list:

TABLE 4: LEGISLATION PASSED SINCE 1960 WHICH HAS AFFECTED THE WORK AND DUTIES OF THE POLICE

(ENGLAND AND WALES)
Movement of Animals (Records) Order 1960
Cycling on the Highways Regulations 1960
Road Traffic Act 1960
Poison Rules 1960
Indecency with Children Act 1960
Motor Vehicles (Tests) (Regulations) 1960
Betting and Gaming Act 1960
Road Traffic and Road Improvement Act 1960
Noise Abatement Act 1960
Motor Vehicles (Test) (Exemptions) Regulations 1961
Dangerous Drugs Regulations 1961
Restriction of Offensive Weapons Act 1961
Mock Auctions Act 1961
Summary Jurisdiction (Children and Young Persons) Rules 1961
Licensing Act 1961

Criminal Justice Administration Act 1961
Commonwealth Immigrants Act 1962
Air Guns and Shot Guns etc. Act 1962
Lotteries and Gaming Act 1962
Betting, Gaming and Licensing Act 1963
Children and Young Persons Act 1963
Licensing Act 1964
Police Act 1964
Betting, Gaming and Lotteries Act 1964
Malicious Damage Act 1964
Obscene Publications Act 1964
Scrap Metal Dealers Act 1964
Drugs (Prevention of Misuse) Act 1964
Road Vehicle Lighting Regulations 1964
Dangerous Drugs Act 1965
Criminal Evidence Act 1965
Rent Act 1965
Race Relations Act 1965
Firearms Act 1965
Road Safety Act 1967
Criminal Law Act 1967
Sexual Offences Act 1967
Road Traffic (Amendment) Act 1967
Criminal Justice Act 1967
Dangerous Drugs Act 1967
Commonwealth Immigrants Act 1968
Firearms Act 1968
Theft Act 1968
Clean Air Act 1968
Gaming Act 1968
Transport Act 1968
Vehicles and Driving Licenses Act 1969
Children and Young Persons Act 1969
Police Act 1969
Indecent Advertisement (Amendment) Act 1970
Road Traffic Disqualification Act 1970
Vehicles Excise Act 1971
Courts Act 1971
Criminal Damage Act 1971
Road Traffic Act 1972
Deposit of Poisonous Waste Act 1972
Criminal Justice Act 1972
Misuse of Drugs Act 1972
Hallmarking Act 1973

Administration of Justice Act 1973
London Cab Act 1973
Heavy Commercial Vehicles (Controls and Regulations) Act 1973
Employment of Children Act 1973
Powers of Criminal Courts Act 1973
Road Traffic Act 1974
Rehabilitation of Offenders Act 1974
Rabies Act 1974
Policing of Airports Act 1974
Emergency Powers Regulations 1974
Safety of Sports Grounds Act 1975
Public Service Vehicles (Arrest of Offenders) Act 1975
Children Act 1975
Evidence (Proceedings in other Jurisdictions) Act 1975
Guard Dogs Act 1975
Mental Health (Amendment) Act 1975
Lotteries Act 1975
International Road Haulage Permits Act 1975
Unsolicited Goods and Services (Amendment) Act 1975
Road Traffic (Drivers' Ages and Hours of Work) Act 1976
Sexual Offences (Amendment) Act 1976
Motor Cycle Crash-Helmets (Religious Exemption) Act 1976
Lotteries and Amusements Act 1976
Licensing (Amendment) Act 1976
Fatal Accidents Act 1976
Explosives (Age of Purchase Etc) Act 1976
Domestic Violence and Matrimonial Proceedings Act 1976
Dangerous Wild Animals Act 1976
Police Act 1976
Prevention of Terrorism (Temporary Provisions) Act 1976
Race Relations Act 1976
Protection from Eviction Act 1977
Passenger Vehicles (Experimental Areas) Act 1977
Minibus Act 1977
Licensing (Amendment) Act 1977
Criminal Law Act 1977
Administration of Justice Act 1977
The Bail Act 1977

NORTHERN IRELAND

Companies Act (Northern Ireland) 1960
Dogs Act (Northern Ireland) 1960

Attempted Rape Act (Northern Ireland) 1960
Litter Act (Northern Ireland) 1960
Radioactive Substances Act 1960
Mental Health Act (Northern Ireland) 1961
Restriction of Offensive Weapons Act 1961
Commonwealth Immigrants Act 1962
Electoral Law Act (Northern Ireland) 1962
Drugs (Prevention of Misuse) Act 1964
Road Traffic Act (Northern Ireland) 1964
Protection of Depositors Act (Northern Ireland) 1964
Magistrates' Courts Act (Northern Ireland) 1964
Criminal Injuries (Amendment) Act (Northern Ireland) 1964
Criminal Evidence Act (Northern Ireland) 1965
Backing of Warrants (Republic of Ireland) Act 1965
Factories Act (Northern Ireland) 1965
Dangerous Drugs Act 1965
Criminal Justice Act (Northern Ireland) 1966
Fisheries Act (Northern Ireland) 1966
County Courts Act 1959 (Reprint to 1966)
Transport Act (Northern Ireland) 1966
Dangerous Drugs Act 1967
Criminal Law Act (Northern Ireland) 1967
Criminal Justice Act (Northern Ireland) 1967
Road Traffic Act 1967
Road Traffic Act (Northern Ireland) 1967
Registration of Clubs Act (Northern Ireland) 1967
Road Transport Act (Northern Ireland) 1967
Children and Young Persons Act (Northern Ireland) 1968
Criminal Procedure (Committal for Trial) Act (Northern Ireland) 1968
Criminal Justice (Miscellaneous Provisions) Act (Northern Ireland) 1968
Treatment of Offenders Act (Northern Ireland) 1968
Criminal Injuries to Persons (Compensation) Act (Northern Ireland) 1968
Livestock (Protection from Dogs) Act (Northern Ireland) 1968
Trade Descriptions Act 1968
Road Traffic Act (Northern Ireland) 1968
Firearms Act (Northern Ireland) 1969
Judgements (Enforcement) Act (Northern Ireland) 1969
Theft Act (Northern Ireland) 1969
Motor Vehicles and Refuse (Disposal) Act (Northern Ireland) 1969
Fire Services Act (Northern Ireland) 1969
Protection of Person and Property Act (Northern Ireland) 1969

Post Office Act 1969
Air Navigation Order 1970
Criminal Injuries (Amendment) Act (Northern Ireland) 1970
Explosives Act (Northern Ireland) 1970
Police Act (Northern Ireland) 1970
Prevention of Incitement to Hatred Act (Northern Ireland) 1970
Printed Documents Act (Northern Ireland) 1970
Public Order Act (Northern Ireland) 1970
Road Traffic Act (Northern Ireland) 1970
Radiological Protection Act 1970
Misuse of Drugs Act 1971
Immigration Act 1971
Criminal Injuries to Property (Compensation) Act (Northern Ireland) 1971
Firearms (Amendment) Act 1971
Historic Monuments Act (Northern Ireland) 1971
Licensing Act (Northern Ireland) 1971
Public Order (Amendment) Act (Northern Ireland) 1971
Carriage Act 1971
Evidence of Alibi Act (Northern Ireland) 1972
Miscellaneous Transferred Excise Duties Act (Northern Ireland) 1972
Vehicles Excise Act (Northern Ireland) 1972
Welfare of Animals Act (Northern Ireland) 1972
Detention of Terrorists Order (Northern Ireland) 1972
Explosives (Northern Ireland) Order 1972
Prosecution of Offences (Northern Ireland) Order 1972
Trade Descriptions Act 1972
Firearms (Amendment) (Northern Ireland) Order 1973
Road Traffic (Amendment) (Northern Ireland) Order 1973
Emergency Provisions Act 1973
Supply of Goods (Implied Terms) Act 1973
Prevention of Terrorism (Temporary Provisions) Act 1974
Biological Weapons Act 1974
Northern Ireland (Young Persons) Act 1974
Fines (Northern Ireland) Order 1974
Criminal Jurisdiction Act 1975
Northern Ireland (Emergency Provisions) (Amendment) Act 1975
Diseases of Animals (Northern Ireland) Order 1975
Diseases of Animals (Amendment) (Northern Ireland) Order 1975
Armed Forces Act 1976
Prevention of Terrorism (Temporary Provisions) Act 1976
The Animals (Northern Ireland) Order 1976
The Treatment of Offenders (Northern Ireland) Order 1976

The Criminal Damage (Northern Ireland) Order 1977
Rabies (Control) Order (Northern Ireland) 1977
Criminal Law (Amendment) (Northern Ireland) Order 1977
Northern Ireland (Emergency Provisions) Act 1973 (Amendment) Order 1977
The Police (Northern Ireland) Order 1977

SCOTLAND

Road Traffic Act 1960
Noise Abatement Act 1960
Mental Health (Scotland) Act 1960
Restriction of Offensive Weapons Act 1961
Mock Auctions Act 1961
Criminal Justice Act 1961
Commonwealth Immigrants Act 1962
Licensing (Scotland) Act 1962
Betting Gaming & Lotteries Act 1963
Deer (Scotland) Act 1963
Children and Young Persons Act 1963
Police Act 1964
Emergency Powers Act 1964
Drugs (Prevention of Misuse) Act 1964
Criminal Evidence Act 1965
Race Relations Act 1965
Rent Act 1965
Lost Property (Scotland) Act 1965
Police (Scotland) Act 1967
Criminal Justice Act 1967
Deer (Amendment) (Scotland) Act 1967
Social Work (Scotland) Act 1968
Firearms Act 1968
Clean Air Act 1968
Gaming Act 1968
Transport Act 1968
Race Relations Act 1968
Sale of Venison (Scotland) Act 1968
Vehicle and Driving Licences Act 1969
Children and Young Persons Act 1969
Police Act 1969
Indecent Advertisement (Amendment) Act 1970
Game Act 1970
Vehicles (Excise) Act 1971

Misuse of Drugs Act 1971
Road Traffic Act 1972
Road Traffic (Foreign Vehicles) Act 1972
Deposit of Poisonous Waste Act 1972
Criminal Justice Act 1972
Gaming (Amendment) Act 1973
Hallmarking Act 1973
Heavy Commercial Vehicles (Controls & Regulations) Act 1973
Employment of Children Act 1973
Powers of Criminal Courts Act 1973
Road Traffic Act 1974
Rehabilitation of Offenders Act 1974
Rabies Act 1974
Policing of Airports Act 1974
Prevention of Terrorism Act 1974
Safety of Sports Grounds Act 1975
Children Act 1975
Evidence (Proceedings in Other Jurisdictions) Act 1975
Guard Dogs Act 1975
Lotteries Act 1975
International Road Haulage Permits Act 1975
Unsolicited Goods and Services (Amendment) Act 1975
Conservation of Wild Creatures and Wild Plants Act 1975
Diseases of Animals Act 1975
Criminal Procedure (Scotland) Act 1975
Salmon and Freshwater Fisheries Act 1975
Road Traffic (Drivers' Ages and Hours of Work) Act 1976
Motor Cycle Crash-Helmets (Religious Exemption) Act 1976
Lotteries and Amusements Act 1976
Explosives (Age of Purchase) Act 1976
Dangerous Wild Animals 1976
Prevention of Terrorism (Temporary Provisions) Act 1976
Race Relations Act 1976
Bail Act 1976
Freshwater and Salmon Fisheries (Scotland) Act 1976
Licensing (Scotland) Act 1976
Sexual Offences (Scotland) Act 1976
Passenger Vehicles (Experimental Areas) Act 1977
Minibus Act 1977
Criminal Law Act 1977
Administration of Justice Act 1977
Roe Deer (Close Seasons) Act 1977

Every Parliamentary Bill and the 2,000 annual Statutory

Instruments ought in future to have to contain a statement of any additional cost and manpower its provisions entail for the police.

Civilian assistance

Relief could also be extended by using more civilians to assist the police with certain parts of their work. The total number of civilian staff used by police forces in England and Wales including London increased from 10,984 in 1960 to 34,119 in 1977. The number of traffic wardens rose from 338 in 1961 to 5,087 in 1977. Since the introduction of traffic wardens, London's traffic has doubled in volume but its average speed is now 5 m.p.h. faster – principally, in Scotland Yard's view, due to the effect of the wardens. These are easier to recruit than regular police officers, because they are not subject to such strict requirements of physique and age. In London, where financial cutbacks have reduced the number of traffic wardens to 1,500, Sir David McNee estimates that 2,500 are needed even to enforce adequately the present waiting restrictions. The recent reduction makes no financial sense, as the burden of each warden's salary is more than offset by the penalty revenue he or she produces. Their work could easily be expanded to cover more duties at peak hours, when at present regular officers have to be brought in off the beat twice a day. (It is interesting that in Algeria Boy Scouts have been doing traffic duty on one day a week when the regular policeman has his rest-day, and even have powers to arrest and fine.) In addition, this policy would increase the interest of the wardens' role – its present negative and limited nature is responsible for a high rate of early resignations. In Scotland, where some wardens voluntarily carry personal radio sets, David Gray, the Inspector of Constabulary, would like to see them 'become the eyes and ears of the police as an auxiliary [though] we would be shattered at the idea of them developing into a separate traffic corps'.

There is a need as well for more civilian clerical staff, who are also not so difficult to recruit as uniformed men and women. The average direct annual cost of employing a civilian in 1977 was £3,200 and for a traffic warden £2,895, compared with £4,953 for a police officer excluding his rent allowance or housing costs (a disparity which is now greatly increased by the 1978 police pay award). Overall civilians are more economical as well because they do not need to qualify for the exceptionally early and generous pension which is awarded to policemen after twenty-five years service. More of them could save trained detectives the valuable time the latter spend often laboriously typing their reports with one finger. After the Second World War Bradford attached two shorthand-typists to each division to act as secretaries to the CID: as a result, the time the detectives were able to spend in the actual investigation of crimes increased from 55 per cent to 85 per cent, and the clear-up rate rose accordingly. Despite the Oaksey Committee's recommendation that this should be followed everywhere, it has not yet been done. One English police officer voiced a frequently heard complaint when he said, 'When I joined this force it was 196 strong and now it is about 350, yet there are no extra men out on the beat. All these additional men have been swallowed up by paperwork and the specialist departments. That's the chief problem with the job now: you're tied down with paperwork when you should be out on the beat.' Manhattan police – perhaps slightly hyperbolically – estimate they spend 40 per cent of their working time in court work and procedures, and a further 40 per cent in their station-houses doing paperwork. Scene-of-crime officers, whose job is meticulously to search for clues, are now often civilians who are too short or whose eyesight (ironically) is considered too poor for them to qualify as regular policemen. They form a crucial link for the success of forensic science: Edmund Lochard of Lyons University in his theory of 'criminal interchange' suggested that someone committing a crime nearly always unwittingly leaves some clue at its scene and takes some particle (for example of blood, earth, or paint) away with him.

In Ayrshire, at the suggestion of management consultants, twenty civilian girls run 'police shops' linking the public's calls to available mobile policemen: this experiment initiated by the then chief constable Quintin Wilson saves £27,000 a year and spreads the workload more evenly between the Ballantrae officer's previous average of 10 offences a year and the Auchinleck one's 102. Unfortunately, civilians, traffic wardens and cadets were all made priority targets for cut-backs during the economic restraint of 1976–77.

TABLE 5: CIVILIAN POLICE STAFF, CADETS, AND TRAFFIC WARDENS (ENGLAND AND WALES OUTSIDE METROPOLITAN LONDON)

Year	*Civilian staff*	*Cadets*		*Traffic wardens*	
		men	*girls*	*men*	*women*
1967	13,110	3,377	521	2,048	897
1968	13,726	3,018	447	1,973	927
1969	14,722	2,945	525	2,044	1,030
1970	15,135	2,975	615	2,229	1,229
1971	16,387	3,247	737	2,468	1,405
1972	17,057	3,359	676	2,656	1,645
1973	17,749	3,237	721	2,493	1,868
1974	19,563	3,511	929	2,291	1,861
1975	20,355	3,163	986	2,402	1,961
1976	20,189	2,117	847	2,270	1,792
1977	19,814	1,108	588	2,008	1,547

There have recently been suggestions that 'civilianization' should in fact be further extended by, for example, using specialized family service units to intercede in family disputes – 'domestics', as policemen term them – whose incidence occasions many more calls to the police than robberies do. But any new extension of civilian duties meets increasing opposition from Police Federation members, ostensibly because of reasons such as the confidentiality of some of the information dealt with, but in reality because of the threat civilians present to the service's professionalism and quasi-union bargaining power. Civilian scene-of-crime officers are denounced as being 'the thin end of a wedge leading to back-door entry to the CID', and the Federation told the government flatly that a plan for a traffic corps to take over all traffic work from the police was 'not on'. Civilians employed on police work are criticized by regular officers both for undercutting them and for being paid more than them – PC Stewart Reeves of Cheshire cited one civilian with three years' service whose pay was greater than that of a detective-constable after eight years. David Gray, HM Chief Inspector of the Scottish police, points out:

> Resentment is increased when it is found on occasion that the civilians sometimes need not do night duty or work at weekends when policemen are expected to cover for them; and that when they are on stand-by night duty they may be entitled to very substantial allowances to which the policeman is not entitled and which have the effect of making police remuneration appear poor in comparison. The effect on the efficiency of the service in the event of withdrawal of civilian labour is also regularly raised and here we are able to explain that sufficient police presence and expertise is retained in all operational branches of the service to ensure adequate police coverage should an emergency occur.

(Civilian police drivers did indeed go on strike in August 1978.) Several policemen will also admit privately that they covet quiet civilian-type jobs such as being an usher in court, particularly in the years approaching their retirement.

The rise of private security companies

The spectacular recent growth of private security companies can be seen as one reflection of the inevitable gaps in the service provided by the police through shortage of men and equipment. To some people, this rapid expansion of unaccountable private armies is a more insidious threat to democracy than any tendency towards a stronger national police would be; to others, it appears merely a return to the situation of the centuries prior to professional policing – and one, moreover, financed by an accurate private levy which saves the public's taxes and rates, since those whose business particularly needs protection pay the protection money. The chairman of Securicor, Britain's largest security company, argues that companies that 'create temptation' by assembling large amounts of valuable assets for profit should themselves pay to protect them, rather than expect others to do this for them. Some security companies have now spread their operations across national boundaries throughout the world: one British company for example has flourishing subsidiaries in Iran, South Africa and Thailand. France now has at least 32,000 private guards in over 200 firms; Italy more than 40,000 armed men in 500 private organizations; West Germany twice that number. In Britain there are well over 41,000 guards (the private equivalent of uniformed policemen), backed up by a further 33,500 managerial and security staff, in 800 firms in addition to more than 20,000 men employed in private detective agencies (parallel to private CID men) or in private firms' security forces. (There are also fifteen small police forces attached to government departments or other public authorities, such as the 4,800-strong Ministry of Defence police, the Atomic Energy Authority police, and the 2,000-strong British Transport Police. They have many of the attributes but few of the advantages of the regular police and their standards and conditions vary considerably.) The private commercial firm of Securicor alone transports over £60,000 million in cash each year and now has 23,000 employees, compared with 3,000 when I wrote *The Police* in 1963 and fewer than 1,000 men in 1960. By mid-1978 its turnover had risen to £60 million, and its half-time profit had grown by 22 per cent to £2.4 million. *The Times* reported that 'Guarding private property is a function where the group sees itself progressively taking over the role of an over-stretched police force'. The security industry in Britain estimates its turnover exceeds £180 million a year and that, in addition to 2,000 armoured vehicles, its total manpower of over 148,000 is now comfortably greater than that of the police themselves. Candidates for deportation in the detention centre at Heathrow Airport are guarded by private officers from Securicor, hired by the Home Office on a £300,000 annual contract. The Foreign Office employs several private security firms such as Security Express and KMS, to provide bodyguards for Embassy staff abroad. Over these firms, unlike in most other countries, there is in Britain no public control whatsoever. Any ex-convict can start one: there is no licensing of firms, no requirement about minimum standards or training, and (unlike the screening required for midwives or taxi-drivers) no checking of whether their employees have a criminal record. Two men set up a security company immediately on their release from Strangeways Prison. Several men who had been sacked from some docks for dishonesty were hired by a security firm to guard the same premises. One firm was run by a man with eight convictions, mainly for violence. Errors about employees can occur even in the police – as when the murderer Christie was enrolled as a Reserve policeman despite his nine previous convictions ranging from fraud to violence – but some security companies, facing keen competition in striving to meet an apparently inexhaustible market, reputedly ask fewer questions than others. Criminal gangs have been known to plant 'moles' or 'sleepers' inside security companies, who then pass them inside information. One man employed by a firm to guard currency at Heathrow had fourteen previous convictions, including several for armed robbery. He, and £2 million of currency, disappeared. A Midlands policeman told of another case: 'I was on duty late at night, and I saw a man in a police uniform with a dog. I thought at first he was a dog handler. Then I got close and I recognized him. He was a man I'd knocked off once for housebreaking. He and his brother had started a security firm. I told the chief constable, but there was nothing we could do.'

Low pay often accompanies low standards. Security firms' drivers, on a basic weekly wage that can be as low as £50, annually move more than £23,000 million of cash in Britain. It is not surprising that a proportion succumb. Group 4, Britain's second largest security company but the largest in Europe, has proposed that – as in Sweden – prospective employees should first be required to obtain a certificate themselves from a police station which absolved them from having a criminal past. At present such records are confidential and kept from employers though, as one man involved in this field explained, 'There is no doubt there is an old-boys' network which sometimes helps us to discover whether a man has a criminal record, but it is wrong that we should be placed in this situation.' The Rehabilitation of Offenders Act, which expunges many offences from a person's record after a given number of years, has added a new complication. It is widely believed that the reasons why so many former police officers are attractive to security companies includes their knowledge of criminal records. Security

Express at one time would only employ ex-policemen; Securicor has thirteen former chief constables on its staff. The links with the police mean that ambushes of bank-robbers can be arranged; but it is deplorable that private security companies can offer better inducements than the public police service itself.

In the same year that William Fargo was joining Henry Wells at the American Express Company to start the first modern security firm, Pinkerton's, the original private detective agency, was also being founded in America in 1852 – ironically by a former labour agitator from the Gorbals who had been forced to flee across the Atlantic because of his involvement in the Chartist movement, and who had become the first detective of Cook County, Chicago. Begun as a result of the failure of the US's national and local administrations to provide an adequate police service, Pinkerton's uncovered a plot to assassinate President-elect Lincoln in 1861, and laid the basis of the Federal secret service; but it soon became popularly – and unpopularly – politically identified with the interest of its big business clients. What is the standing of security firms today? Private detective firms in particular are little loved by the police, and many officers are suspicious of anybody who like themselves wears a uniform. Sir Douglas Osmond, recently the chief constable of Hampshire, has said that the use of private security men to deal with industrial unrest or to patrol social functions such as pop festivals is totally alien to the British way of life. The National Council for Civil Liberties has protested at such firms using dogs to clear gipsies and squatters, and at the British government itself employing them to guard detention centres and immigrants at Harmondsworth. Private security firms and detective agencies should be subject to an independent board for complaints just as much as the regular police. Robert Kilroy-Silk MP believes that

> increasingly they are taking over traditional police functions, even to the extent of escorting prisoners. It is the private police who offer the greatest potential dangers. Mercenaries of big business, they go where the work is. And if that involves undercover work in trade unions, infiltrating

and reporting on the loyalty of employees, or breaking up strikes, student sit-ins, squatter occupations or gipsy encampments, they will do it. Increasingly they tread on ground the police would avoid, as when evicting students from Hornsey College in 1968. All police forces need to be placed firmly in a constitutional framework and be subject to rigid controls. With minor exceptions, this condition is met by the official police. The private police, one of whose functions is the invasion of individual privacy, are subject to few limitations. Britain is almost alone in not having laws on licensing of private detectives and security agencies.

The private firms are very anxious to avoid any threatening image. They have stopped the carrying of truncheons, since a case in 1973 when Isle of Wight magistrates ruled that these were offensive weapons. Group 4 (unlike Securicor) is ending its dog patrols; and all employees are told to leave arrests to the police. If such firms extended their outlook to employ some fraud specialists they would not be felt to be so anti-working class. It is true that, by undertaking much monotonous guard duty, private security firms enable the regular police to concentrate more on the kind of police work that requires initiative, and on their social service role. But a properly supported police service should be able to undertake both commitments: the prevention of crime is, after all, the original task they were given. To defray cost, some extra guard duties might perhaps – as suggested by George Terry, when chief constable of Sussex – be undertaken by police officers on a fee basis, on the same basis that they now do at football matches. The Singapore government at present runs its own commercial security agency, but there can be no justification for using private companies to do regular policing; and meanwhile their proper licensing and some system of public accountability are long overdue.

Another response to the overstrain on the regular police was Glasgow's proposal in 1977 to engage fifty-eight uniformed vigilantes, at a cost of £300,000 a year. The US at present has over 800 private vigilante forces. But at their worst, such movements can turn into lynch-mobs. Although self-policing by a community – which in city life has disappeared – is one ideal to be aimed at, Devon and Cornwall's chief constable, John Alderson, has suggested that Specials are preferable to vigilantes as an expression of this: he proposes there should be two or three on each beat under the command of the neighbourhood beat officer, supplying him with local knowledge and support. Insurance companies, who employ their own detectives on large claims, have lately increased their rewards – often 10 per cent of the value of stolen goods – and are able to pay informers more than the police (for whom £100 is an exceptional reward) can offer. Senior police officers frequently criticize those insurance companies who allow themselves to be blackmailed into paying a reward for stolen articles in the absence of the conviction of the culprits. 'In this way the criminal benefits from his crime without the added risk of finding a receiver for the goods he has stolen.' Such informers, who can be dangerous as double agents and may be motivated by rivalry or by desire for a sense of importance, are examined in more detail in Chapter 7. In both Britain and the US, the police have been known to turn a blind eye to illicit gaming places, bars and brothels on the understanding that their operators act as police informants, and seven informers in London are currently under continuous police protection.

Scientific crime-control

The CID in many parts of the country would like more, and more modern, equipment. No police force in Britain owns a helicopter; although the New York police possess several, when the Metropolitan force needed one to search for the kidnapped Mrs McKay, they had to borrow one with the help of the *News of the World*. Experience has shown their value for traffic control both in cities and on motorways, as well as for aerial photography and searches. When provided with a direct radio link to patrol cars, they can also be used for crime prevention as an 'eye in the sky' on the movement of valuable consignments. Here is one field for the supporters of the present fragmented pattern of forces to show that co-operation between them is as satisfactory as they allege, for it is well known that several chief constables would like helicopters but that their local authorities have not felt able to afford one. A unified or regionally-organized force could be equipped with a helicopter or a light plane in each region of the country. One chief superintendent said, 'Portable radios are the best thing that's ever happened to the police' – they have lessened the need for some of the acres of minutiae that policemen learn parrot-like in training – but some of their value is lost because they are not fitted with encryption (scramblers) for reasons of cost. Their messages can be picked up on most standard VHF radios (my own gramophone mysteriously and irritatingly also receives police calls), and are easily capable of being jammed. Sometimes criminals have been known to broadcast false messages on police wavelengths. Although listening into police transmissions is technically illegal, on one occasion when a house in Hampstead was burgled five news reporters were able to arrive there twenty minutes before the police. Another impediment is the secretarial facilities for many detectives, which remain archaic: often several busy sergeants and inspectors have to wait for the one ancient typewriter they have to share. The use of dictaphone-tape-recorders, audio-typists and photocopiers could ease this bottleneck. Forensic laboratories are also under such pressure that sometimes they are able to concentrate on only the most serious cases and have little or no time to do any research other than on an *ad hoc* basis. Most scientists understandably prefer to work elsewhere at higher salaries and in occupations where they do not have to spend their time waiting around to be attacked in courts, or work in such cramped conditions: the antiquated laboratory at Nottingham is so short of space that some of its work has to be carried out on the roof of the police station that houses it.

One of the most senior officers at Scotland Yard described the conventional criminal record system to me as being 'on the point of collapse'. Some offenders have in the past been tried in magistrates courts before their description and fingerprints have been able to be manually processed (the Criminal Record Office's staff are frequently too overworked to deal with telephoned inquiries), so that a defendant who is wanted for arrest elsewhere in the country may be freed before his file can be traced, perhaps under one of several assumed names. Although many habitually do so, not all criminals are helpful enough only to offend in their own locality. For several years to come it will still be necessary to check regional CROs – some of which are very patchy – as well as the national one. It will be at least another five years before single fingerprints are capable of identification by a computer: the new British police computer is programmed only to compare complete sets of the ten prints of people convicted of those offences for which fingerprints may be taken. One police superintendent commented, 'With computers the need here is for a national system, but I fear that a piecemeal system has been built up so that today we have a hotch-potch of equipment in separate forces with interfacing facilities virtually non-existent.' Chief inspector Fraser of Merseyside, on secondment at the Police College, also greatly regrets the lack of progress towards a national network, and the fragmented way in which each chief constable has been allowed by the Home Office to make use of computers each in his own fashion.

A record, which might take a detective several months to find in conventional files, can be printed-out by a computer in less than six seconds. To guard against breakdown, most of their vital equipment is duplicated. Prior to the computers' arrival, it used to take weeks to identify a print like that left on a ransom note by Leslie Whittle's killer; or ten days for information about a stolen vehicle to reach police forces throughout the country: now a car has been known to be recovered before its owner has finished his report of its theft at a police station. The national police computer in Britain was first programmed with the criminal index, fingerprints, names of vehicle owners, and a list of stolen vehicles. Names of wanted and missing persons were added in 1978. Later it is planned to include details of stolen cheques and credit cards, lists of other stolen property, and the names of disqualified drivers. Experiments are being made to test its value in sifting clues and the information received in cases of murder and other serious crimes. The speed of the computer link also provides a psychological fillip for officers' morale by giving them a feeling of being in touch. In America police forces such as the one at Dade County in Florida also make use of computers by, for example, data-processing accident reports so as to produce instant analyses of causes and blackspots, which enables accident prevention measures to be taken; immediately classifying crimes according to characteristics and locality by means of a punched card system (which is an invaluable aid because the great majority of criminals are traditionalists and rarely change their methods); and regularly making an operational time analysis of all cases, calls and communications, so that the force's crime prevention and law enforcement plans can be continually reassessed and, if necessary, recast. But the British have hesitated at the idea of adopting some similar scientific developments, for fear of public resistance to 'Big Brother' techniques: Scotland Yard goes to great lengths to stress that its computers are 'for police, not for government, use'. West Germany's immigration officers are able to make an immediate check of any information required about travellers by inserting their passports into the impol system, which was developed by a British firm but has not yet been installed in Britain. The US expects to have computer terminals installed in half its police cars by 1980. In Britain, so far ten patrol cars in Bristol and six in Sussex have been fitted with Mufax equipment which can receive transmissions of photographs, documents and maps. But the British national police computer is now overloaded: there is no room on the present model for the names of disqualified drivers, and until a new replacement machine is installed in 1979, officers have been asked not to use the missing persons list extensively.

Technological development probably represents the police's one short-term hope of getting on top of the rise in crime. Further advances are inevitable. But there also is a negative price to be paid by the police. Technological advances increase the bureaucratic and impersonally statistical part of the police's work: at the same time as widening the demands made upon them by the public as the latter are educated to use their facilities, the new technical aids make policemen feel they are working on an assembly line, and have less of the craftsman's job-satisfaction in using their independent initiative and personal contact with the public.

Experiments are now also being made at the central research laboratory at Aldermaston and elsewhere with electronic 'sniffers', which are able to detect the vapour given off by some explosives and drugs more reliably than a dog can; 'night vision' devices developed by the army; infra-red rays for detecting forged inks, and also in aerially searching for fresh graves; underwater Asdic detectors; laser micro-spectral analysis to identify specks of material; the X-ray fluoroscopes for inspecting baggage, which have become familiar at airports; new chemical processes which enable finger-, palm- or toe-prints to be recognized on paper, fine fabrics, certain kinds of clothing and plastics (through the reaction of sulphur dioxide with the fatty acids left by human fingers on an absorbent surface); high pressure liquid chromatography and radio immunal assay, which are being developed to detect drugs; gas chromatography to analyse debris from a fire; and holographic interferometry whose sensitivity can identify data such as footprints on some types of carpets. Each individual's blood, semen, saliva, and ear-shape are distinguishable and may shortly be able to be identified. In the case of blood, fourteen different and distinct classifications are so far recognized; the rarest factors found in eight of the classifications, based on blood constituents like enzymes, would narrow their origin to five people in 100 million. Every individual firearm similarly leaves some marking on a cartridge case or bullet which scientifically can be shown to have come from that weapon alone. Recently for the first time in Britain a man was convicted on the evidence of the prints left by his gloves (no two pairs of which leave the same marks – though since most intelligent criminals know that prints can be taken from the inside of gloves, few experienced hands keep their gloves after committing a crime). But 'the problem of public reaction' has, to not all police officers' regret, stayed the suggested use of electrified water jets or of high-intensity sound or stroboscopic light for riot control; and the human fallibility and simple boredom of their operators has led to the abandonment of continuous covert television surveillance of streets by the police. Nevertheless, the inevitably increasing use of such devices as night-cameras, radar, video-cameras and listening aids, needs independent monitoring to ensure it is never abused.

The public's methods of police avoidance are also entering the scientific era. In the United States, sales of electronic radar detection boxes for motorists – marketed under names such as Fuzzbuster – now exceed one million a year. Police reaction to such technology is mixed: the state of Virginia has banned their use by law, but a Kentucky state trooper detachedly commented: 'The idea of radar is to get motorists to slow down. If these buzzer boxes also do that, we are probably accomplishing as much as a speeding ticket would.'

Strengthening research and the central Inspectorate

In the past the police, rightly recognizing the value of human experience, local knowledge, and common sense, have not always taken easily to science. Fingerprinting had been used in India for a hundred years before it replaced Scotland Yard's methods of anatomical measurement following the terrible miscarriage of justice in the case of Beck, who was wrongly identified by twelve witnesses (and whose years in prison also contributed to the establishment of the Court of Criminal Appeal). Fortunately the Police Federation in general accept they have nothing to fear from new scientific advances, and indeed welcome them as upgrading their occupation. In the same way as fingerprint evidence almost inevitably ensures a conviction, the maximum use of scientific equipment like radar and breathalysers would reduce the area of attack on the police in courts – to the benefit of everyone except the guilty. In the United States, videotaped confessions are increasingly being used as evidence in trials. The possibility might also be investigated of filming drunk motorists. The Swiss traffic police save much dispute by providing drivers with immediate photographs of traffic offences, which show the speed meter reading and the number plate of the vehicle. The Israelis have developed a new machine which analyses voice prints and is capable of identifying who, for example, is making a ransom demand on a telephone. More research remains to be done in the use of infra-red spectrophotometry, televising and taperecording evidence. There should be a much wider international exchange of methods and experience of crime prevention and treatment: often many individual countries are laboriously seeking the same solutions, in the same way that separate local forces in Britain are making identical elementary experiments. Fragmentation of research and of the capital necessary for it has been a recurrent handicap resulting from the number of different forces in Britain, and in other countries whose police is organized locally. The total annual research budget for the police remains minute compared to the amount spent weekly on the armed forces. Quadrupling the budget could well produce, at the lowest, economic dividends in reducing the cost of crime to society.

The central Inspectorate's visits to forces are at last becoming more professional and less of a formality; up until recently they have been so cursory and well advertized in advance that one police officer said that 'by the time the band had played at the parade, buttons had been inspected, the most promising recruit had had his hand shaken, and the papers laid out on top appreciated, the visit was over.' (Even that was an improvement on the technique of earlier days when, for example, Carlisle's force were inspected by being lined up on the station platform as the inspector's train passed through.) But it is unfortunate that the Metropolitan force – easily the largest and almost a fifth of the country's total strength – is still not included in the national inspection. This is a cardinal omission when knowledge about advances made by other forces often depends largely on its informal dissemination by the Inspectors. The Inspectorate in any event still has the power only to suggest improvements or standardizations to chief constables; it is part of the Home Office, but has no formal authority. Many people think it would also be strengthened by the addition of, for instance, a professional efficiency expert who could advise on administrative improvements, an accountant who could suggest savings in costs, an educationalist to discuss ways in which to make training better, a scientist to coordinate research, and a lawyer who could look at faults in criminal legislation as well as patterns of complaints.

The Inspectorate, reinvigorated under Sir Colin Woods, could become the centre of a radical strategy to share nationally the improvements made by the police in different parts of the country, in the way that the Police Foundation promulgates advances in the US. Perhaps the biggest waste of police time which they could tackle is the inefficient court procedure, which can cause a busy officer to travel and wait around for six hours in order to make a one-minute remand appearance. Hundreds of magistrates' courts are daily filled with policemen waiting perhaps half a day to read from their notebooks about some trivial incident which is not disputed by a defendant whose own time is frequently too valuable for *him* to trouble to attend court. Similarly, in Crown courts, scores of experienced CID officers waste many hours waiting to read out in a few words the previous history of an accused. The power to give a ticket and to impose a fine on the spot when a fare-evader or a motorist admitted an offence would save hundreds of police hours in court every day. Many magistrates' courts would also save a considerable amount of everybody's time if depositions no longer had to be laboriously written out in longhand. The second priority might be a frontal attack – with the help of efficiency experts – on paperwork, which CID men say now takes up almost 40 per cent of their working lives. In every single traffic case, for example, it is necessary for the officer concerned to write a report in the accident book, seek statements, and then type them out with his own comments and summary. He must then prepare copies of plans and photographs, organize medical or forensic evidence, and check records (criminal, employers', and Service) besides the insurance policy and car and driving licences. Finally, he may have to prepare the brief for the prosecution – as well as serve the summons, call on and notify witnesses, and perhaps liaise with another police force if the defendant is not a local man. The third subject the Inspectorate should always be watching is the optimum size, burdens and boundaries of police areas. Due to reorganizations, a number of police headquarters are now sited in inconvenient places. A fourth reform programme the Inspectorate could propose would be the modernizing of unnecessary or badly-conceived legislation. If, for instance, the roadfund licences on motor vehicles were replaced with a proportionate rise in petrol-tax, this – besides catching the 1.2 million cars which escape tax, and being fiscally fairer for everybody by raising revenue in direct relation to road use – would it is estimated save 236,000 police hours annually in Britain. The ultimate aim should be not just to simplify our laws by speedier implementation of the recommendations of the Law Commission, but eventually to codify them in simplified laymen's language.

To keep in touch with areas where reforms are needed, it is

essential that senior police ranks meet and talk with the men on the beat as much as possible, and do not become mere distant administrators: other chief constables could benefit from following leaders like John Alderson who themselves join foot and car patrols in order to experience practical problems at first hand. Savings can be effected by a policing policy which recognizes, for instance, that separate areas require different policing on differing weekdays and at different periods of the day and night. In the US, a variety of solutions are being tried: New York is using specialized police teams such as the Family Crisis Intervention Unit; Detroit's Beat Commander approach is experimenting with a different strategy, enlarging the tasks of patrols instead of dividing and delegating them; while Washington DC is giving priority to community links, with its Pilot District Project where an elected citizen board links civilian volunteers to police patrols. The continued use of horses and dogs, as in Britain, on the other hand is of more doubtful value to the police: the former can panic (even if their riders do not) with dangerous consequences, while the arrival of the latter invariably results in a rise in tension. Other police forces in Europe emphasize preventative measures such as minimizing the amount of cash in transit; or training civilians to recognize and report emergencies (an amazing number of people who telephone a genuine report to the police fail to give, for example, the relevant address). In America, the Citizens Band radio system enables twenty million people to make two-way radio calls to the police with information, but the government still refuses to allow such a system in Britain. Each of these approaches could be evaluated and their lessons learnt. Other intelligence which the Inspectorate could help to be shared could include the psychological knowledge which policemen – especially in Sweden, Holland, Germany, the US and Israel – have learnt in dealing with incidents such as sieges, kidnappings, and people who barricade themselves in.

Perhaps the most contentious administrative judgement to be made concerns the correct strength for the police. The government White Paper in January 1978 admitted that, even at a time when there are over 1.5 million unemployed, there are now 4,900 fewer police officers in England and Wales than had been predicted a year before. The numbers of the service have

TABLE 6: ANNUAL ESTABLISHED AND ACTUAL POLICE STRENGTHS IN GREAT BRITAIN

	Authorized Establishment	*Strength*	*Percentage deficiency of strength on official establishment*
1938 (year end)	68,759	66,863	2.8
1945 (year end)	69,247	69,715	0.7 surplus
1946 (year end)	73,433	61,385	16.4
1949 (year end)	79,371	68,215	14.1
1950 (year end)	80,174	70,597	11.9
1959 (mid-year)	87,373	80,495	7.9
1960 (mid-year)	88,743	80,899	8.8
1961 (mid-year)	89,893	82,674	8.0
1962 (mid-year)	92,159	85,750	7.0
1963 (mid-year)	95,456	88,605	7.2
1964 (mid-year)	98,474	89,674	8.9
1965 (mid-year)	103,059	91,658	11.1
1966 (mid-year)	113,208	94,333	16.7
1967 (mid-year)	117,281	97,324	17.0
1968 (mid-year)	119,186	99,828	16.2
1969 (mid-year)	119,016	100,361	15.7
1970 (mid-year)	119,043	102,032	14.3
1971 (mid-year)	120,043	104,491	13.0
1972 (mid-year)	121,374	108,398	10.7
1973 (mid-year)	123,010	110,320	10.3
1974 (mid-year)	126,340	111,109	12.1
1975 (mid-year)	129,018	115,019	10.8
1976 (mid-year)	129,451	119,756	7.5
1977 (mid-year)	130,130	119,968	7.8
1978 (mid-year)	130,435	118,328	9.3

been increased (though there was a net loss in 1976) – but crime has risen faster still.

Part of the higher numbers is attributable to reductions in the length of the working week, and makes for no increase in effectiveness. Only some 30 per cent of officers are now on duty at any one time. Ray Buxton when he was chief constable of Hertfordshire, estimated in 1974 that at least another 10,000 men are necessary for the adequate everyday policing of England and Wales: since then the problems have multiplied. In mid-1978, Scotland was 1,348 officers (10.38 per cent) under strength, more than the Royal Ulster Constabulary's shortage of 639 (9.83 per cent). Overall there is currently one police officer in England and Wales for every 420 people in the population. The comparable ratios in other countries (bearing in mind national differences in the definition of policing) were:

TABLE 7: DIFFERENT NATIONAL POLICE/POPULATION RATIOS (1972)

Netherlands	1:702
Denmark	1:619
Japan	1:612
Sweden	1:596
West Germany	1:544
Canada	1:533
US	1:500
Luxembourg	1:485
France	1:366
Italy	1:336
Belgium	1:323

Comparing some of the countries at the head and the foot of this table, there would if anything appear to be an inverse correlation between strength and performance. Certainly numbers alone cannot guarantee a good police service.

The crisis in London

But the key to the problem in Britain is that the most crime-ridden (in qualitative as well as quantitative terms) area of all – Metropolitan London – remains at least 20 per cent undermanned. In Scotland, the two most urban concentrations, Glasgow and Edinburgh, similarly have the highest deficiencies. If 21,000 policemen were needed to cope with 17,000 indictable crimes in Metropolitan London in 1921, how many men should there be to handle the more than half a million crimes being committed there annually today? In fact, while provincial forces in Britain have doubled their strength in the last fifty years, there were actually 600 fewer police officers (though several thousand more civilian assistants) in Metropolitan London in 1975 than there were in 1921 – when the Metropolitan area was smaller, the working week was longer, and crime was less than one twenty-third of its extent today. In 1977, the number of applicants, recruits and net strength of the force all fell. The authorized establishment figure for London has risen proportionately much more slowly than those of the provincial forces. Home Office policy has traditionally been not to grant an increase in establishment to a force unless it has already almost reached its existing maximum. This has meant for areas like Metropolitan London, where the actual strength has recently fallen even further short of the authorized figure, that the latter has become meaningless as an index of actual need. Even so, London's formal 16.2 per cent deficiency of 4,329 officers is as great as the total establishment laid down to police the whole of Merseyside. London in fact now has less than half the number of policemen Paris employs for its population of three million, which itself is less than half Metropolitan London's population. Although the London police force has a creditably successful record against bombers and in sieges, its other crime figures have gone from bad to worse. During 1976, attacks on policemen there rose by 40 per cent, and street robberies increased by over 50 per cent compared with 1975. When the capital is the centre of so much of the major criminality, it cannot be sensible for the case-load of most of its CID officers to be twice that of those outside London. Scotland Yard in addition continually has to lend a number of its best officers for important investigations in the provinces and overseas, as well as having to bear the brunt of national demonstrations and guarding diplomatic visitors, so that its capacity to try to deal with its own enormous problems is permanently interrupted. The previous boast of the Metropolitan force that it can answer any emergency call within three minutes has been jettisoned: a Commander of E Division recently revealed that it sometimes takes twelve minutes even to find an officer. Furthermore, if London policemen did not compulsorily work overtime on three out of their eight monthly rest days, their strength would be a tenth even more weak than it is at present.

What can be done to help the capital's crisis? Sir Robert Mark suggested that all new recruits to the police service should do an initial three years service in London. 'If the amount of money available for police is to be restricted for understandable reasons of national economic policy,' he argues, 'London should use a much greater share of it than hitherto.' Some recruiting might be deterred by the resulting social and geographical dislocation, but many provincial police authorities would probably welcome a moratorium on their own training costs in exchange for a future supply of trained and experienced officers from London and the other conurbations to which the policy might be extended. Other remedies could involve drastically further raising the London weighting allowance (the Edmund Davies committee recommended £650 a year); interest-free loans for deposits on homes for urban policemen, together with 100 per cent mortgages at preferential interest rates to help with the cost of housing; and the merger of the anomalous separate City of London with the Metropolitan force.

The long resistance to pay being weighed according to areas' needs has resulted in a vicious circle of the shorthanded areas' continuing to be overworked and hence unattractive to recruits. But if help for London is not to be at the expense of police forces elsewhere, recruiting overall must be boosted both in size and quality. Chief constables consider it is the way of life and conditions of work which are principally responsible for the vacancies, and that these, unlike pay, cannot be altered. 'The main disadvantage of police life anywhere,' said a former Metropolitan Commissioner, 'is the necessity for duty to cover the whole of the twenty-four hours a day, seven days a week, in contrast to the bulk of the population whose working day is over by 6 p.m.' Nor, chief constables argue, are they able to lower standards of recruitment any further. Too often, however, by 'standard' they are thinking of some physical measurement: the City of London force, for example, which is over 20 per cent below strength still insists on a minimum height of 5 ft 11 in., while 5 ft 8 in. suffices for the rest of London. Today is a far cry from the time when the City had a waiting list of 500 and was able to be highly selective. Many administrative and detective posts in the police might surely be filled by men who fall short of the mandatory requirements of chest measurement. In scientific work, traffic control and car patrols, height is scarcely relevant; even in making an arrest, tallness is not as much help as a knowledge of judo or karate. The minimum height requirement effectively rules out most Asians from enrolling: Gujaratis, for instance, have an average height of only 5 ft 5 in., while Gurkhas – not noticeably refused entry to the British army – have an average of 5 ft 4 in. The Police Federation defend the height rule with the somewhat sweeping assertion that 'there is a tendency for small men to make up by truculence what they lack in authority'. But the conspicuous whiteness of the police is unfortunate on other grounds. (London's 83 black officers – none of them in the higher ranks – are less than 5 per cent of the number they would be if equivalent to the black proportion of the population; while the West Midlands have only 25 black officers out of 5,500, and Greater Manchester a mere 10.) In many US cities, where police jobs traditionally became the virtual monopoly of certain ethnic groups, officers of Asian, Mexican or American-Indian descent are almost unknown. The police must become visibly integrated racially to cope with cities which themselves are partly integrated but which contain several areas of racial tension. The unfortunate experience of the Protestant-dominated police force in Northern Ireland has shown what can happen when a section of the population comes to think of the forces of law as a partisan enemy. Although widespread recruitment of West Indians has been shown to be difficult, a campaign to enlist good Bengali and other Asian candidates (despite their height) would both help police numbers and serve to assuage the latter community's acute isolation and fears.

Policewomen

Women are another major catchment area for recruits that until recently has been largely neglected: if they were recruited to make up even one-tenth of the British force that would result in an improvement in strength of 2,000. Women officers occasion fewer complaints from the public than male ones do, and often succeed in calming aggressive confrontations. For

TABLE 8: ENGLAND AND WALES: COMPARISON OF POLICE FORCES' STRENGTH, DETECTION-RATES, POPULATION AND SIZE
(Source: Home Office)

Police force	*Population (as at 30 June 1974)*	*Acreage (as at 30 June 1974)*	*Authorized establishment (as at 31 December 1974)*	*Offences cleared-up* / *Offences known (April–December 1974)*	*Actual strength* / *Authorized establishment (as at 31 December 1974)*	*Population* / *Acreage* / *Acreage (as at 30 June 1974)*
Name	*Thousands*	*Thousands*	*Number*	*Percentage*	*Percentage*	*Percentage*
Avon and Somerset	1315.7	1185.0	2,868	37.1	91.5	111.0
Bedfordshire	484.3	305.0	890	50.4	90.8	158.8
Cambridgeshire	540.7	842.4	1,023	55.8	96.9	64.2
Cheshire	902.3	575.4	1,770	50.4	91.3	156.8
Cleveland	565.6	144.1	1,411	55.3	93.6	392.5
Cumbria	475.7	1682.4	1,070	55.3	96.6	28.3
Derbyshire	892.3	650.1	1,559	46.0	93.7	137.2
Devon and Cornwall	1327.4	2534.7	2,573	51.8	101.6	52.4
Dorset	570.5	655.8	1,089	45.5	97.2	87.0
Durham	610.9	601.9	1,371	50.5	93.7	101.5
Essex	1339.2	887.7	2,436	46.9	90.8	150.9
Gloucestershire	485.4	652.7	1,007	64.4	96.5	74.4
Greater Manchester	2718.1	318.0	6,600	45.4	85.2	854.9
Hampshire	1545.6	1026.6	2,844	48.2	94.9	150.6

Hertfordshire	799.5	367.8	1,472	50.0	91.2	217.4
Humberside	848.8	867.7	1,910	49.2	89.8	97.8
Kent	1440.8	922.2	2,454	43.7	92.9	156.2
Lancashire	1370.1	751.9	2,880	57.2	100.4	182.2
Leicestershire	829.8	630.8	1,603	58.6	98.6	131.5
Linconshire	519.5	1454.4	1,174	60.4	97.5	35.7
Merseyside	1602.7	160.1	4,317	40.4	95.0	1001.1
Norfolk	650.3	1323.3	1,218	52.1	95.6	49.1
Northamptonshire	496.4	585.0	844	46.4	98.6	84.9
Northumbria	1475.2	1377.1	3,322	51.7	94.4	107.1
North Yorkshire	648.6	2053.1	1,277	53.0	96.6	31.6
Nottinghamshire	981.0	534.7	2,066	61.5	98.3	183.5
South Yorkshire	1317.2	385.6	2,752	47.0	85.3	341.6
Staffordshire	991.1	671.2	2,066	62.5	94.7	147.7
Suffolk	567.3	939.1	1,077	56.7	90.9	60.4
Surrey	732.7	363.6	1,438	46.8	90.7	201.5
Sussex	1274.3	935.7	2,661	60.6	97.9	136.2
Thames Valley	1686.5	1420.8	2,960	49.3	94.1	118.7
Warwickshire	469.5	489.4	876	49.8	90.3	95.9
West Mercia	940.3	1832.7	1,650	57.4	91.0	51.3
West Midlands	2779.7	222.3	6,471	36.2	83.5	1250.7
West Yorkshire	2082.2	503.9	5,103	49.6	87.8	413.2
Wiltshire	506.7	860.1	979	41.2	91.7	58.9
Dyfed-Powys	420.3	2679.4	866	62.2	99.8	15.7
Gwent	440.5	340.0	928	51.5	99.8	129.6
North Wales	596.8	1554.7	1,216	60.0	95.7	38.4
South Wales	1301.7	556.2	2,886	44.9	99.6	234.0
City of London	5.3	0.7	1,028	23.9	77.7	782.9
Metropolitan Police District	7446.6	496.7	26,628	27.7	79.0	1539.5

many years both the Police Federation and most chief officers – for once, shoulder to shoulder – were hostile to their employment. The Federation confidently pronounced that 'the very nature of the duties of a police constable is contrary to all that is finest and best in women'. They limited policewomen's work to escorting and searching women and cases involving children; but since the Sex Discrimination Act, female officers are now allowed to undertake virtually any duty. (Home Office instructions state, 'A man is to search a man. A woman is to search a woman. A woman may search a man below the knee and above the waist, but if the sex of the suspect is in doubt, only a woman is allowed to discover the truth.') Britain had fewer policewomen in 1929 than it had at the end of the First World War; by 1939 there were still less than 280; but the Second World War achieved a breakthrough in their acceptance. There are now 8,000 compared with half that number five years ago. Many male officers are uneasy about this, and not just because of the physical demands of some police tasks. Resistance to them remains greatest in northern forces; the Scottish Police Federation wish the police to be exempted from the Sex Discrimination Act. Opposition stems partly from wider reluctance to accept female equality in the culture of parts of northern Britain, and partly from a fear that a growing proportion of female employees will have its traditional effect of depressing wage levels. The US however still has only some 6,000 females among a total of over 400,000 police officers. Sir Colin Woods's belief is that 'when there is a shortage of officers, it is crazy to ignore half the population. . . . The time will come when one out of every three or four CID officers will be women. There's no earthly reason in particular why frauds or traffic cannot be dealt with by policewomen.' There are now two female chief superintendents in Britain, but as yet there is no sign of a woman chief constable: 'It'll be at least fifteen years before that could be conceivable.' No policewoman wants a return to the separate women's sections. One described her male colleagues' attitude as 'one of acceptance on the basis that we're of a lower stratum. The younger generation who have working wives are better. But a few of the older ones won't accept women, won't work with them or take them in a car.' In 1977 there was in fact a reduction in the number of women holding supervisory ranks in England and Wales. Policewomen (like black recruits) believe they have to prove themselves several times over. 'The truth is,' as one of them said, 'that the idea of equality hurts men's egos.' The combination of a feminine appearance and police uniform (although women officers do not carry truncheons) can produce a conflicting, almost schizophrenic, reaction in many male members of the public – and in eminent policemen as well: Sir David McNee is reported to have said that 'a lady policeman is a contradiction in terms'. The Sex Discrimination Act can only improve women's chances in the police; hitherto they have had a less than one in three likelihood of acceptance, compared with one in two for male applicants. By 1978, a quarter of all new entrants were women, although the proportion of women in the service is still only 8 per cent and is not expected to reach one-tenth at least until 1985. Shift-work makes it extremely difficult for mothers to continue working. As late as 1965 policewomen in Scotland had to resign on getting married, though of those who marry in the force, 70 per cent marry policemen.

But half of male officers who resign from the service also do so within their first two years. Although it is far from a foregone conclusion that increasing pay alone will attract a higher quality of man or woman into the police – role, status and reputation are almost certainly more important factors – doing so is likely to increase the number from which to select. The same applies to graduates: a good graduate will not necessarily be a success as a policeman. But it is a reflection on the reputation the police service has suffered from in the past, as well as a self-reinforcing handicap to them in the present, that out of the 500,000 people who graduated in Britain between 1945 and 1965, only a derisory twenty-five entered the police. Despite the current unemployment facing many who complete university degree courses, the London force of 21,000 today contains only 150 graduates; the total for England and Wales is 920, of whom more than 250 graduated while serving in the police.

The current pressure on the police calls for the best use of their available forces, even though the priorities of the public may conflict with those of the police themselves. One useful

TABLE 9: INCREASE IN MOTOR VEHICLES IN THE

Year	Number of offences in England & Wales			(i) Number of offences in Scotland	(ii) Number of offences in N. Ireland
	Pro-ceedings	Written warnings	Total offences		
1960	796,408	245,105	1,041,513	87,020	33,775
1970	1,531,735	238,172	1,769,907	133,527	21,816
1971	1,590,603	238,116	1,828,719	143,841	22,187
1972	1,789,593	242,639	2,032,212	147,904	16,477
1973	1,983,504	239,888	2,223,392	159,448	21,831
1974	2,119,364	222,310	2,341,674	166,938	22,577
1975	2,142,011	222,239	2,363,240	166,973	24,568
1976	2,216,111	264,572	2,480,683	154,064	27,433
increase:	178%	7%	138%	77%	−18%

(i) Number of offences made known to the police where one or more persons were apprehended, cited or warned.
(ii) Number of convictions.

approach has been pioneered by Gordon Wasserman at the Home Office, adapting the PPB – programming, planning and budgeting – system of the US Defence Department. This aims to match the maximum amount of police resources to the most crime-prone areas at the most crime-prone times. Its method is to systematize deployment by attempting to express the current aims of policing policy in terms of specific functions, and to analyse their cost, thus presenting police leaders with a range of policy options in quantifiable terms.

In 1977/78, England and Wales spent £1,101 million on its police (of which £891 million was accounted for by salaries and wages), compared with £989 million in 1976/77, £820 million in 1975/76, £640 million in 1974/75 and £496 million in 1973/74. (The search for Leslie Whittle's killer alone cost more than £2 million.) The cost of the increases recommended by the Edmund Davies committee in 1978 is a further £250 million.

'NITED KINGDOM, AND RELATED OFFENCES 1960–76

Total ɔffences	*Number of vehicles registered (round figures)*				
	England	*Wales*	*Scotland*	*N. Ireland*	*Total*
,162,308	N/A	N/A	684,000	227,000	—
,925,250	13,078,000	729,000	1,124,000	372,000	15,303,000
,984,747	13,569,000	754,000	1,134,000	383,000	15,840,000
,196,603	14,124,000	792,000	1,181,000	380,000	16,477,000
,404,671	14,907,000	836,000	1,252,000	N/A	—
,531,189	15,084,000	868,000	1,274,000	379,000	17,605,000
,554,781	15,283,000	860,000	1,304,000	384,000	17,831,000
,662,180	15,593,000	878,000	1,313,000	403,000	18,187,000
149%	69%	71%	92%	77%	68%

With so many competing demands for education and health upon a static or declining national budget, the police service cannot continuously and automatically expect major increases in its precept. Regretfully, a number of police in rural areas – whose population is declining and whose inhabitants have always been more self-policing than urban communities – should be redeployed to help the crisis in the major conurbations. Almost 80 per cent of Britain's inhabitants now live in urban areas, and 35 per cent in six conurbations which are characterized by growing mobility and lack of neighbourly links. The undermanning of city forces is a false economy, especially when the bill for permanent substantial police overtime is costed. The meagreness of research is another mistake: the police at present spend only 0.3 per cent of their annual budget on research and development, compared with the Ministry of Defence's mean annual level of 10 per cent.

(The cost-benefit of our whole approach to law enforcement needs to be radically re-examined: in 1977, one case involving the theft of £14,350 occasioned legal fees of over £313,900.) While the traffic work of the police in Britain costs £35 million annually, the price of road accidents is estimated to be over £970 million and of traffic congestion £920 million; but the real damage that road casualties and crime can cause, in human terms, is incalculable.

In the US it has been suggested that if victims of crime could sue the state for any resulting damage, this would give the government an incentive to adjust expenditure to the point at which its cost was equalled by the marginal benefit. Since the bulk of serious crimes are committed by professionals, even a small improvement in the clear-up and conviction rates might well lead to a significant brake on crime. But it should never be lost sight of that focusing simply upon such statistics pays no regard to other, perhaps more important factors: it would be an error if the police or the public, in fear of the statistics, came to value detection before prevention, short-cuts above liberty, mere efficiency above true effectiveness. Such boundaries are discussed in the next chapter. Since the real condemnation of crime is that it attacks people's liberty, it would be its ultimate triumph if we only defeat it at the cost of losing our own liberty. A good policeman remains a human handling humans, a craftsman not an oppressive bureaucrat. As John Alderson underlines, the true remedies can only lie with the community:

> I have often thought that the creation of a professional police has tended to make the general public less interested in dealing with crime. The attitude of 'Oh, it's a police matter and nothing to do with me' has arisen from this and is against our traditional attitudes. It seems to me that we shall have to get back to committing the public to helping the police to deal with crime much more than they have done in recent decades. It needs a massive programme of public education and I do not think we do the public any great service by pretending that we, the police, can cope when clearly we cannot. The so-called battle against crime is a matter for the whole of society and not just for the police.

FOUR

Freedom, and Freedom from Crime

'Salus populi suprema est lex'
Cicero

'It is excellent to have a giant's strength
but it is tyrannous to use it like a giant'
Shakespeare, *Measure for Measure*

A hard but cool new look at the legal powers of the police is long overdue. The Anglo-Saxon preference has always been to keep these too weak rather than to have them too great. John Stuart Mill commented, 'In England there has always been more liberty, but worse organization, while in other countries there is better organization, but less liberty.' But there is a less understandable pride in this country in keeping the limits of these powers uncertain, capriciously enforced and nowhere properly defined; between what the police may, and may not, do there is a critical no-man's-land whose boundaries are still disputed and regularly and lengthily fought over in the courts.

It is time that this inflammable, expedient, but potentially dangerous uncertainty was cleared up. At present, policemen complain that their work has become more difficult because members of the public are increasingly aware of their rights. In the past the police have been used to relying largely on bluff, when, for example, inviting someone to come or remain with them for questioning. How many people are aware that, except in motoring and Official Secrets cases, a person questioned by the police is under no legal obligation to supply his identity or address, or even to make any reply – whatever his social or moral duty may be to help the police? Equally few people know that, unless they are formally arrested, they have no obligation to comply with any police request to accompany them to a police station, and that legally at any time they are entitled to leave there as soon as they wish. Nor is it common knowledge that nobody, under arrest or otherwise, can be compelled to take part in an identification parade. A suspect can demand one, but this right is increasingly unavailable to young black suspects: the police in Lewisham and some other areas say that it is becoming impossible for them to organize identity parades, because young blacks, due to their refusal to cooperate with the police, will not any longer volunteer to line up. Neither can a police officer, who gives no specific reason for the request, require any car driver to stop. Lord Scarman summarizes the laws applying to public order as 'uncertain, archaic and undeveloped'. What incontrovertibly is an anomalous absurdity is that police powers at present vary in different parts of England: the police have the power by local legislation to stop someone on suspicion in London, Birkenhead, Birmingham, Burnley, Hertfordshire, Hull, Newcastle-on-Tyne, Oldham, Rochdale, St Helens, and Salford – but not anywhere else. Either such a power is necessary throughout the country, or nowhere. Similarly, laws protecting badgers give a right of search; but there is no such right when murder is suspected. One very senior police officer said, 'There's nothing wrong with the law as it is, you can always get round it'. For example, although for many offences a magistrate's warrant is needed before an arrest can be made, the police are known to arrest people unlawfully on 'catch all' holding charges such as – if indoors – 'being found on premises for an unlawful purpose, contrary to the 1824 Vagrancy Act', or – out of doors – 'insulting behaviour likely to cause a breach of the peace'. The need for administering a caution is similarly on occasions pragmatically evaded by arresting a suspect on some minor spurious charge, and then drawing him into conversation about the real crime – about which there is no technical legal need to caution him since no charge has been made. It would be a healthier situation if the police were given whatever clearly defined powers are considered necessary for them to do their work, and then never permitted to evade or exceed their limits.

Which powers the police should possess is a matter of the highest importance, and one that arouses correspondingly strong feelings. It is all the more necessary that the subject should be approached calmly and rationally, and that emotive but scarcely helpful words such as 'un-English' – employed with equal facility and lack of definition by anarchists and authoritarians alike – should be embargoed. The onus of justification should, I suggest, always be on those who suggest that the police should possess any particular power. The criteria by which each power should be tested are (1) will it jeopardize any innocent man? and (2) if not, will it increase our freedom from crime? Henry Fielding (the Chief Magistrate of Bow Street in the eighteenth century who formed a small body of 'thief-takers') stated in his *An Inquiry into the Causes of the Late Increase of Robbers* that the ideal was a system which 'alike opposes those wild notions of liberty that are inconsistent with all government, and those pernicious schemes of government which are destructive of true liberty'; but this does not carry the argument much further.

Jeremy Bentham, the great juridical philosopher who believed that the object of any law should be to augment the total happiness of the community, was in favour of police for preventing and ensuring the punishment of crimes, but stipulated that 'no method of prevention should be employed, which is likely to cause a greater mischief than the offence itself'. He said that police were 'destined to prevent evils and provide benefits', but only on condition that their powers were clearly laid down. In this, as in some of his other suggestions – full legal aid, proper compensation for victims of crimes, and identity marks for people – he was in advance of our present position.

Penal reformers, from Bentham and Romilly down to Lord Gardiner, have advocated that the route to reducing crime lies in making its punishment more certain rather than more severe. (Probably the only influence which deterrent sentences have is in inverse proportion to the gravity of the offence: they may have some effect on, for example, minor motoring offenders.) Research shows that the overwhelming majority of first offenders who are caught are not recorded as offending again; this is not only the strongest, but virtually the only clearly established, factor that is so far known to discourage crime. Certainty of detection must be one *sine qua non* whatever views are held as to the subsequent treatment of the criminal. Peel's belief in 1829 that a proper police force would result in – and is a necessary prerequisite for – penal reform remains equally true today. The endless debate between those who would reform and those who would punish offenders pales beside the fact that in the majority of cases there is no chance to do either.

We would be unwise ever to forget that rights and liberties, once curtailed perhaps as the panic result of some exceptional incident, are (like riders of tigers) rarely recovered. 'The mood and temper of the public with regard to the treatment of crime and criminals is one of the most unfailing tests of the civilization of any country. A calm, dispassionate recognition of the rights of the accused – and even of the convicted – criminal against the State . . . marks and measures the stored-up strength of a nation,' said Winston Churchill, speaking as long ago as 1910. A society's real defence against crime survives or fails not due to any efforts of its police, but depends on the attitudes of its public opinion. The view of Professor James R. Wilson of the United States is that 'basically crime can only be reduced by fundamental social changes'. A certain amount of crime is inevitable as the price to be paid for any lines drawn for the structure of society; some people indeed believe its incidence is a necessity, part of the initiative of free enterprise, and certainly preferable to having an over-efficient police force. The majority of opinion today has probably come to agree that the enforcement of morality is no longer society's – or hence the police's – job. But on the other hand too often people's attitude to almost any offence resembles not so much apathy as that of spectators enjoying a harmless game: too many adults irresponsibly view crime in sporting terms rather than attempt to study its real implications. Idiotic can be the only description of a public attitude that allows intoxicated car-drivers to escape simply because they were caught in random testing. Men or women who would be ashamed to steal from an individual see little wrong in defrauding the whole community as represented by a nationalized industry or the tax collector or customs. But people as well as society can be dehumanized: we should not forget how easily the Nazis persuaded so many educated men and women of their right to commit ever more horrific crimes against their innocent neighbours. A dehumanized attitude to crime can reveal poverty of sympathy and imagination, and leads to results like the Genovese and Sidoli cases described in Chapter 1. It is easy to admire some crimes' panache or daring; it requires more effort to recall the less glamorous results of many offences: the unhappiness, fears, and the mental or physical effects upon victims' families.

Reforming the crimino-legal system

The institution of the police cannot be looked at or reformed in isolation from the whole crimino-legal system, or from society's attitude to deviancy itself. This became increasingly clear when discussing the present crisis, in the previous chapter. To decide which powers the police should have, it is necessary to consider the entire process from investigation to trial and appeal, and – above and beyond that – the acceptability of the criminal code and penal system. English legal traditions are characterized by giving a great deal of protection to an accused in court, but by contrast they provide few definitive safeguards to suspects during police inquiries prior to being charged. It is unproductive to consider the reform of one part – as the latest Royal Commission has been asked to do – in isolation from the remainder. The whole crimino-legal process is overdue for fundamental reassessment of its justice and practicality. One basic idiosyncrasy in the Anglo-Saxon tradition is that the 'adversary' system of trial is never an inquiry to discover either the truth of what happened or the best outcome, but is a skilled competition to put up the better story. (A study by the Institute of Law and Social Research of 17,000 arrests for serious crimes made by the Washington DC police in 1974 found that more than 70 per cent of the arrests did not lead to conviction. It is possible, but not very likely, that all 70 per cent were innocent.) It was a British judge who rightly gave the warning 'This is a court of law, not a court of justice.' But similarly, the pre-trial procedure is more a dual of bluff between police and suspect than an inquiry with checks or safeguards. Detective chief inspector Soady of Durham recently stated that legal aid has made it increasingly unlikely that the police can any longer obtain convictions merely on the basis of an accused person's admissions or identification by a witness; corroboration by some scientific evidence is now crucial. 'Fifteen years ago we would have got a conviction on identification alone. Today that would be disputed and the case thrown out of the window. The old conventional ways of securing a conviction have largely gone.' One day perhaps a national legal service will serve both prosecution and defence independently of both the government and the police; and the criminal process itself will focus on what really happened, as it does elsewhere in Europe – but without the delays known on the continent. The British system itself is scarcely swift justice now, to the detriment of witnesses, defendants, and police. People who are later acquitted frequently spend several months awaiting trial; and one recent criminal case lasted for six months, with weary jurymen listening to twenty-four defence counsel taking twenty-seven days for their speeches. To minimize waiting for everybody, where there are serious backlogs of cases courts should be arranged in the evenings and on a two-shift system; and the over-ample and rigid vacations of the Bar and Bench should be further rationalized in the interests of the rest of the community. At present expensive court-room space which is in short supply lies unnecessarily empty; and if magistrates' courts were to list the approximate starting time of cases, witnesses would not have to hang about so long and might be less reluctant to volunteer evidence.

A few juries may acquit perversely because of a wish by some of their members to pay off an old score – real or imagined – against the police. They can also be unwilling to convict because they have no say in the sentence and distrust what the judge may impose – unlike a magistrate, who can combine a finding of guilt with the choice of a lenient penalty. The acceptability of laws, and hence of law-enforcement officers, can be affected by the punishments imposed on violators. Many people blame the police unfairly for laws they did not make and which they themselves may little like. It is not the police but parliamentary inertia and the public's lack of political interest which should be blamed for the fact that today, in 1978, a person can still be sent to prison for fourteen years for wounding cattle, compared with only two years for cruelty to children; for five years for stealing electricity, compared with a maximum of only seven years for stealing a child; for ten years for damaging property (life imprisonment if by arson), compared with merely five years for exposing a child's life to danger. The maximum penalty for the gravest case of corruption – two years – is no more than that for the offence of fishing in concert without a licence. Continual revision is needed to keep our criminal statutes in line with present-day values: many still reflect the proprietary and philistine values of their eighteenth- and nineteenth-century landed and mercantile creators, preserved by an uncritical reverence for tradition.

Sir Robert Mark suggested to me that if the penalty for drunken driving were clearly known to be restitutional work or a rehabilitation camp as in Scandinavia, rather than consignment to a prison-system pronounced obsolescent in Victorian days, the undoubted perversity of juries in such cases would very likely diminish. Wrongful acquittals are to be regretted, as Professor Glanville Williams QC of Cambridge points out, not only because a dangerous criminal may be left loose in society, but also because if social agencies can do anything for a person's rehabilitation, the sooner an offender is justly convicted the earlier such rehabilitation can start. It is the certainty of conviction which ultimately deters crime, not merely the certainty of detection which is often claimed to do so. Wrongful acquittals have already been diminished by the introduction of majority verdicts and the rule that alibi defences must be disclosed in advance so that they can be checked; Mark more controversially believes that the caution and the right to silence will be abolished also in the next six years. But the institution of the jury – whether perverse or perceptive – remains an essential democratic safety-valve against oppression by law or government (opponents of the controversial Incitement to Disaffection Bill of 1934 successfully argued to *increase* its summary penalty from three to four months' imprisonment in order to enable defendants to request trial by jury rather than by establishment-minded magistrates). 'If it is remembered that the prime function of the criminal law is to encourage and sustain civilized conduct, to declare and confirm the basic moral code,' Professor Alexander Bickel of Yale Law School reminds us,

> then the justice and evenness of its administration, the decent and civilized calm and self-consistent manner in which it is brought to bear are crucial to the attainment of its objectives, and are of a much higher order of importance than considerations of the speed and effectiveness with which we can process large numbers of cases to a successful enforcement conclusion.

It should not be impossible to reconcile the liberalism of Professor Bickel with the utilitarianism of Professor Williams.

The current and previous Metropolitan Commissioners' proposals

The professional burglar or robber in Britain is estimated to have a better than two out of five chance of escaping arrest, and if he is caught probably an approximately two out of five chance of acquittal. In America – where some juvenile criminals who cannot read or write can recite their Supreme Court rights word-perfectly – the odds are even longer: only one in five of those who commit serious crimes are arrested, and only one in twelve is convicted. An attack upon this state of affairs was recently instigated by the eleventh report of the Criminal Law Revision Committee in 1974 and subsequently was championed by Sir Robert Mark. 'It is part of the English character that we prefer illusion to reality; that we prefer to look at the past rather than to the future,' he claims; more specifically, that

> it is, of course, right that in a serious criminal case the burden of proof should be upon the prosecution. But in trying to discharge that burden the prosecution has to act within a complicated framework of rules which were designed to give every advantage to the defence. The prosecution has to give the defence advance notice of the whole of its case, but the accused, unless he wants to raise an alibi, can keep his a secret until the actual trial. When the police interrogate a suspect or charge him they have to keep reminding him that

he need not say anything. If he has a criminal record the jury are not ordinarily allowed to know about it. Most of these rules are very old. They date from a time when, incredible as it may seem, an accused person was not allowed to give evidence in his own defence, when most accused were ignorant and illiterate. There was no legal aid and, perhaps most important, if someone was convicted he would most likely be hanged or transported. Under these conditions it's not surprising that the judges who made the rules were concerned to give the accused every possible protection. But it is, to say the least, arguable that the same rules are not suited to the trial of an experienced criminal, using skilled legal assistance, in the late twentieth century.

What changes would he make?

In the short term, I want only two things. First, the abolition of the caution: 'You are not obliged to say anything unless you wish to do so, but what you say may be put into writing and given in evidence.' This has never been of the slightest value other than to the guilty and the criminal lawyer. Secondly, the limited compellability of the accused, by which I mean that the prosecution should have the right to invite him to enter the witness box to listen to questions without there being any liability to punishment for unwillingness to answer. There would, however, be a right to direct the attention of the jury to his failure to answer. Both these changes were advocated by the distinguished members of the Criminal Law Revision Committee, and opposition to them has been emotional rather than logical. The two changes are, of course, directly related and should not be considered separately. The intention is that the credibility of the accused should be related to his spontaneity rather than to that period of reflection and professional consultation between his original interrogation and trial, a period which has produced not only some cases of inexplicable silence but also some of the most predictable, ingenious and highly paid fiction of our time. . . . He is not required to disclose his defence before his trial and thus can – and frequently does – adduce false evidence which the prosecution does not have the opportunity to disprove. If he does give evidence he may

> lie with comparative impunity for it is widely known that in this country it is not the practice to prosecute for perjury if there has been no miscarriage of justice; nor is it the practice, if the accused is found guilty, to reflect that aspect of his defence in his punishment.

Mark decided that to have any hope of change, he would have to campaign publicly. He also agreed that 'there is, I think, a price that we in Great Britain must pay for public acceptance of changes of this kind. We must first accept that no punishment by criminal process should be irrevocable. In other words, the death penalty should not be restored. Second, we must be willing to accept a high degree of supervision of and accountability for our own handling of criminal cases and of complaints.'

Mark sincerely believes that 'nothing I have suggested would in my view increase by one iota the likelihood of the conviction of the innocent.' But the problem is that while it is true, as he says, that 'a high proportion of those who commit crime are unintelligent, weak or otherwise defective people who know nothing of the rules governing investigation,' many innocent people who are accused may similarly be inarticulate, subnormal or merely confused. The protagonists of reform claim that this would be the best way to curb police malpractice through reducing officers' frustration; Mark says,

> I disagree with those who describe the two further changes as increasing the powers of the police. On the contrary, I think they would do much to reduce police malpractice created by the present position. In time, there would be a tendency for most interrogation to take place in open court rather than in a police station . . . Unwillingness to make the law more effective will inevitably provoke demands for harsher punishments and will increase the pressures on the police to use arbitrary methods. You can already see this in the United States . . .

The Criminal Law Revision Committee's proposals – the result of eight years' labour – were however greeted with hostility which condemned them at birth, partly because they appeared at a time when the extent of London police corruption was starting to be exposed. A destructive vicious circle resulted. The police, by breaking the current rules, make civil libertarians unwilling to trust them to operate any less onerous ones. And governments' inability or refusal hitherto sufficiently to improve the police's pay or numbers resulted in first, the police being unwilling to cooperate on other reforms, and second, in the Home Office hesitating to press such controversies on the police.

The Prevention of Terrorism Act 1974, introduced as a result of the IRA's extension of their bombing campaign to the mainland of Britain, gave the police temporarily increased powers of arrest and detention. Although described as 'Draconian' by the then Home Secretary in order to assuage public feeling in the wake of the Birmingham bombing, its effect was comparatively minor (ironically, the IRA had hoped to provoke far tougher panic measures from Westminster which might have alienated public opinion), and there has been no evidence that the police have abused the temporary powers they were given. None the less it is essential that the desirability of changes should be assessed not in the light of any emotive or untypical crimes, but rationally and according to more permanent criteria.

In July 1978, Sir David McNee, the present Metropolitan Commissioner, returned more bluntly to the need for more and better-defined powers for the police. In evidence to the Royal Commission on Criminal Procedure he warned that 'society must also realize that it is not right to expect the police to obtain the necessary powers by stealth and force'. He pointed to examples such as the fact that suspected hooligans entering a football ground at present cannot be searched for weapons without their consent, and asked that the powers of search which now apply to stolen goods might be extended also to cover at least articles which may cause injury to persons, and that spot searches should be permitted if 'by reason of a person's presence at a particular location, an officer believes that such search may assist in the prevention of a serious crime or danger to the public' – for example, at a railway station after a bomb has exploded. He also requested an increased power to obtain bank accounts and the names and addresses of reluctant witnesses: to obtain a blanket fingerprinting order, covering a particular area, from a High Court judge; and to be able to take an arrested person's finger-, palm-, toe-prints and photograph for identification or to compare with those linked with offences. He proposed that for certain offences a court should be allowed to make an order for a person to provide relevant samples of blood, hair, semen or saliva. Less justifiably, even in the view of many police officers, he also suggested that the police might be allowed to detain a suspect for seventy-two hours before charging him.

Decriminalization

Overall reform must start with the weeding out of any dead or dubious wood in the criminal code, in order that the remaining law should command as wide public assent and support as possible – and thus enable the hard-pressed police to concentrate upon the undubitably criminal core. Crime has been defined as a great variety of human acts whose only common feature is that they are currently prohibited by law for a variety of reasons. Views change about what a crime is, not only from one generation to the next, but also contemporaneously across national frontiers. To attempt to kill oneself was a criminal offence from 1854 until 1961 in England, but not in Scotland. In sixteenth-century London, people could be executed for eating meat on Fridays (the idea of eating fish on certain days, originally a religious custom, was in fact strictly enforced to help the national fishing industry). Some activities, such as duelling or slave-owning, are admired in one generation but attract the condemnation of the next. Scarcely three of the ten biblical commandments are enforced by the criminal law in Britain today. Lending money for interest was forbidden by the medieval Christian church, but has long been the chief occupation and ambition of respected pillars of the City of London. Present-day police officers often feel embarrassment at enforcing – usually very reluctantly – the anachronistic laws that still survive relating to Sunday observance. A hundred and fifty years ago Sir Richard Mayne, London's first Commissioner, was reluctant to jeopardize the authority of the police by having them enforce laws about Sunday trading and public houses, because they lacked public support.

A fresh start today could be made by abolishing 'victimless' crimes such as blasphemy, pot-smoking and incest between consenting adults. Other sex laws are also misguided, not just because they are unenforceable (Ulysses Grant's opinion was that he knew of no method to secure the repeal of bad or obnoxious laws so effectively as their stringent execution) but because, in Morris's and Hawkins's words, 'No social interest whatsoever is protected by desultory attempts to impose upon persons adherence to patterns of sexual behaviour arbitrarily selected from the great variety which forms our mammalian heritage.' In France, and several states of the US, wives can still be imprisoned for adultery. Charges of 'insulting behaviour' are redolent of a hierarchical and more authoritarian bygone era: prosecutions for such conduct – regarding, for example, nudity – can make the law today appear a Victorian ass by attempting to regulate taste and manners. The laws against sleeping rough, begging and soliciting similarly now seem obsolete; while the one against fortune-telling, if fully enforced, might end most racing, pools and City columns in the newspapers. The Street Offences Act 1959 still glaringly discriminates between male and female morality, and labels a woman a 'common prostitute' before she has been convicted, and without anyone allegedly offended by her importuning them ever having to give evidence. 'Disorderly houses' have no victims because no one is in them involuntarily. And the haziness of the picketing laws leads the police unnecessarily into political controversy and violence.

Some laws are culpable because they cannot be understood by potential offenders; others are unenforceable while a third group of venerable and vague offences are otiose, if not potentially dangerous. Thus creating a threat to the sovereign's peace by 'insulting behaviour', and the common law offence of 'committing a public nuisance' are both dangerously unspecific and tentacularly reminiscent of the army's catch-all charge of 'dumb insolence'. As the commentary to the American Law Institute's Model Penal Code observes, 'if disorderly conduct statutes are troublesome because they require so little in the way of misbehaviour, the vagrancy statutes offer the astounding spectacle of criminality with no misbehaviour at all.' The former are liable to be used by over-officious conformists to try to control a wide variety of harmless or only slightly annoying non-conformity; the latter by over-zealous social cosmeticians to sweep social problems from visibility. The operation of indecency laws should be restricted to cases when a member of the public has specifically and reasonably complained of being offended: police officers should stop wasting their time spying in public lavatories or pruriently pouncing on lovers to arrest them for performing in their car acts which would be perfectly legal inside a private house. Another charge which is frequently associated with injustice is 'sus': the offence, under section 4 of the Vagrancy Act of 1824, of being a 'suspected person' frequenting a street or highway 'with intent to commit an arrestable offence'. The original rationale of the offence, which derives from some fifteenth-century statutes, accords with Blackstone's precept that 'preventive justice is upon every principal of reason, of humanity and of sound policy preferable in all respects to punishing justice.' But in this particular instance, the requirements of proof are so chimerically low and the difficulties of refuting the charge so onerously great, that it is wide open to abuse. To prove it, it is only necessary for two police officers to allege they saw the accused person – who may have a previously excellent character – acting suspiciously on two separate occasions, which need be only minutes apart. (Looking in two shop-windows has been held to be enough to convict.) The first establishes the alleged offender as a suspected person, the second constitutes his offence; he is charged not with attempting to commit an offence – which would necessitate some subjective *mens rea* –, but with being a suspected person who ostensibly intends to commit an offence. There is no right to have such cases determined by a jury. The temptations such a charge can present to police officers are obvious, and have not always been resisted. In addition, Home Office figures show that 42 per cent of people picked up on 'sus' are black, although blacks make up only some 3 per cent of the population in Britain. There is no logical necessity for any such statutory offence, because the law of attempt would cover any circumstances in which a person's conduct is sufficient to support 'beyond reasonable doubt' an allegation of criminal intent.

The other equally criticized manifestation of preventive justice is the power under the even more antiquated Justices of the Peace Act 1361 of binding someone over 'to keep the peace and be of good behaviour' – an order which continues to be made in Britain some 8,000 times a year. If the person in question declines to agree, or is unable to find suitable sureties, he or she can be sent to prison for six months – without ever having done anything wrong or committed any offence: all that is necessary is merely to be suspected of being about to do something undesirable in the opinion of a police officer and magistrate. The Vagrancy Acts of 1824 and 1935, which punish homeless people for wandering abroad without visible means of support or for sleeping out without permission, are equally arbitrary and oppressive: by making a crime of poverty they not only harm those already disadvantaged, but also politically and socially damage the criminal law itself – together, inevitably, with its enforcement officers. Such arbitrary statutes are too nearly reminiscent of the present offence in the Soviet Union of 'hooliganism', which is defined as all 'intentional acts which seriously disturb public order and show a clear disrespect for society'. Overcriminalization is potentially a dangerous weapon which can at any time be selectively wielded against unpopular defendants in other countries besides communist ones.

Identification

Such amorphous laws are sometimes defended as being necessary to allow the police to arrest and question people they suspect; but it would be better if the police, instead of having to resort to subterfuges often biased against the poor, were given authority to stop any person they reasonably suspect of committing or having committed a crime, and to require him to provide his identity together with an explanation of his suspicious conduct.

Certain of the powers of the police at present are too wide, or too vague; in other respects, additions could be made which would not conceivably prejudice any innocent person. It is difficult to see that many people, unless they had just committed a crime, could reasonably object to telling a police officer their name and address; yet the police at present are frequently handicapped by having no power to discover these elementary facts. For instance, a policeman who sees some people committing misdemeanours is often helpless because he is neither able to order them to wait so that he can charge them, nor does he have any means of discovering who they are. If everybody carried an identity card as they did in war-time, it would be possible to name not only bodies and the injured, but also lost or abandoned children, and people found suffering from loss of memory who sometimes at present have to be kept unnecessarily in hospital for weeks. Such a card could save lives if it recorded the blood-group and vaccinations of the owner, or whether he or she suffered, for example, from diabetes or epilepsy. It could also state what their wishes were regarding transplants after death. It is essential to know the correct name – and hence the history – of a person, in order to be able to give him the appropriate treatment, whether medical (including mental) or penal.

In addition, the likelihood of being asked to prove one's identity would discourage credit-card or cheque frauds and other forgeries. In order to obviate the possibility of false papers, in some parts of India it is necessary to give one's fingerprints before cashing a cheque. The objection that identity cards can be easily forged can be met by adding fingerprints. These are the one totally infallible means of identification. No two fingers or toes are ever identical, even belonging to the same person or otherwise identical twins. Neither do the characteristics of the ridges of skin ever change; if a person mutilates this skin, the ridges regrow exactly the same as previously. Prints are in fact the marks formed by a thin coating of grease which covers every finger. At present in this country, when a man is acquitted his fingerprints are burnt in the 'confidential waste sack' – even if the police are certain of his guilt and even if he gave his fingerprints voluntarily. It is hard to see what any law-abiding person has to fear if his prints are kept in a permanent record. Because they are the most scientific, they are therefore the most impartial, form of evidence possible. They could be used to authenticate birth and death certificates, or bank savings and pension books. If everybody had their prints taken at an early age (they are clearly formed before birth), the idea of that being any more degrading than being photographed would disappear; if they were filed in a computer, they would be the greatest possible deterrent to crime throughout a person's life. A complete fingerprint register could further justice by helping rapidly to clear innocent suspects; it would constitute the best safeguard against the forgery of any document; and it could save many thousands of police man-hours which could then be deployed against crime elsewhere. It is patently impossible for the police to memorize all missing and wanted people, as in theory they are expected to do. Larceny, housebreaking, and receiving – the crimes in which prints are most commonly found – normally make up more than 80 per cent of all indictable offences, and are just those crimes which the police are now least able to clear up.

It is difficult to see how the duty to be correctly identified can be described as an infringement of civil liberty. Instead it is the opposite, for the correct scientific identification of the real culprit may avert a miscarriage of justice. There is a similar case to be made for a court to be able to order tests of saliva, semen, or blood, for their results might all contribute towards the accurate establishment of innocence. (If there were night courts as there are in America, which could see intoxicated drivers immediately on arrest and order a medical examination, a great deal of dispute would also be saved.) Chief Superintendent Bowley of Nottinghamshire would also like to see a law which would enable courts to call for press films or photographs of public disorder, in order to ascertain accurately what occurred. Overall, the more indisputable evidence there can be before a court, the greater possibility there is of justice being done. The reaction of the Home Office to the Devlin Committee Report on Identification has been disappointing. New instructions for the conduct of identity parades have been drafted to replace the previous ones, but have not been given any statutory force, and can therefore be ignored with impunity.

Search

The right to remain anonymous or wrongly identified is defended with a passion which is exceeded only by an Englishman's traditional emotion about the sanctity of his home. Although other officials (such as gas, telephone, water and electricity inspectors) may do so, by law the police are not allowed to enter private premises, or to search them for stolen property or evidence, without an invitation from the owner – improbable in cases of guilt – or a warrant issued by a magistrate for a limited number of particular offences. Whereas in Canada police can search for drugs without a warrant, in Britain the police are not enabled even by the recent Prevention of Terrorism Act to search for explosives or firearms without a warrant, and have fewer powers in this respect than VAT inspectors. Chief inspector Michael Turner of Kentish Town points out that policemen have no right even to patrol many council estates, since these count as private property: 'If we were walking up a tower-block staircase and someone took exception to our presence, we would have no right to be there, and we would have to leave.' Nor is it legal for them to search a car or motorist without some concrete suspicion. Speed of search is obviously of the essence if stolen property or vital evidence is to be recovered; but the difficulties under which the police at present labour is illustrated by their experience that if they guard a house while obtaining a search warrant they are laying themselves open to an action for defamation. One detective superintendent at Scotland Yard said that he did not often apply for a warrant 'because the publicity it attracted was fatal'. With so little stolen property being recovered at the present time, forty-nine years would seem long enough to wait for the 1929 Royal Commission's recommendations to be implemented – especially if it was coupled with a provision that speedy compensation must be paid for any damage caused. The Royal Commission stated that 'it had long been the practice of the police' to search arrested people's homes without any warrant, and that this 'is, in the main, necessary and proper in the interests of justice and cannot be regarded as in any way an undue infringement of the rights and liberties of the subject'; yet despite their recommendation that this should be 'regularized by statute' it still is not legal. Most policemen will frankly admit that it continues to happen frequently.

Pitt's famous eighteenth-century rhetoric – that 'the poorest man may in his cottage bid defiance to all the forces of the Crown. It may be frail, its roof may shake; the wind might blow through it; the storms may enter; the rain may enter. But the King of England cannot enter. All his forces dare not cross the threshold of the ruined tenement' – is already a hollow sham: in England and Wales government departments have 188 different statutory powers to enter and search premises or homes. It is virtually only the police who need to resort to hypocrisy or inevitably are tempted to trickery. Fraud investigations are frequently stymied by the Catch-22 situation that it is only through an application to the High Court that the police can get permission to examine a company's books, but the High Court will not give the go-ahead without evidence – and the evidence as often as not lies in the books the police want to examine. Delay obviously invites an intelligent criminal to alter or destroy evidence so that it is irrecoverable. Lord Denning MR pointed out in the case of Ghani v. Jones in 1969 that

> No magistrate – no judge even – has any power to issue a search warrant for murder . . . nor to dig for the body. Nor to look for the axe, the gun or the poison dregs. The police have to get the permission of the householder to enter if they can; or, if not, to do it by stealth or by force. Somehow they seem to manage. No decent person refuses them permission. If he does, he is probably implicated in some way or other. So the police risk an action for trespass.

More recently, in the case of Jeffrey v. Black (1977), the present Lord Chief Justice has given the Divisional Appeal Court's imprimatur to the general run of illegal police searches by holding that evidence obtained thereby will not be disallowed as evidence other than in 'very exceptional circumstances'. It would be greatly preferable if instead the police were given those powers which are adequate and proper, and then made to stick within them. In Poland today the police are obliged by law to have an impartial witness present when they search someone's house, as a protection against the planting of evidence: in this respect, other countries can learn from Poland.

Arrest

The 1929 Royal Commission's other unanimous recommendations for regularizing 'detention for questioning' have also not yet been acted upon. The result is that the police again have to continue to resort to methods such as bluff, threats or 'holding charges'. Contrary to what a surprising number of officers believe, or claim to believe, they have no power to detain without arrest. (Urban police officers are inclined to arrest on many occasions when rural officers, with a more stable population, would use a summons.) Every newspaper report that someone has been 'detained for questioning' is legally inaccurate – though after the Aldershot bombing, one man was so held for four and a half days. (An American Civil Liberties Union study of 2,038 cases in Chicago in 1956 found that more than 50 per cent of police prisoners had been held without charge for more than seventeen hours.) If the police force a man to go to the police station against his will, without arresting him, they risk an action for false imprisonment; but they are often reluctant to arrest and charge him, because from then on he is not allowed to be questioned. An arrest is an unlawful act and must be capable of being specifically justified: the public interest is not sufficient reason. The police are permitted to enter a house to arrest someone for an offence carrying a maximum penalty of more than five years imprisonment, but not for a lesser one. Police officers themselves agree that if they were given adequate legal powers they would not have the excuse of frustration for resorting to extra-legal methods. A senior commander of the London CID recalled that on one occasion he ordered his officers to lock up all ninety people who were in a bar until one of them talked about a shooting that had taken place there; and that on another occasion in 1975 he unlawfully had to order a murder suspect to be detained for five days until a sick witness was well enough to identify him. Some police officers argue that the only real power they possess is to be able to inconvenience a person who refuses to cooperate with them. 'If we stuck to the letter not one in ten of those in prison would be there', and 'If we fully observed the Judges' Rules, we would be tying one hand behind our backs, and the public would be the first to howl at us because we never convicted anybody', are typical police views. But arguments that 'we have to break the law to enforce it' are too reminiscent of other people who claim to 'abolish democracy in order to save it'. Nor is having to rely on public ignorance of legal rights a sound basis for law enforcement.

A completely new public attitude is required about several issues involving crime and the police. A start should be made with the tragic scandal of road casualties. Every year over 7,000 people meet violent death and 80,000 are injured seriously on the roads of Britain alone: an annual total of killings six times greater than those in all the years of the recent troubles in Northern Ireland. Yet this receives infinitely less public concern than the yearly total of less than 190 known murders, or even the country's 2,000 serious drug addicts: resistance continues to safety-belts, and lethally drunken drivers continue to be acquitted on ludicrous grounds. The British opposition to allowing the police to conduct random breath-tests (as they do on the mainland of Europe) epitomizes the public attitude of regarding even serious crime as a game: no innocent and safe driver would have anything more than a brief delay to fear from such a test, whereas they themselves as well as innocent pedestrians could owe their lives to its intervention or deterrent effect on other drivers. A similarly illogical antipathy to camera-evidence – often the best proof of truth in court – is shared both by the public and the police themselves, who have been known to smash the cameras of journalists recording demonstrations.

Failure to report any crime, however serious, is not an offence. Members of the public have no general duty to help the police, though if an officer specifically asks for assistance and a by-stander unreasonably refuses, he can be prosecuted. The CID were opposed for a long time in the last century on the grounds that they were 'snoopers'. This 'sporting' attitude stems from the days of revulsion against the earlier barbarity of the criminal law and its methods. But anybody who takes a romantic view of crime today should sit in a criminal court and see its true human consequences – in the injuries, broken families, and the fear and suspicion it can arouse in people. It would be to the benefit of everybody if justice could be made more of a science and less of a sport. Crime, and being suspected of it, are both serious matters; a suspect is not a fox or a pheasant: he is entitled at his trial to something other than luck.

The main protections of the citizen against police oppression are his ability to apply to the courts for *habeas corpus* to stop wrongful imprisonment, and to sue a police officer who has exceeded his powers. However, unless he has some corroboration, a complainant's word is rarely accepted against that of the police. A defendant in a criminal trial faces a further serious risk from our rule that any criminal history which he has is liable to be revealed in court if he makes an allegation against a police witness. This threat introduces a disagreeable element of gambling into a trial, and should be abolished. It is a fundamental part of justice that a man is tried for the matter he is accused of, and not for the smear of his previous history. The fact that a man has a criminal record should not deny him the right to speak of anything irregular that has happened to him – especially as almost all police misconduct takes place against known criminals. Neither does it necessarily follow that the word of such a man is worthless – some of the most criminal people are truthful, yet some of the most law-abiding are recidivist fantasists.

A delicate but distinct border-line has been drawn by judges between the police's permissible use of informers and the illegality of their employing *agents provocateurs* – for whom the British, typically, retain the foreign name. Neither the police nor their informers may create a crime in order to trap criminals: James Callaghan when Home Secretary issued a circular which stated that 'no member of a police force and no police informant should counsel, incite or procure the commission of a crime.' Nevertheless such an action necessarily often takes place in, for example, cases of the sale of goods in contravention of the Food and Drugs Act or the Trade Descriptions Act. On the other hand, officers or informers are permitted to participate in offences already being committed in order to obtain evidence for a conviction. Informers play a key role in much crime detection: one CID inspector said, 'A detective is as good as his informers allow him to be. In many cases you have nothing to go on at all until the informer comes in.' Dispute continues as to what degree of encouragement by an informer would constitute 'entrapment', which in the US constitutes a complete defence to a criminal charge. CID men argue that if plans for the crime have already been made, it is virtually impossible for the police not to allow the crime to take place: otherwise a prosecution would have to rely entirely on the mere word of the informer – whose identity would be exposed – set against that of his accomplices who would deny everything.

Telephone taps

Another difficult issue is the covert interception by the police of telephone calls and letters. The police are allowed, if they can show a cast-iron *prima facie* case of a serious crime, to intercept telephone calls. In 1957 a committee of Lord Birkett, Lord Monckton, and Mr Patrick Gordon-Walker examined the present practice and approved it. They were unanimous in declaring that 'so far from the citizen being injured by the exercise of the power in the circumstances we have set out, we think the citizen benefits therefrom.' Its value is demonstrated by the fact that in 1957 every interception but one led to arrest. The present position is, however, a compromise: the personal approval of a Secretary of State has to be obtained for each individual case, so that authority is sought only rarely – about 160 times a year by the police in England, considerably more in Northern Ireland due to the Emergency, and for several years in Scotland not at all. In the US there are some 700 taps authorized by the courts annually, nearly half of which take place in New York, and another quarter in New Jersey. In Britain, official authorization is not required when a subscriber whose telephone is being tapped – such as a line from a public call-box in a pub – has given his permission. A thorough tap requires a relay of intelligent officers listening round the clock, and can be monotonous work. The Campaign for Nuclear Disarmament, suspecting they were being surveyed, once arranged a fictitious picket on their telephone; only plain-clothed Special Branch officers attended it. The lines to the central listening post under Chelsea Barracks in London have been trebled in the last decade, but informed sources say that the number of taps has hardly increased. Every paranoiac or status-seeker claims that his telephone is tapped, but the listener has no means of knowing this: clicks on the line are due to other causes.

But a senior judge would undoubtedly be a more appropriate person than a politician to give such authorization. Since Home Secretaries refuse to answer questions on the matter, the present system provides no democratic safeguard through Parliament to compensate for its political dangers, and in the US President Carter has recently abandoned his prerogative power of ordering electronic surveillance, which in future can only be authorized by the warrant of a Federal judge. On the other hand, if we accept the Birkett committee's recommendation that the criminal and the wrong-doer should not be allowed to use services provided by the state for wrongful purposes quite unimpeded, and the police, the customs, and the security services ought not to be deprived of an effective weapon in their efforts to preserve and maintain order for the benefit of the community, it is difficult to see why such a weapon should be used so little. It is permitted with varying safeguards elsewhere: for example, in the United States, Italy, Austria, Scandinavia, Switzerland, Germany, and France. Oddly enough, the police do not require permission to film secretly whereas they do to record a telephone conversation. It is possible to argue that no innocent person need worry if his telephone is being tapped, and that wider use of this power could prevent many cases of business fraud and blackmail – two of the hardest crimes to prove before considerable damage has been caused. But if the police are to have this power at all, it is essential that the information obtained is never passed to any outside body, as the Birkett committee criticized Lord Tenby for having permitted when he was Home Secretary. Regrettably, the private use of most bugging devices and phone taps is not illegal, although fortunately in Britain this is extremely difficult, for technical reasons – unlike in America, where it is used by commercial rivals. Whether an intercepted conversation should be admitted as evidence at a trial is a separate question, which presumably depends on proof that the method of recording was reliable and that the entire conversation is before the court. At present the results of telephone taps are never produced in court, but are only used by the police to assist them in obtaining other evidence. Consequently, courts never have any opportunity of ascertaining whether a tap was authorized or not.

For similar reasons, only a senior judge should be allowed to authorize the interception of letters. At present the Home Secretary sanctions this on some two hundred occasions a year, but the safeguards regarding the privacy of the mail are even weaker than those regarding telephone taps, since the Post Office Act of 1969 empowered and indeed required the new Corporation 'to do what is necessary to inform designated persons holding office under the Crown concerning matters and things transmitted or in the course of transmission' by the Post Office. Consequently in its Private Office, the Post Office steams open or X-rays the contents of letters regularly: about half for suspected criminal cases and half for suspected politically subversive purposes. Sometimes a needle is pushed through an open corner at the back of an envelope and then rotated to furl the letter round itself so that it can be extracted. There is an engaging tradition of amateurism about this operation: not long ago, a senior trade unionist was surprised to find that the official form authorizing the interception had been inadvertently included in a letter delivered to him.

The Judges' Rules

The most discussed and disputed actions of the police occur when they question suspected people. In general they have no power to compel any witness or suspect either to disclose any fact within his knowledge or to answer any question. The conditions necessary before any statement or confession is admitted as evidence in a trial are laid down not by Parliament but by the High Court judges. These 'Judges' Rules' were first formulated in 1912, after two policemen had been censured by two different judges, one for 'cautioning' a suspected man and the other one for not doing so. In desperation, the then chief constable of Birmingham wrote to the Lord Chief Justice asking for elucidation and advice. His reply, drafted after a special meeting of the judges but without any consultation with Parliament, the police, or the Home Office, forms the Rules, whose text as amended in 1964 is printed as Appendix A in this book. They are an attempt to strike a fair balance between the rights of a suspect and the interests of justice, but they do not have the validity of law, and breaches of them are frequently but erratically condoned by courts. Sir Henry Fisher in his report on the Confait inquiry stated that some of the Judges' Rules and directions did not seem to be known to police officers and members of the legal profession. The National Council for Civil Liberties believe that new rules with statutory backing should be devised, and that any evidence obtained in breach of them should be excluded from trials. There is a certain ambiguity about the present Rules, but probably their main defect is that they are so complicated that they are unlikely to be observed. However, it is even more doubtful whether the three 'cautions', on which the Rules are principally based, fulfil any useful purpose: does the well-worn formula really prevent any innocent person from making a false confession? In the absence of physical or mental pressure (in conjunction with which no 'caution' will make any difference) wrong confessions will only emanate either deliberately or, more commonly, from the mentally ill. On neither of these categories is the caution likely to have any effect. And, as a detective inspector asked, 'After a flying tackle on an armed thief, what sane person seriously expects us to solemnly caution him?' Not only is it a chimerical safeguard but, when it is scrupulously administered, it must often cut off possibly valuable information – relating perhaps to other crimes or the whereabouts of stolen property – which a guilty man is anxious to volunteer in explanation of his actions. Is it in the public interest that really voluntary and accurate confessions, or even the significance of false statements, are excluded from being evidence merely because of the absence of the traditional shibboleth? As Jim Jardine of the Police Federation of England and Wales points out, 'The suspect knows he is dealing with a police officer who is investigating a crime. That in itself warns him to be careful of what he says.' The real safeguards we need in order to be satisfied about a statement are first, that it was made voluntarily, and secondly, that it is recounted or reproduced accurately and in full. The present arrangements are unsatisfactory in that they fail to meet completely either of these minimal requirements.

There are strong arguments that people who are in custody should not in any event be held under the control of the police. Because there is no legal right to detain someone for questioning, there is at present no legal limit on how long he or she may be so held. In France, suspects may be detained *incommunicado* for a maximum period of forty-eight hours, though after twenty-four hours a prisoner has a right to medical examination. The US, Canada and Denmark allow a maximum period of twenty-four hours; Japan, Austria, Holland and Israel, forty-eight hours; Finland, seventy-two. The whole crucial area of detention for questioning is, as Professor Michael Zander of the London School of Economics says, completely fudged in the present Judges' Rules. The Thomson committee in Scotland in 1975 suggested a new power for the police of limited arrest without warrant for up to six hours, but proposed as a *quid pro quo* that suspects' statements would only be admissible in court if the interrogation had been taperecorded, and that in cases begun with indictment, the record of the interrogation should be put to the accused for challenge or agreement before a sheriff. Rightly, the committee concluded 'society must make up its mind whether or not such things as detaining and questioning suspects are acceptable, and either prohibit them, or legalize them under suitable safeguards.'

Confession statements

John Mortimer QC suggests that 'police interrogation is in urgent need of reform and present inept and unconvincing ways are costing thousands of unnecessary pounds a year in wasted legal aid fees.' One solution would be to allow questioning only when an impartial third person is present; whether he was a solicitor, magistrate, independent shorthand-writer, or even a bystander, he would be able equally to verify fairness and to protect the police from unjust allegations. At present suspects who are poor sometimes receive less justice than rich people who have more chance of solicitors' attendance. A number of solicitors say they would be prepared to join a panel who could be summoned to be present during questioning at any time. It would neither be necessary nor desirable to allow them to interrupt or advise silence; their mere presence would be enough to ensure fairness. In a case in 1950, the Court of Criminal Appeal approved notes taken by a shorthand-writer at an interrogation as being the fairest and best record. If the administrative difficulty of getting reliable people to be present at all hours of the day and night proves insuperable, the alternative is to develop and install a tamper-proof form of taperecorder that could reproduce the questions, together with the pauses and the tone of voice – although it might miss other factors only discernible to the eye. It is true that suspects may be reluctant to inform on confederates or associates if they know that their words are being recorded, but locked cassettes or clock-mechanisms can make taperecordings more reliable court evidence than notebooks or even photographs. In due time, a video-taperecorder will no doubt be used. One method of forestalling allegations of subsequent tampering would be if at every interrogation there were two machines, so that each party could take into possession his own recording until the trial. This is analogous to the present system for handling blood samples, and the expense would probably be less than that of the time saved in counsels' disputes about confessions and 'verbals' at jury trials. If it is objected that the full recording would be too long or incoherent for a jury to follow, the solution would be to make it all available to the defence, so that they could refer to any particular part if they wished.

The Judges' Rules – which should be extended to cover fingerprinting and police photography – advise the police to allow everybody to write out their own statement (one experienced judge who was charged with a motoring offence not long ago significantly insisted on doing so himself in the policeman's notebook). When the police do the writing, it becomes hearsay evidence by being translated into police language. Even honest policemen tend to write down their interpretation of what – and indeed not infrequently what they wish – had been said. Questions and answers cannot result in a truly spontaneously voluntary statement, because they dictate the general direction of the statement, and are themselves determined by the questioner's ideas. When the questions are edited out of the statement, the whole tenor of the conversation is altered – without the court generally being aware of this. In addition, the defendant and witnesses often forgo points they wished to state because these did not fit in as replies to any of the questions they were asked. As far as possible, therefore, statements should be in the speaker's own verbatim words. If the Judges' Rules are thought to ensure fairness, their principles should be applied to cover the questioning of witnesses as well. But, as one senior judge rightly comments, 'They do not lay down what the police may or may not do at the police station to obtain information, provided it is proved in court by some other means.' The Home Office has issued some 'administrative directions' to all police forces regarding their methods of taking statements, though, like the Judges' Rules, these are not part of the law. The outcome of a great number of criminal cases hinges much more upon obtaining a confession than upon anything that happens in the course of the trial. The Criminal Bar Association proposes that 'until a watertight system of recording can be devised we think that any note made of an alleged verbal reply to questions, by an accused, or a copy thereof, should be shown to the accused at the earliest practicable time after the making of the note. He should be invited to endorse the note as being accurate or to make any comment upon it that he wishes. Any such comment should be recorded if possible by the accused himself. If this procedure were followed we feel much of the dispute that centres around alleged police "verbals" would be avoided and much time saved.'

American judges have taken a much firmer and more consistent role in defining constitutional rights. In the 1966 case of Miranda v. Arizona, the US Supreme Court by a five to four decision prohibited the questioning of a suspect in custody unless a lawyer is present, or the suspect expressly waives this right. The majority of the court in addition concluded that interrogation in an isolated setting in a police station constituted a formal compulsion to confess. There was greater sympathy with the prosecution in the early years of the subsequent Burger Supreme Court, but recently the court has ruled more often in favour of defendants than prosecutors: in 1978 for example it refused to allow any exception to the requirement for a search warrant, even at the scene of a murder. Mr Justice Goldberg stated in Escobedo v. Illinois (1964), 'If the exercise of constitutional rights will thwart the effectiveness of a system of law enforcement, then there is something very wrong with that system'. Excluding good evidence is a crude instrument for trying to enforce police fairness. From the point of view of justice it would be far better rationally to reform and define the police practices. In British courts, confessions have been ruled inadmissible because they followed the interrogator saying 'You had better tell the truth', 'I think it would be better if you made a statement and told me exactly what happened', and even because a social worker present advised the defendant, 'Do not admit something you have not done. But it is always the best policy to be honest. If you were at the house, tell the officers about it'. For a variety of reasons, people none the less have certainly been known to make false confessions to the police. One case dealt with by the NCCL concerned a young man employed in a garage in West London as a petrol pump attendant. The garage reported to the police the loss of £50 and the man was arrested and held at the police station for six hours. By the time he was released the police had a written confession from him and he was charged with stealing the money. The garage then discovered that the money had never been missing at all and that they had been mistaken. In fact the man had confessed not only to a crime he had not committed but to a crime that had never occurred at all. He told his solicitor that while in police custody he had been slapped round the face and had been threatened that unless he confessed his mother and wife would be implicated. It was then that he agreed to make a written confession. A much more serious case was that of Confait which involved three South London youths convicted respectively of murder, manslaughter and arson after confessing their guilt to the police. Three years after the conviction – and only due to a sustained campaign led by Christopher Price MP – the Court of Appeal decided that on the medical and scientific evidence they could not have been guilty. Although Sir Henry Fisher later took a third and different view, this episode should finally silence agitation for the return of capital punishment. Yet other cases have shown how people confess to crimes merely to stop police questioning or to enable them to be released from the police station – and this can happen even where there is no improper behaviour by police officers. Often these people wrongly assume that it will be an easy matter to withdraw their confessions at a later stage. There is a great deal of psychological evidence to show that people generally have the urge to talk in situations where they are expected to talk, as part of the general sociological phenomenon of people often fulfilling the roles expected of them. In the criminal process this is intensified by the whole range of fears generated by arrest, interrogation, isolation, and the physical control of the situation by the interrogators. Most people are in a very frightened state at a police station. Sympathy, anxiety, silence, exhaustion, bluff, cajolement, insinuation – and especially the alternation of these pressures – can, according to psychiatrists, eventually lead almost anybody to say what he thinks his listener wishes to hear.

The Judges' Rules are unheard of by most laymen, and are publicly displayed in few police stations. But even if they were, they have been at their most weak and virtually meaningless with regard to a detained person's right to contact his solicitor. This 'right' has until recently only existed on sufferance when the police are prepared to grant it, and has therefore been in practice totally unenforceable. Detained people recount that the police's replies to their request to contact their lawyer often take the form of 'You've been watching too many films' and 'If you try to be funny, we can be funny too.' The Fisher report in 1978 revealed a wholesale disregard of this rule within the Metropolitan police force: 'The existence of Administrative Direction 7 was unknown to counsel and to senior police officers who gave evidence before me. In the Metropolitan Police District it is not observed.' A 1972 study of 130 prisoners revealed that 108 had not seen a solicitor and that 74 per cent said that the police had refused them permission to do so. Yet in the Briggate Mill insurance fraud trial in 1976 Mr Justice McKenna excluded incriminating answers that an accused made after the police had denied him access to his solicitor, and the Court of Appeal upheld a similar approach in the case of Lemsatef in the same year. The police reluctance is primarily due to the fact that a solicitor's usual advice to his client is to say nothing. In July 1977 a backbenchers' campaign in Parliament (led by George Cunningham MP) for once succeeded and forced the Home Secretary to concede in the new Criminal Law Act 1977 the statutory right of a suspect when he is arrested to have informed 'one person reasonably named by him, without delay, or, where some delay is necessary in the interests of the investigation or prevention of crime or the apprehension of offenders, with no more delay than is so necessary'. Home Office circular no. 74/1978 now states that suspects must be told of this right when they arrive at the police station, by a notice posted in the station or by a leaflet being handed to them. The notification of a reasonably named person (the Home Office cite as 'unreasonably named' persons 'e.g. famous pop star, football player or government minister not being the person's own MP') should be done wherever possible by telephone: and the provisions apply equally to people arrested under the Prevention of Terrorism Act. Chief police officers will have to report regularly to the Home Secretary the number of cases in which they have delayed the exercise of this right for exceptional circumstances.

The police had opposed allowing any such right, on the grounds that it might lead to interference with witnesses, the concealment or destruction of evidence, or the flight of the accused's criminal associates. They have another motive too which is less often publicly bruited. Dr William Sargant states, 'To elicit confessions, one must try to create feelings of anxiety and guilt': being cut off from the comfort or advice of a friend or lawyer is crucial to the police's success in this. But MPs pointed out that section 19 of the Criminal Procedure (Scotland) Act had two years earlier stipulated that 'where any person has been arrested on any criminal charge, such person shall be entitled immediately upon such arrest to have intimation sent to a solicitor that his professional assistance is required by such person, and informing him of the place to which such person is to be taken for examination,' and Cunningham asked what use was the right of *habeas corpus* if a detainee is unable to exercise it because he is unable to let anybody know he is detained.

The right to remain silent

Some senior London detectives, backed by the Superintendents Association, say they would willingly abandon any evidence obtained by oral questioning, if in return an accused person should give up the right to silence. In English-speaking countries witnesses can be subpoenaed to appear in court, but they are under no obligation to answer any question that might incriminate them – often the questions to which their answers might be most valuable. By pleading the Fifth Amendment some men in America have been able to evade conviction for years. In both countries the person who is actually charged with a crime enjoys an even greater right: not only need he not answer, but he need not even be questioned in court if he does not so desire. This is the high-water mark of the 'sporting' attitude in the law. Support for the rule (which is not an ancient one) seems to have originated in reaction to the days of torture, when suspects were almost invariably uneducated men facing the death penalty. It has been widely criticized since. The American National Commission on Law Observance in 1931 stated that they considered that this privilege 'has come to be of little advantage to the innocent and a mere price in the game of criminal justice.' Bentham described the rule as 'one of the most pernicious and most irrational notions that ever found its way into the human mind', and went on

> If it is wished to protect the accused against punishment, it can be done at once, and with perfect efficacy, by not allowing any investigation ... If all criminals of every class had assembled and framed a system after their own wishes, is not this rule the very first which they would have established for their security? Innocence never takes advantage of it: innocence claims the right of speaking, as guilt invokes the privilege of silence.

Moreover, he pointed out, the rules applied by English courts do not in fact play fair, because the accused is not able to prevent his written words, or his conversation recounted by other witnesses, from being admitted as evidence:

> Thus, what the technical procedure rejects is his own evidence in the purest and most authentic form; what it admits is the same testimony, provided that it be indirect, that it has passed through channels which may have altered it, and that it be reduced to the inferior and degraded state of hearsay.

More recently Sir John Foster, QC, told a committee on the Preliminary Examination of Criminal Offences organized by Justice:

An argument was put forward that it was bad luck on inexperienced offenders who often did not know their rights and gave themselves away, while the old lags, knowing they need not say anything, remained silent and secured acquittals. I would have thought that the bad luck was on the community that a sentimental sporting rule for which there was no justification should enable guilty men to escape.

He went on to claim that if the English rules had been applied at the Nuremberg Trial, not one of the defendants would have been convicted. Revocation of them, he argued, would make the English criminal trial 'less of a game or a contest and more of a serious inquiry as to the true nature of the crime and its real perpetrator'; it could even at times operate to the benefit of a defendant because 'if he has to go into the box the whole is more likely to emerge, which may throw light on some feature of the case and possibly lead to an acquittal or a diminution of the gravity of the offence (e.g., from. . . . murder to manslaughter) or to the establishment of some mitigating factors.' This fuller picture would, at the least, give the judge material to help him to be able to decide the most constructive sentence.

At present, on the other hand, the right to silence permits a skilful lawyer to leave the jury with a wholly misleading impression of events, without there being any opportunity to test or challenge it. Out of court, few innocent people are aware of its existence, whereas experienced criminals are able to make use of it. The abandonment of this rule would not be the revolutionary or unprecedented innovation that its supporters contend. Already people are liable to be convicted if they refuse to disclose information concerning offences under the Official Secrets Acts, or even if they do not divulge who was driving their car at the time a road traffic offence was committed. Even in public examinations in bankruptcy, the debtor has no right to silence. If the principle is acceptable in these cases, it is strange that it is not thought 'sporting' in cases of rape, kidnapping or murder. Sir David McNee has proposed to the Royal Commission on Criminal Procedure that two new forms of caution shall be given by police officers:

I suspect that you have (specify offence). You will be asked questions about it. If you are prosecuted later and have not answered the questions now, the court will be told of your failure to answer, and your evidence may be less likely to be believed.

Just before a person is charged, a second caution would be administered:

> You are going to be charged with ... If there is anything that you have not already said that you think shows that you are innocent, you should tell me about it now. If you hold it back until you go to court, your evidence may be less likely to be believed.

Professor Glanville Williams, who is a powerful advocate for the abandonment of the present right to silence, believes it would not be necessary to have any penalty for refusal to answer; he would only require an accused person to listen to questions put to him by counsel for the prosecution. If questioning was transferred to the public court in this way, it might be unnecessary to admit as evidence any statements whatever obtained by the police – which would thus remove from the arena a major source of dispute. Sir Patrick Hastings said that 'voluntary statements' are never voluntary, and should never be admitted in evidence. In India, following a period of disquiet about confessions, the British in 1872 introduced a new Evidence Act which has been retained since Independence. This permits the police to interrogate for purposes of investigation, but does not allow any resulting statement to be admitted in court. Instead, statements which will be admitted may be made at any time before a magistrate. Lord Shawcross, among others, suggested the adoption of a similar practice here, but one eminent jurist with great experience of its working in India comments, 'There was always the suspicion that the confessing accused had been threatened or cajoled into making a confession, and tutored as to the answers he was to give when asked by the magistrate why he wishes to confess'. A policeman, who has lately returned from there, says succinctly that 'third degree used to go on while the magistrate was asked to wait'. From this it is plain, not that the principle is necessarily wrong, but that the safeguards are not enough. 'The ideal,' Lord Devlin has stated, 'is an impartial investigator whose only duty is to bring the true facts to light.' Can we expect policemen, whom we require to be ardent in the pursuit of criminals also to fulfil this role?

Some recent cases have resulted in the suggestion that the prosecution should have greater legal powers to ensure the presence of witnesses at court: by being, for example, able to extradite them. Extradition, whether or not extended to witnesses, should cover all except political offenders, instead of the present somewhat arbitrary categories. Several trials show the necessity for protecting witnesses, but it would be unjustifiable interference to take them into custody, as a few people advocate: in the United States, two unfortunate law-abiding sisters spent six months in gaol because they were unable to raise a large bond.

In most Continental countries, the *juge d'instruction* can examine people who are believed to have relevant information in addition to the suspect himself. In some jurisdictions these people can be penalized if they refuse to answer questions. This system has two major advantages over our own 'accusatorial' method. First, it is to society's advantage to learn as much as possible concerning the reasons for every crime – an aspect which often totally fails to emerge in English courts. Secondly, and of even greater importance, the more thorough the investigation of a crime, the less chance there is of a wrong conviction.

Computerized records

Different but equally important issues are raised by police records. In Britain there are now more than 220 different functions of central government which involve computerized personal information about identifiable individuals. Fifteen thousand metres of tape are not capable of storing a twenty-page dossier on every man, woman and child in the World. In theory, the Metropolitan police delete the criminal record of a juvenile after ten years, and an adult's (except for sexual offences) after twenty years, if he only has one conviction; otherwise they do so when he reaches the age of seventy. A number of police forces unofficially advise some employers – and especially their ex-police security officers – about prospective employees' records; the conviction of a teacher, civil servant, lawyer, doctor, dentist, nurse or magistrate is automatically notified to their appropriate employing or professional body. In the United States, the police have sometimes been known to purchase credit reports; criminal record information is usually given to the police forces of friendly nations when they request it. The potential for abuse is obvious: the FBI's files, which under Edgar Hoover contained details of many people's non-criminal weaknesses and indiscretions, were described by Senator Joseph Clarke as a potential threat to American democracy. Newspapers regularly demonstrate how easy it is for experienced outsiders to obtain data from records by telephone; regrettably, it is not a criminal offence to get confidential information by deception. The NCCL also receives a number of complaints that the police privately inform employers about offences (especially sexual ones) committed by their employees or prospective candidates for a job. In 1977 workers occupying the Reinforcement Steel Services factory at Greenwich found a memorandum that revealed inaccurate and obsolete information about two union activists at the factory, which had been supplied by a Scotland Yard officer. As records inexorably become more detailed (criminal files may soon extend to data of blood, saliva, semen and voice), it is all the more important that a member of the public should be able to verify their accuracy concerning himself: a computer or human error might – unknown to the victim – blight his whole life. Since the Consumer Credit Act of 1974 all consumer credit agencies in Britain must on payment supply a copy of any file kept on a customer by the agency. In principle, individuals should, perhaps in return for compulsory fingerprinting, have the right to see, challenge and correct all their own files, with the exception of some police and national security records which might be verified through an independent third party. Non-governmental civil liberties representatives should sit on a Data Protection Authority which would watch over the whole field of the collection and storage of personal information, and ensure for example that it was never employed against political opponents. The NCCL has proposed the additional safeguards that no system should store information about a person's politics, religion or sexual activity except in connection with a violation of criminal law;

that information given for one purpose should never be used for another without the individual's knowledge and consent (the UK governmental data banks); and that the international transfer of personal information must be controlled, since a confederation of German detective agencies recently moved their data bank to Luxembourg to avoid new West German legislation to regulate this field.

Police discretion

Perhaps the most powerful of all the police's roles is their exercise of discretion about whether or not to prosecute somebody they believe has broken the law. In this they assume a function which is quasi-judicial rather than executive – and one which can have a considerable effect. For example, in Manchester in 1955 there was only one prosecution for male importuning, none at all in 1956 or 1957, and only two in 1958. At the end of 1958 a new chief constable arrived, and prosecutions for this offence rose rapidly: from 30 in 1959 to 105 in 1960, 135 in 1961, and 216 in 1962. Apart from the local police area's policy, each station officer, when he weighs evidence to decide if there is a *prima facie* case and whether or not to accept a charge, has a role not far different from that of a continental examining magistrate. Both stages of the discretion whether to prosecute happen to be innocent of any legal authority, though naturally their exercise is the subject of few formal complaints. But the decisions involved can give rise to many other problems. An arrest or detention later judged to be illegal can involve the payment of heavy damages, and the policeman on duty has neither the time nor the opportunities to consult law-books which are available to those who may later sue him. In making up his mind, he has to take account of the relative considerations of his own, the local police authority's, and the local Bench's or a public jury's views, as well as the policy of his superior officers. Many policemen say that the most difficult part of their work is to know when to enforce the law and when to turn a half-closed eye. Since crimes are only certain acts 'believed to be socially harmful by a group of people which has power to enforce its beliefs', there sometimes are substantial minorities who disagree with a particular measure. It is doubtful whether a majority of people in this country today approve of the present law on Sunday observance, or on licensing, although each is defended by politically powerful groups.

Every year, hundreds of thousands of traffic offences are dealt with by a verbal warning, besides those resulting in a written caution (also without legal authority incidentally) – a far greater total than those which lead to a summons. This discretion is not easy to distinguish from the power to impose an on-the-spot fine, which is often resisted on the grounds that the police and the judiciary have separate functions in this country. But frequently it is the apparent comparative unfairness of being prosecuted or having their car towed away which is most resented by people who realize they are guilty, but see others escaping with impunity. Sometimes they are irritated because they remember a different policy in the same place in the past, or cannot understand why night parking in a street requires lights in one city and not in another. The factors such as accident rates, varying perhaps at different times of the day or week, which influence the police's policy, and any alterations to the policy itself are rarely made known to the public. The impossibility of properly enforcing some regulations may well encourage a general disregard for the law by diminishing people's respect for the concept both of law and of themselves as law-abiding persons. Ineffectual restrictions probably cause more harm than good by weakening natural self-enforced controls: they certainly have added to the difficulties of the police. The proportion of young offenders who are cautioned varies in different police forces from 2 to 70 per cent. Research about criteria and effects are obviously overdue. Scotland involves independent trained 'reporters' in such decisions.

But with the growth in the number of administrative offences, and the shortage of manpower which is compelling the police to give selective priorities to the enforcement of laws, the incidence of their discretion has increased. It also extends to more serious offences, and in the view of Lord Denning MR, cannot be challenged: 'I hold it to be the duty of the Commissioner of Police of the Metropolis, as it is of every chief constable, to enforce the law of the land. . . . He must decide whether or not suspected persons are to be prosecuted. . . . But in all these things he is not the servant of anyone, save of the law itself. No Minister of the Crown can tell him that he must or must not . . . prosecute this man or that one. Nor can any police authority tell him so. The responsibility of law enforcement lies on him. He is answerable to the law and to the law alone'. (R. v. Commissioner of Police of the Metropolis, *ex parte* Blackburn, 1968.) Indictable offenders known to the police are cautioned for a wide variety of reasons: perhaps because it was a first offence, or because there was too little evidence or because an employer was reluctant to prosecute. A limited number of offenders escape prosecution by providing information about other criminals. Many American police officers admit they are affected by an offender's sex appearance, race, background and cooperativeness in deciding whether to press a formal charge. Policemen cannot hope to be immune to some of the same influences which Lord Justice Scrutton described as affecting judges: 'I am not speaking of conscious impartiality; but the habits you are trained in, the people with whom you mix, lead to your having a certain class of ideas, of such a nature that, when you have to deal with other ideas, you do not give as sound and accurate judgements as you would wish.' The overloaded system of justice in the United States would in fact collapse totally if 90 per cent of criminal defendants did not plead guilty, which means that most cases involve some sort of deal being agreed between the police, defendant and prosecutor. Although police discretion in some cases is supplanting the function of judges, it is often exercised for humane reasons. A few forces have a policy of warning children up to four or five times before bringing them to court. Some rigorously prosecute offences which are brought to light by blackmail, whereas others make a principle of not doing so. One force, when a man lost his wife after twenty years of devoted marriage in a car accident for which he was acquitted of dangerous driving, then stonefacedly sought to exact a pound of flesh by prosecuting him for careless driving; but other forces observe a 'nearest and dearest' rule whereby proceedings are waived against a driver when it is considered that he has been punished enough by the death of a relative. In most borderline cases when the police decide in favour of prosecution, charges are sometimes brought for considerations of deferrence or in order to meet public feeling rather than solely to achieve a conviction. Current popular moves have their effect too: in a democracy, policemen remain members of society and can hardly fail to be influenced by community views.

The basic premise of the British and some other police forces, that they are the executive branch of the law totally separate from the judiciary, is inevitably compromised by the considerable discretion they have to exercise. In the US, out of every 100 youths arrested, only twenty reach a court; the police's judicial role is therefore far greater than any judge's or jury's. The decision to prosecute is a serious penalty for the person concerned, even if he should subsequently be acquitted, and particularly so if he is held in custody pending trial. When decisions are taken privately and in secrecy either to ignore some offences or not to bring other detected ones before a court, the police will inevitably be accused of condoning wrong-doing, and may be suspected of unfairness and partiality. Yet as A. E. Wilcox, the former chief constable of Hertfordshire, says, the law cannot be enforced indiscriminately, even if it must be administered impartially. Wilcox, whose work *The Decision to Prosecute* is a blend of compassion and commonsense, performed a public service by lifting the veil on the kind of criteria which influence senior British policemen. He said that, even though they have sufficient *prima facie* evidence, the police may decide against prosecution because of administrative convenience or a law's obsolescence or because an infraction was merely technical; or by reason of the youthfulness, old age or mental condition of the offender, or from fear that a child witness might be harmed by the ordeal of a trial. He points out that sometimes there are good grounds for reticence about the reasons behind a decision: 'It would be cruel, for instance, to disclose that no action had been taken because the offender was in the last stages of an incurable disease. The main object, however, is lest it be adduced as a precedent on future occasions.'

In cases of perjury, a prosecution is generally only brought when the perjury has resulted in an innocent person being put in danger of conviction. The police also never prosecute for example a fire service driver who has gone through red lights as long as he took care not to endanger others, and this blind eye received the Appeal Court's imprimatur in Buckoke v. GLC in 1971. A former chief constable of Warwickshire, Commander Kemble RN (retd), once tried a policy of prosecuting every motorist without exception who exceeded the speed limit in his area, but before long was forced to abandon the attempt. Other policemen scarcely regard even serious motoring offenders as criminals. Technically, it is an offence to wash your car in the street; to fail to sign your driving-licence; to shake a door-mat in the road after 8 a.m. – but a police officer said it would be 'asking for trouble' even to caution someone for doing such things. It is often easier for a neighbourhood beat or rural police officer to exercise discretion than for an anonymous urban one to do so, since the former can judge something of the longer-term character of many of the people he deals with. Antagonistic defaulters are significantly more likely to be arrested than polite or deferential ones. Most policemen will also admit that they are more inclined to leniency for women offenders, and estimate that they let off with a caution nearly twice as high a proportion of females as of males. Snobbery now plays less part than it did: to the question, 'Now look here, my good man, don't you know who I am?' most policemen delight in rejoining 'No, and I want your address as well.'

Yet if the law is invariably enforced as impartially as is generally claimed, it is difficult to see why Sir Edward Carson or F. E. Smith were never proceeded against for sedition or under the Unlawful Drilling Act during 1912–14; political considerations do not always seem to be excluded. More recently, there have been a number of complaints from mainly left-wing publication sellers that they have been prohibited or arrested for obstructing the highway when for example religious vendors have been allowed. In addition, senior officers have a wide discretion over the public's right to assemble and meet, especially in London under Sections 52 and 54 of the Metropolitan Police Act 1839 (Section 54 makes it a blanket offence wilfully to disregard any direction of the Commissioner of Police for preventing an obstruction). But recent Commissioners have been anxious to limit the police's involvement in political controversy by emphasizing that the decision whether to ban a particular meeting or march should be taken by the Home Secretary rather than themselves. When the police decide which demonstrations to allow and which to break up or prosecute, they are inevitably exercising an executive function, as John Arden showed in *The Workhouse Donkey*. It would probably be better that such decisions should be made, accountably, by local authorities or parliamentary ministers; even at the risk of political bias, for politicians can at least be challenged and changed.

On other occasions magistrates and judges have criticized officers for bringing prosecutions even when these have succeeded: in 1970, Mr Justice Cusack described one prosecution as 'a sheer act of cruelty'. Besides the actual decision of whether to prosecute, the police exercise further formidable powers in selecting which specific charges to prefer, and can influence the likely sentence both in this way and by means of the way in which the evidence is presented. Many offences can be described by alternative charges of contrasting gravity: for example, as a riot or unlawful assembly. When the police bargain over bail or the gravity of which charge they will bring in return for information, this is a rough form of justice but one that is obviously vulnerable to corruption or abuse. There are also wide local variations over, for instance, the prosecution of sexual offences, demonstrations or assaults. The police pre-try a suspect in exercising their discretion, but this can equally be said of the public when they decide whether to report an offence; the importance of the lay role in social control is often overlooked. Nevertheless laws such as those concerning obscenity or picketing, which involve opinions more than facts can put the police in an invidious position, quite apart from the fact that a decreasing number of policemen today are content to accept unquestioningly the laws they are charged to uphold.

Public Prosecutors

It is wrong that a politician, the Attorney General, should have anything to do with prosecutions, just as it is wrong that the Lord Chancellor should be both a politician and a judge. A more standardized prosecution policy towards some crimes is obtained through the office of the Director of Public Prosecutions, who takes charge in some 8 per cent of the most serious criminal cases. Many people would prefer an extension of his function so that all prosecuting decisions were removed from the hands of the police. This would not only lead to a more consistent policy for laws which are made nationally, but also probably save the police work and at the same time improve their relations with the public. Each offence would still receive individual consideration, but according to standard criteria instead of the varying idiosyncrasies of different chief constables and local authorities. When the police are personally involved in conducting a prosecution, they are with rare exceptions less likely to adduce any evidence favourable to the accused, whereas an independent prosecuting authority can filter the evidence with greater objectivity and detachment and instruct the police to investigate alternative explanations. Sir Henry Fisher, the former High Court judge who investigated the Confait case, says that the police do not see it as their duty to initiate inquiries that might suggest they had got the wrong man, and that at present no one outside the police 'regards it as his duty to spur the police on to question the case and to follow lines of inquiry which might be inconsistent with it.'

Most police argue against a system of public prosecutors on the grounds of expense, and that the police's knowledge of local conditions and opinions is a virtue – whereas Justice takes the opposite view that it is a disadvantage to be influenced by the fear of public criticism. In Scotland, from whom England could usefully learn on several legal matters, each court has a procurator fiscal (popularly known to his clients as a 'persecuting physical') who decides on and conducts prosecutions, and who periodically meets with his colleagues in order to discuss policy. The English and Welsh system is now the only one in Europe where the interrogation of suspects, the interviewing of witnesses, the gathering and testing of scientific evidence, the selection of evidence to be laid before the court, the decision as to what charges shall be brought and the conduct of the prosecution may all be entirely under the control of the police. Critics of the present English system would in any event like all prosecutions to be brought in the name of the Crown instead of an individual police officer, and think that policemen should not be seen either conducting prosecutions or acting as ushers in courts. This might cause the expression 'police court' to die out in practice as well as in theory, as well as lead to a considerable saving of police manpower.

In the United Kingdom, because there is no written constitutional protection, such liberty as there is, dearly won, should be jealously guarded. But criminal activity cannot avoid being a public as well as a private matter. To put it at its lowest, each one of us is statistically much more likely to be a victim of crime than to be wrongly accused of having committed one. Complacency about crime is often at the expense of the most vulnerable in society; it is low-income families who suffer most from criminal violence. Sir Robert Mark argues that it is the dedicated criminal who is most likely to benefit from the loopholes in the present system, which is 'effective only in dealing with the compliant, the weak, the stupid, the illiterate and the spontaneous wrongdoer . . . it is ineffective to an alarming and harmful extent in dealing with the non-compliant – those who set out to break the law and are able, by experience or through advice, to exploit its weaknesses.' Yet a revised system should make just as certain that the weak and stupid innocent are not convicted. Provided safeguards are indisputable, there is no conflict between police efficiency and civil rights. The reverse is true – one of the civil liberties is freedom from violence and crime. Every civilized society must have powers to protect itself from destroyers. If vigorously scrutinized, such powers in themselves can add to the maintenance of civilization and the true freedom of the individual. The police ought not to be handicapped in their efforts to prevent or detect crime while the criminal has every modern method at his disposal. But equally, as Professor Harry Street of Manchester University said in 1978, 'No longer should the police have to rely on deception to accomplish their tasks.' There is a natural reluctance – especially a political one, which we shall meet again in the next chapter – to alter or increase the powers of the police. But their present situation is unsatisfactory on every count: it is anomalous, capricious and indefinite, as well as calculated unnecessarily to expose them to damaging disputes. The police should not be in a position which causes them to complain about an increase in knowledge of the law. It is even worse – just as many people believe that in America the Fifth Amendment is responsible for condonation of third-degree methods – when the ineffectiveness of their legal powers is used as an excuse for the police themselves to ignore the law. At present, some police powers in Britain are too great – such as those of a senior police officer under the Public Order Act 1936 to take such measures 'as appear to him necessary for the preservation of public order' which cannot be challenged in the courts; and the legality of policemen colluding when writing up their notebooks should be forbidden. Other powers, however, could be extended: for example, as the NCCL has proposed, the police should be able to arrest men served with Court injunctions to stop them battering their wives. One compromise would be to allow some of the extended powers senior police officers request only in cases involving the most serious categories of crime, such as violence; and in return to insist on independent surveillance of police interrogation. At the other end of the scale of offences, fixed penalty tickets, with the option that these could be contested in the courts, could be used for minor offences such as speeding in order to allow the police and courts to concentrate on more serious crimes. (But in Britain, emotive resistance to changes such as a fingerprint register should never be underestimated. Even a census is viewed with a tradition of suspicion. When in 1753 an MP called Potter tried to introduce a Bill for registering the annual numbers of births, marriages, deaths and of the poor in the country, he was resisted by William Thornton MP with the words 'I hold this project to be totally subversive of the last remains of English liberty.') The present powers of the police have been described by one policeman as 'a game devised by gentlemen to be played by rogues'.

Rightly, it is a cardinal principle of British justice that it is better to let ten guilty men go free rather than to convict one innocent person; but the aim should be to see that, as far as it is humanly possible, neither happens.

FIVE

State and Police: National or Provincial?

'The danger of unbounded liberty and the danger of bounding it have produced a problem in the science of government which human understanding seems hitherto unable to solve'
Dr Johnson

'A student of the political institutions of any country desirous of understanding the "ethos" of any country's government can hardly do better than make a close study of its police system, which will provide him with a good measuring rod of the actual extent to which its government is free or authoritarian.'
J. Coatman

Many people in England and Wales are not aware that the police there are still divided into forty-three independent forces, each with its own CID and separate police authority. These vary in strength from less than 850 in Warwickshire to over 20,000 in Metropolitan London. Fifty years ago there were almost 200 different forces. In theory, the enforcement of law in Great Britain has always been local. Apart from a brief period under Oliver Cromwell there has never been a national organization charged with that duty; today control is further divided between central and local authorities' responsibility for the adequacy and efficiency of the forces, and the power of their chief constables to direct them. The present situation is a compromise resulting in at least one constitutional anomaly: the Home Secretary is responsible to Parliament for policing Metropolitan London and answers parliamentary questions about this, without being able to exercise any operational authority over the Metropolitan police. Although the Home Secretary's views will be respectfully listened to by the police, he is unable to give a simple order about policy or even priorities; when a recent Home Secretary suggested that the police were giving too much attention to homosexuals in lavatories ('some of my best friends are homosexuals'), senior police officers replied that their friends disliked being accosted. The United Kingdom's caution is also evidenced by its separating facets of other countries' Interior or Justice ministries, so that it has different government ministers responsible for prosecutions, for the judiciary, and for police and prisons.

British suspicion of a national police force is an old one, recently reinforced by the twentieth-century experiences of Germany and Russia. Originally it found its roots in national xenophobia: early English opponents continually muttered about Fouché, Naples, or Austria. 'Since we are so happy', Cibber said in 1739, 'as not to have a certain power amongst us which in another country is called the police, let us rather bear this insult than buy its remedy at too dear a cost.' In Louis XIV's and Fouché's Paris, Frederick II's Prussia, Joseph II's Austria, one of the police's main purposes was to gather intelligence about public opinion. For a long time the English refused to admit any word which meant 'police' into their language. Even after they had adopted the French word the *British Magazine* in 1763 was writing: 'From an aversion to the French . . . and something under the name of police being already established in Scotland, English prejudice will not soon be reconciled to it.'

How valid is this feeling today? It is difficult to forget that Goering who was Minister of Police under Hitler, wrote in *Germany Reborn*:

> It seemed to me of the first importance to get the weapon of the police firmly into my own hands. Here it was that I made the first sweeping changes. Out of thirty-two police chiefs I

> removed twenty-two. Hundreds of inspectors and thousands of police sergeants followed in the course of the next month.

It was only because this had first been done that Hitler was able to use his gangs to establish a dictatorship. Yet all but fifteen out of the 100 Gestapo men in Coblenz in 1938 had also served in the police of the Weimar Republic, a service which had specially prided itself on having high democratic standards and being non-political, but which was to succumb to exasperation at public disorder. Between 1925 and 1932 the police lost control of the streets, as the political centre did not hold and fell apart between the extremes of right and left. When in turn the communists seized power in Czechoslovakia in 1948, their first demand was for control of the police force. The crisis of the coup came when a majority of the coalition cabinet ordered the communist Minister of the Interior, Nosek, to stop packing the police with communists, and he refused. Yet, in fact, the Nazi Gestapo (Geheime Staatspolizie – the state secret police) and SS (Schutzstaffel) of Himmler, the Tsarist Ochrana, the Soviet Cheka, OGPU, and NKVD, the Fascist OVRA of Mussolini and the Ton Ton Macoute of Duvalier were all political and not civil police forces, usually created by an authoritarian leader and owing personal loyalty to him.

Would Britain benefit from having one unified police service? Several Western European countries which are far from totalitarian possess national police forces, including Eire, Denmark, Finland and Norway. Belgium and the Netherlands have both national and local forces; Switzerland's is mainly cantonal, with a few Federal policemen: Sweden's is based on local communes, although like Britain's it is becoming increasingly standardized by central government. Apprehensively, West Germany has only a very few federal Bundesgrenzschutz, mainly guarding airports and the frontier. By its constitution, control of the police is entirely in the hands of the eleven Länder. There have been repeated complaints that a criminal who crosses the border between one Land and another has a good chance of escape. France by contrast has two national police organizations: the 100,000-strong Police Nationale under the Minister of the Interior (including the 15,000 tough and detested anti-riot CRS), and the 65,000

Gendarmerie Nationale under the Defence Minister. A third Minister, of Justice, controls the work of the detective police through the public prosecutors and the *juges d'instruction*. There is a similar contrast in Spain between the reputation of the 65,000 members of the Guardia Civil (whose operations are mainly confined to the country and small towns); the 8,000 plain-clothed Cuerpo General; and the 40,000-strong Policia Armada riot police, whose role has traditionally been a repressive one. In Italy, the Corpo Carabinieri, paid from the Defence budget, are trusted more than the Minister of the Interior's badly-paid Pubblica Sicurezza police, whose links with politics – including the extreme right – are still suspected to be close. (There is, though, no simple polarization there: in riots the sympathies of some left-wing intellectuals such as Pasolini were with the police as sons of the poor rather than with their middle-class student opponents.) In the USSR, the police militia owe a dual allegiance both to the Ministry of Internal Affairs and to their own local soviet. Elsewhere, New Zealand has one national force; Australia has Federal and State forces, but none for smaller localities; in Canada, Quebec and Ontario have their own provincial forces, while the remainder is policed by the Royal Canadian Mounted Police – often on contract to municipalities. Democratic checks and balances reach their apogee in the United States, which has 40,000 autonomous police forces, one – the FBI – administered by the Federal government, 50 by States, 3,000 by counties, each with its sheriff, 1,000 by cities, 20,000 by townships and 15,000 by villages and boroughs. Dissatisfaction with these local forces is far greater than with the FBI or the State police (the FBI, all of whose men incidentally are graduates, is almost the only one untainted by politics; while on the other hand some forces, such as at Houston, appear to be virtually autonomous). But of the country's 420,000 full-time law enforcement officers, less than 26,500 are Federal and only another 45,000 are State police: the remaining 80 per cent are employed by local bodies. A single county such as St Louis contains more than a hundred separate police agencies within its borders. The average American police force has a total of ten officers: many have but a single one. The overall result, varying from 4.04 police officers per 1,000 citizens in Boston to 1.07 in San Diego, bears little correlation to crime or comparative need; and, unlike in Britain, an American officer's jurisdiction ends with the boundary of his own police district. Patrick Murphy, a former Police Commissioner of New York, says that the police system in America 'doesn't even deserve to be called a system – it is so grossly ineffective, antiquated, poorly managed and fragmented. The US police departments do not work well together, or cooperate or communicate well with each other, and the criminals know this.'

In 1962, the British Royal Commission was unanimous in coming to the conclusion that the creation of a national police service would not be either 'constitutionally objectionable or politically dangerous'. They stated that the stigma of a 'police state' derives, not from a nationally organized police force, but from the totalitarian nature of a government which if it came to power 'would without doubt seize control of the police however they might be organized.' One Commission member, Dr Goodhart went further: 'The danger in a democracy does not lie in a central police that is too strong, but in local police forces that are too weak.'

In the event of a coup . . .

People in Britain who fear a national force because of the risk of its political abuse overlook the fact that the government already has close links with easily the most powerful force in the police, concentrated strategically in London. A government which so wished could seek to arrest the opposition's MPs by means of the Metropolitan force. A Commissioner who refused to do this might be dismissed by the Home Secretary and replaced by a stooge. In addition, the Home Secretary and cabinet have under their control the main Special Branch, which is the nearest equivalent we have in this country to a 'political police'. How many police officers would obey such an order is an interesting question to which we might learn the definite answer only too late. In France in 1958 it was a march of policemen to the Palais Bourbon that signalled the fall of the Fourth Republic. In Britain the police, despite not being armed, have a special importance because for a long time this has not been a military country. What would the average British policeman see as being his duty in the event of UDI in

Northern Ireland or Scotland, or a coup by the army or a dictator? In the majority of cases, it would almost certainly be to continue his function: in the words of the Chief of Police in Genet's play *The Balcony*, 'Order must be restored; traffic flow, jay walkers must be crushed.' Policemen themselves give an estimate that if it were a right-wing coup, some nine out of ten of them would remain at their posts; if a left-wing one, perhaps six out of ten. Even in the event of an overseas invasion, most policemen would believe their basic loyalty was to remain on duty and mitigate the effects on civilians – although, unlike members of the armed forces, they are allowed to resign. When the German Nazis occupied the Channel Islands in the Second World War, the British policemen there continued at their posts. In Britain, much would depend on the lead given by the Metropolitan Commissioner (who becomes a civilian when appointed), on how a coup were presented: if it were decked out – like many coups – as being in order to preserve law and order, police support at first might well be almost unanimous. Many, probably most, policemen because of their work come to see obedience and solidarity as the highest good. If a government or even an illegal regime (as in Rhodesia) passed oppressive or discriminatory laws, a considerable number of policemen would still conceive it their duty to enforce them.

The legal position is that a police officer's powers are not delegated to him. He is an independent officer of the Crown and is held personally responsible for his actions. It was decided in Fisher v. Oldham Corporation in 1930 that he exercises, at his own discretion, statutory rights independently of any contract, and this was reiterated by Lord Denning in R. v. Metropolitan Commissioner *ex parte* Blackburn in 1968. On the other hand, the Home Secretary appoints not only the Commissioner, but the DPP and the senior officers in the Metropolitan police. In 1978 the heads of both the Eire and the South Australian police were suddenly dismissed by their respective governments. And a former Conservative Home Secretary explained to me that while prosecutions as of the Shrewsbury pickets were not instigated by any directive from above, they were in some cases influenced 'by a change of atmosphere'.

The Fédération Autonome des Syndicats de Police, an

association representing 400,000 European policemen, drew up a draft ethical code at Royan in 1973. In June 1975 a seminar on an international code of police ethics was convened by Amnesty International at the Peace Palace in The Hague, Holland. Its participants included members of police forces, police authorities and national and international police organizations from eight European countries. At the end of the meeting several conclusions were unanimously reached in what is now known as the Declaration of The Hague. Its fifth point stated:

> Police officers and all others covered by this code have the right to disobey or disregard any order, instruction or command, even if lawfully made within the context of national legislation, which is clear and significant contradiction to basic and fundamental human rights, as described in the Universal Declaration of Human Rights. They have a duty to disobey or disregard any order, instruction or command summarily to execute, torture or otherwise to inflict bodily harm upon a person under their custody. They also have the duty, where they have carried out orders, instructions or commands which they believe to be otherwise in clear and significant contradiction to basic and fundamental human rights – such as lengthy detention without effective judicial supervision – to protest against the issuance of such order, instruction or command.

Some means will have to be determined to safeguard police officers who denounce abuses, especially by their superiors. It would be interesting to give every police officer a questionnaire to see at what degree of illegality in an order he would (a) refuse to obey, (b) resign, or (c) resist. On the other hand, how many would help carry out an order to torture a suspect for information, if this were described as a 'deep interrogation technique'?

The classic method by which past police states have been created is by means of political police being built up into a national force parallel to the traditional service. This political force then takes over criminal prosecutions, while the ordinary police are subordinated into a reserve force. Recently elements of the political police in Italy and of the CIA in the United

States have shown how easily they can become self-governing and unaccountable. The power of access to and control of police files can become a weapon for terrorizing government itself, as Stalin's and Hitler's purges demonstrated; totalitarian regimes have themselves been taken over by the very police with whose help power had been first seized.

The police and the army

A second key factor is the always somewhat uneasy relationship that the police have with the military. Sir Robert Mark says that the British have 'a growing distaste on the part of both army and people for the involvement of troops in the homeland in a peacekeeping role, and this has become traditional'. If a Commissioner or chief constable invokes the aid of the military, a crucial change in authority takes place, because members of the armed forces – unlike police officers – are servants of the government. (The UK Atomic Energy Authority's armed police force, which has been formed to guard atomic plant against terrorists, is even less publicly accountable; whereas the armed services' actions are answerable to Parliament through the Defence Minister, the AEA's special constabulary answer only to that authority, which is an appointed and not elected body.) In 1976 Robert Mark told Leicester University:

> The prospect of invoking military force to deal with industrial disputes or political demonstrations has never been contemplated during my thirty-nine years service and there are, so far as I know, no plans at all for such a contingency. Having made that clear perhaps I can be equally frank in telling you that there have always been plans for invoking military aid to help us deal with civil disasters such as floods, rescues and so on and that latterly there has emerged a need for contingency plans for military aid to deal with situations in which defensive armour, sophisticated weaponry and specialized training might minimize loss of life in dealing with armed and dangerous men inspired by political motives; in other words political terrorists as distinct from armed criminals.

When servicemen are used in civil emergencies such as for firefighting or clearing materials during a dock-workers' or dustmans' strike, it is the task of the police and not the army to deal with any violence that the servicemen may encounter. But when in 1972 the chief constable of Birmingham had to march his 700 policemen away from Saltley coke works rather than risk a confrontation with 6,000 trade unionists, this persuaded Edward Heath secretly to set up a permanent National Security Committee (which in 1975 was renamed the Civil Contingencies Committee) to consider contingency plans for military aid to the civil power. Its two main areas of concern were first, the maintenance of supplies and services during a prolonged confrontation with labour, and second, how best to counter terrorist threats. To combat the latter, the committee decided what help units such as the Special Air Services Regiment (SAS) could give the police; and joint police-military exercises took place – including an ambitious one at Heathrow Airport in 1973, and a similar joint police-army-RAF anti-terrorist one at Edinburgh Airport in 1978. In the same year, the US army were supplying armoured vehicles, reconnaissance planes and advisers to the civilian police operation against American Indians in the siege at Wounded Knee. In response to the increase in hijacking, by 1977 such liaison had become international: in October of that year the UK government lent two SAS specialists to West Germany to help with the latter's rescue of the Lufthansa aircraft hijacked in Somalia. If the British police are to remain nominally unarmed and civilian in character, such limited cooperation with commando units will be inevitable to deal with exceptional violence.

The only safeguards of a democracy against the abuse of police power are the independence of its courts, and the accountability of its government to a freely elected Parliament. The Police Act 1964 in Britain shrank from implementing the recommendation of the Royal Commission that the Home Secretary and the Secretary of State for Scotland should be made fully responsible in Parliament for their respective countries' police. The result of the present situation was described by some witnesses to the Royal Commission:

> The present fiction that, because he (the Home Secretary) does not control them (police forces), he should not be

answerable for them seems to result in us having the worst of both worlds, in that control is in fact exercised by anonymous Home Office officials whose conduct cannot be examined or questioned.

The reality of the present position is a classic example of the traditional British love of compromise, which to many outside eyes can appear hard to distinguish from a muddle. The Home Office, for example, at present sends out over a hundred circulars annually to chief constables, which Parliament has no means of discussing and local Councils no right to see. There is no subject of greater importance for Parliament to be able to discuss than the police. Yet although the Ministers of Education and Health are answerable to MPs for matters in their fields, despite the automony of their departments locally, the Home Secretary remains not responsible for any police forces outside the Metropolitan area. The most he can do is to ask for a report, which leads to the anomaly that he can be effectively questioned about a police matter which happens to take place for example in Dagenham, but not about one in Hornchurch, because that falls just the other side of the boundary of the Metropolitan police area. Even within the latter, his answerability appears circumscribed: when questioned by an MP why the Metropolitan police had collected the car registration numbers of people attending an anti-apartheid meeting in London in the autumn of 1977, the Home Secretary, Merlyn Rees, replied, 'It would not be appropriate for me to give chief officers detailed advice on operational matters.'

When Henry Brooke, the Home Secretary at the time the last Royal Commission reported, declined its proposal that he should be fully answerable to Parliament for the police, he stated that he could not have the 'responsibility without the power'. He was unwilling to take the necessary power presumably because to do so was instinctively unacceptable politics. The root of the problem is how to reconcile Parliamentary ability to control the police with safeguards which would prevent any possible abuse from governmental direction. If this difficulty proves, as the Home Secretary contended, insoluble, the alternatives are to transfer either the responsibility for or the direction of the police to an administrative authority which is separate from the central government. One possibility is to give the responsibility for the police to somebody from outside politics who is acceptable to all parties, as has been done for the FBI in the US.

The compromise solution, often adopted at present, is to diffuse the power between many different hands. The political justification for the United Kingdom's fragmentary system of police organization is that it provides a number of independent chief contables and police forces who can act as counter-balancing checks to the Government's control of the Metropolitan force. As Dr Geoffrey Marshall of Oxford University described it at a European conference in 1975, 'In the actual direction of operations against civil disturbance the forty or so chief constables of Britain exercise a semi-sovereign prerogative. Its foundation may be shaky but it may be the least of the evils.' If the police were reorganized in regional units, which most people think would also result in greater efficiency, the same safeguard would remain. But before examining the arguments for or against any form of unification, we must first see how true it is that, as one chief constable said, 'we are much more nationalized now than people think, only we don't call it that.'

The process of uniting the police in this country began very slowly, apart from Peel's foresight in making the Metropolitan police area so large. A Select Committee, with Peel himself as chairman, had reported in 1822 that:

> it is difficult to reconcile an effective system of police with that perfect freedom of action and exemption from interference which are the great privileges and blessings of society in this country, and your committee think that the forfeiture or curtailment of such advantages would be too great a sacrifice for improvement in police, or facilities in detection of crime, however desirable in themselves if abstractly considered.

Although another committee under Edwin Chadwick recommended the union of county police forces in 1839, they remained independent of central control. But in 1856 the government was given powers to inspect them, in return for a financial grant of half the expenditure of each force. The number of Inspectors remained at three, and the annual inspections of some 200 forces were consequently cursory up to 1945. But it was the other side of the bargain, the grant, which proved to be the Trojan horse, and it remains the greatest weapon of the Home Office today. As the cost of the police grew, the Home Secretary found that his power to withhold the government's contribution was pressure that no local authority could withstand. Grants have been withheld from police authorities on seventeen occasions since 1922 (the last being from Cardiganshire in 1957); each time the desired result was soon obtained. The threat alone proved sufficiently effective in a further eighteen cases, most recently against York and Stockport in 1965. But the sanction – though not uncharacteristic of this country – is a blunt instrument. The cure is worse than the ailment: if a serious problem were to arise in a police area, cutting off half its finance would scarcely be likely to improve the situation. It could result in chaos for a district which is only incompetent, if the local police authority retaliated by refusing to appoint any police force at all.

A major advance towards rationalizing standards was made in 1919, when the Home Secretary acquired powers in the 'policeman's Magna Carta' to regulate pay, clothing, and conditions of service, although attempts to standardize criminal records were not made until just before the Second World War. The Home Office now also provides certain 'common services' for all forces, including, for example, regional forensic science laboratories, and the Police College at Bramshill. The last Royal Commission urged that the policy and standards of recruitment, which are at present decided by each separate force, should also be centrally organized. In addition, many police would prefer that other facilities, such as detective training and driving schools, had a common standard by being provided centrally or regionally.

The pattern of the Home Secretary possessing in practice far more control than he is accustomed to acknowledge publicly is shown in the method of the appointment of chief constables. Technically, this is the prerogative of each police authority, but the Home Secretary must approve – and consequently can veto – every selection. One result has been that he is now able to impose a national policy that (unlike in the US) no chief constable shall be appointed who either comes from outside the police service, or who has spent all his career in the force to which he has been appointed chief constable. Similarly, although the Home Secretary is not specifically empowered to dismiss a chief constable, in effect he has been given this power by section 29 of the 1964 Act, which enables him to require a police authority to call upon its chief constable to retire in the interests of efficiency.

The last Police Act left the local police authorities with very few powers, other than financial control over the number of men and the equipment for their local force. Some authorities are prouder than others of the economy with which they run their police. The budgets certainly vary widely. The variation of expenditure, even between authorities of similar size and population density, per officer in 1975/6 ranged on communications equipment from £95 to £218; on uniforms from £33 to £87; and on vehicles from £66 to £153. The House of Commons Public Accounts Committee in August 1978 urged central government to investigate this situation, but the Home Office fears that the police and authorities would regard a detailed inquisition as an unwarrantable intrusion into an area where constitutionally they have discretion. Councils at the present time are under strong pressure to pare down their rates generally. It is wrong that essential services, such as the police or education, should be in any way dependent on local wealth or politics. Rates may be a healthier form of taxation than the penalizing of earnings, but even though it is particularly appropriate to finance the police who protect property by means of the rates, there would be a clear gain from allocating the budget centrally according to actual needs by means of a national plan.

The case for the present system of local forces

'Doubtless all arbitrary powers, well executed, are the most convenient, yet let it again be remembered that delays, and little inconveniences in the forms of justice, are the price that all free nations must pay for their liberty in more substantial matters.' The jurist Sir William Blackstone with these words was justifying complacency about our legal system, but they equally explain our instinctive aversion to a national police force. Democratic control, once it is lost, would not be regained without a terrible struggle. As Chinese people say, 'He who goes for a ride on a tiger can never get off.' Sir Robert Mark opposes a national force because he thinks it would undermine confidence in the impartiality of the police, since they would come to be seen as servants of the executive. But the present system of separate police forces in this country continues also because of positive enthusiasm for local control, as well as from fear of central domination. At a time when administration seems to be increasingly impersonal, local police forces give people some hope of participation, and in a field where personal relationships are vital for the success of the police themselves – even though too close local ties can be a disadvantage for impartial policing. However, any institution such as the jury system which enables people to feel that they are helping to govern as well as being governed, deserves to be welcomed. Not only are people able to gain civic experience on local police authorities, but to be self-policing is one of the eventual ideals of an open society.

If the case for the present system is accepted, as it was by all except one member of the last Royal Commission, there is equally an argument for extending it to the Metropolitan area, which is the only one in the country that at present does not have any democratic police authority. Londoners at present have no say in determining the police rate they pay in the Metropolitan area. This is the heaviest in the country, partly because the services of Scotland Yard subsidize other areas, and partly because of the large burden of national police duties (such as guarding diplomats) carried by the capital. If the Metropolitan police were brought under either the GLC or a special *ad hoc* Police Committee of the London borough councils, Scotland Yard's national services might be transferred to the Home Office. An additional reason for making such a change is that the present large Metropolitan police bureaucracy suffers from having no direct formal liaison with the London public. Parliament cannot be said to exercise the democratic control over the Metropolitan force that a local police authority would; occasionally it finds time to discuss a complaint, but it is never able to consider questions of general policy. Some police officers think that the Metropolitan area is too large and unwieldy altogether. It is interesting that the Metropolitan Commissioner is paid £18,883 a year (which the Salaries Review Board recommends should be increased to £26,000), compared with £13,000 for the man who appoints him, the Home Secretary.

Chief constables, with very few exceptions, want to preserve local forces. One of them in the West Country said:

> It is an interesting trend today to push ultimate responsibility higher and higher. Having watched and participated in central and local government, I am certain that the individual gets a better crack of the whip at a local level, where a certain amount of flexibility can be used, than he will get from central government where all decisions are reached on rigid principles.

Although the late Dr Goodhart and Sir Eric St Johnston argued that local associations will continue even if the police are reorganized on a regional basis, there remains in the minds of councillors a dread of larger bureaucratic control. (To other people this may seem little different from local bureaucratic control.) Neither the Home Secretary nor Parliament can prevent a chief constable from acting in an improper manner that falls short of illegality or inefficiency. There is no power to stop a chief constable from using objectionable methods or political discrimination – perhaps resulting from unconscious prejudices. Fortunately, however, examples of this type of complaint are extremely rare; and although local tyranny is no less obnoxious to those affected by it, it is unlikely to last so long as a national one – because in the last resort it is easier to correct.

Since there cannot be too much protection, the ideal solution might be to have answerability at both local and Parliamentary level. Local authorities, on the other hand, oppose any move towards unification because of pride in their links with the police service in their district. They also argue that competition between chief constables has a healthy effect. (It is true that one case of corruption in a police force only came to light because the railway police, who were making their own independent inquiries, became suspicious when they failed to receive any cooperation from the regular local force.)

As in many other matters concerning the police, so little research has been done that it is common to find the same arguments being used by both sides. The supporters of smaller forces claim that the fact that their chief constable is able to know personally most of the men under his command benefits morale and promotion; their opponents claim it has just the opposite effect. Many of the more ambitious policemen would welcome a unified force because of its increased opportunities for promotion: 'Those who want to stay local, could', one constable said, 'while the others would be able to get on.'

There is similar disagreement about the effect on recruiting. Proponents of the present system argue that loyalty to the local force stimulates recruiting, and that a man from Dorset, for instance, would hesitate before joining an English or even Wessex force because of uncertainty where he might be posted. Their opponents argue that national recruiting would be better than the present position, where, they claim, good recruits are being lost who are unsuccessful in joining their local force, yet who still may be better than those being accepted elsewhere. (The system of recruitment by separate forces has resulted in some cases of a police constable who has been discharged by one force being taken on by another.) Forces in some parts of both England and Scotland at the moment have their full establishment and to spare, while many others have long lists of vacancies.

Police authorities

A separate criticism of the new police authorities established by the Police Act is that many people feel it is quite wrong for magistrates, who must appear impartial in their judicial capacity, to form one third of the membership of such committees. The ostensible justifications for this are first that they are familiar with some police work; and second, that they can provide some safeguard if the local council is formed exclusively from one political party – a situation which is the most frequent seed-bed for corruption. The dangers of party political control are evident in the US: political hierarchy (alternative to the service one) develops within the ranks of the police, generating antipathy from opposition rivals and a network of informers on politically dissenting members. Although politically organized systems of policing have been defended on the crudely democratic grounds that they are one means of ensuring that the police are acceptable and responsive to the voters for the sake of their political masters, few people who have had any experience of such systems endorse them. Once the police become identified with a particular government, they know that they themselves are in danger when that government falls, and develop a vested interest in resisting or averting a democratic transfer of power. Nevertheless, professionalism can insulate the police from sensitivity to their public as well as from undesirable political and corrupt pressures, and some better new ways must be found to combine democratic responsiveness with independence from party politics.

Another school of critics point to the weak control that is exercised by some police authorities; this may be the result of a general lack of informed public interest in the police and their problems. 'I think the present idea that we have local control of the police is a constitutional sham. All that can be said for the present system is that it is not centrally controlled. It is certainly not locally controlled,' Tom Iremonger, the former MP has said. The police authorities are able to exercise little democratic control because they meet so rarely – most usually, only four times each year. One councillor who had also been a MP gave as his opinion that many police authorities do not even know what limited powers they have, and are afraid to exercise any: 'They never see the Inspector or his reports, and so don't get adequate information.' Furthermore a chief constable commented, 'I don't think any member of my police authority has read the Police Act and I hope none of them does.'

One improvement would be to have a neighbourhood police council for each sub-division's area, because subsequent amalgamations and local government reorganization have upset the balance of the democratic structure architected by the 1962 Royal Commission and the resultant 1964 Police Act. Tony Judge, the editor of *Police*, emphasizes that what is required is not interference in the administration of the force so much as improving its non-political accountability to a wider community, and suggests that one possible basis for such a solution might be to extend the role of community relations councils.

The case for unification

Those who want a unified force argue that such a move, far from being a threat to democracy, could bring the police more effectively under parliamentary supervision. They deny that it would mean that any police officer would be transferred across the country unless he so wished. And they contend that a different chain of command need not affect good local traditions: most divisional superintendents have always been encouraged to work as closely as possible with their own neighbourhoods. Military regiments, for example, retain their own identities even though they form part of one national army.

For policemen, unification would certainly result in more equally distributed opportunities for promotion; at present it is not easy to get transferred to another force. The gain in operational efficiency, the reformers claim, would be enormous. Not only would it cure the problem of the inadequate capital and specialist facilities of fragmented forces, but it would also obviate the difficulties and friction caused by their boundaries. (Several motorways for instance now cross a number of different police forces' and even regional crime squads' areas.) They argue that the modern development of criminal organization, transport and means of escape has now made further police reform necessary, in the same way as the Industrial Revolution previously eclipsed the parish constable system. This view echoes most of the words introducing the earlier reform, contained in the preamble to the 1829 Metropolitan Police Act:

> The local establishments of nightly watch and nightly police have been found inadequate to the prevention and detection of crime, by reason of the frequent unfitness of the individuals employed, the insufficiency of their number, the limited sphere of their authority, and their want of connection and cooperation with each other.

Liaison between separate forces can never, one chief

constable argues, be as effective as command. Another former chief constable, who would like to see a unified force introduced forthwith and not gradually built up, said that most forces do cooperate but that a few cases of personal friction can destroy the whole system. Detective officers in some forces are reluctant to share criminal information which they may depend on for their promotion. 'And there's always plenty of coppers who keep details of their best informants in their heads, and die or retire taking them with them,' said one very experienced detective. Other policemen have been known to deposit drunks 'on to another patch' the boundary of the neighbouring force, in the same way as the old parish constable used to drive vagabonds into the next parish. The limits of the present liaison have been exposed by some more serious recent cases. A warning about the bomb which later exploded at the Old Bailey in 1973 was delayed because of a fault in communication between the Metropolitan force and the City of London force. The arrest of Judith Ward, who was convicted for bombing an army coach on the M62, was impeded because the army, police forces and the Special Branch all had separate and incomplete files on her; in the event it was an officer who was a Liverpool dog handler on the beat who in fact apprehended her as a result of his personal suspicion. Most tragically of all, Donald Neilson evaded several separate police forces' intense efforts at detection while killing sub-postmasters in Yorkshire, Lancashire and Worcestershire, as well as kidnapping Leslie Whittle in Shropshire and murdering her in Staffordshire; he was finally fortuitously captured only because he attempted a burglary in Nottinghamshire. 'The muddle,' a leading article in the *Evening Standard* commented, 'poses urgent questions about the way Britain's police are organized.'

An Act passed in Britain during the Second World War did allow a national police force, but was later repealed. Advocates argue that an unarmed police service is unlikely to pose a national threat. A past Secretary of the Scottish Police Federation, who said that he would like one unified force for the whole of Scotland in place of the present eight, pointed out that its size would only be roughly the same as the national Danish or Irish forces, and still less than half the Metropolitan establishment. Superintendent Brian Rowland also argues:

> Until there are uniform standards of procedure throughout the service there can hardly be uniform standards of inspection. There would also be merit in bringing the Metropolitan police within the orbit of the Inspectorate to ensure uniformity and to spread the knowledge and experience gained by that force in policing one of the world's greatest conurbations. The system therefore has evolved whereby there is no central control on many matters which, quite clearly from an efficiency point of view, should have been centralized years ago. To take the simple example of forms and other items of stationery, there is no conformity as regards size, numbering or format. . . .
>
> The future to my mind is very much in the hands of chief officers of police. Contrary to popular belief we are not ruled by one Queen but rather forty-three Kings. Each one is completely autonomous and few agree with each other. In consequence there are tremendous variations within police forces, not all of which can be equally efficient, but none of which seems capable of being challenged. These variations usually exist as the whim of one man and relate to many different matters. To mention a few, the size of divisions, the centralization or decentralization of CID and traffic departments, the role of assistant chief constables and the provision of clothing and equipment come readily to mind. All unfortunately seem to think they are right and in consequence the service suffers. As we move forwards into a more sophisticated society, unless that ring can be broken and the police service given clear guidelines within which it must operate then frankly I have some misgivings. It is the only area within the police service which causes me the slightest concern for the future.

Greater national cohesiveness amongst local forces, even if it stopped short of a unified force under a single command, could bring mutual benefits from the pooling of information and experience, in addition to the standardization urged by superintendent Rowland of matters such as warrant cards and documents (when a carefully-planned standard accident report form was recently introduced, one in five of police forces refused to adopt it). Individual forces' variations in prosecution policies as well make justice dependent partly on the chance of where one lives or is caught: motorists in Suffolk, for example, are estimated to be eight times more likely to be stopped for driving a defective vehicle than those in Merseyside. Two individual chief constables declined to enforce new regulations against motor-vehicle noise; one on the grounds of their impracticability, the other because he thought them unjust. Disparities as wide as these seem to ignore the fact that policemen are officers of the Crown appointed to enforce nationally-made laws, and exercise authority which is derived not from their chief constable but from the Sovereign.

Many policemen talk of a national force as being inevitable one day. Two recent chief constables said they thought that the next Royal Commission would recommend it. When a leader writer in *The Times* wrote that 'whatever Dr Goodhart may recommend, the country is not likely to have a national police force within the foreseeable future', Dr Goodhart tartly replied, 'What is the "foreseeable future" depends, of course, upon one's capacity for foresight.'

There are two future directions for reorganization, short of establishing a national force. First, by the unification of the CID, and also perhaps of the traffic police; or second, by a complete regroupment on a regional basis.

A national CID

Unification of the CID would creat one separate national detective force (similar to the FBI) to concentrate on major crimes and seriously dangerous professional criminals, while uniformed forces remained locally organized. In this way, it is argued, the police could combine the advantages of both worlds: more efficient and specialized organization where it is currently most badly needed, while retaining the local tradition and contacts of the men on the beat. Nuclei for this force already exist in the national specialist bomb, drugs and fraud squads and in the regional crime squads; but since the same major criminal gang can operate in London, Glasgow and Cardiff on successive jobs, the case for a single nationally coordinated detective unit which could piece together knowledge about gang methods seems unanswerable. There is evidence that the successful parts of the 'crime industry' are increasingly often organized in depth: one recent criminal team was composed of eighty-three people, and before it was broken up, had succeeded in stealing and disposing of over £500,000 worth of goods. Reformers would like any sufficiently big crime automatically to be investigated by national detectives: sometimes when, as at present, Scotland Yard has to wait to be called in until the local force has tried and failed, the trail is dead from being three days cold. In France, besides a *brigade mobile* flying squad who can go anywhere, there are agents in every provincial centre who are under the direct control of the Sûreté Nationale.

The operations of a national CID, like those of the FBI, might be restricted to the more serious crimes that are organized across the boundaries of police districts, and which are increasing in number and gravity, even though numerically 80 per cent of the total number of crimes are estimated still to be 'local' ones. It would therefore be necessary also to have local detectives – contacts on the ground play an essential part in detection. Basically, a good detective officer succeeds most because of the quality of his information, which in turn depends on local knowledge coupled with tried and trusted sources. And detectives will to a considerable degree always need to rely on the rest of the police to act as their eyes and ears. The opponents of a national CID say that a hybrid system would inevitably cause even more friction than there is sometimes at present between the CID and the uniformed branch, and that a national CID which had to operate within a framework of locally autonomous forces would face overwhelming difficulties in dealing with those forces. The officers of a national CID would only be composed, one sergeant alleged, of 'ambitious young bachelors or men with broken marriages'.

There is a separate case for the recruitment of members of the detective branch to be distinct from that for other policemen. Criminals – who themselves need no minimum physical specifications – are often able to recognize British detectives by their height. Some of the most brilliant French detectives, who are selected for their ability separately from the police, are not only tiny but also have glasses and flat feet, and would stand no chance before a selection board in the United Kingdom. According to some policemen, a detective needs different specialized qualities because he is working against the minds of criminals, whereas the uniformed man works among the law-abiding public. One former chief constable, an exceptional and humane man, argued that here lay just the danger. He said that detective officers who shared a criminal culture for too long can become too 'CID-minded'. The 1929 Royal Commission reported in similar words:

> Some of the CID (Scotland Yard) evidence which we have heard leaves a somewhat disquieting impression upon our minds. There is, we fear, a tendency among this branch of the service to regard itself as a thing above and apart, to which the restraints and limitations placed upon the ordinary police do not, or should not, apply. This error, if not checked, is bound to lead to abuses which may grow until they bring discredit upon the whole police force.

The former chief constable emphasized that it is more important for the CID to be better human beings than to be better detectives; he had had a policy of automatically returning CID officers, when they were promoted, back to work in the uniformed branch for two or three years.

A national traffic force?

One problem which is certain to increase in the future is the number of traffic offenders. The volume of vehicles is officially expected to double within the next decade and treble by the decade following. The harm they cause is even greater than that due to criminals: every second of the day, careless motorists are estimated to be doing over £500 of damage. A person is injured on the roads every 94 seconds, and another is killed every 78 minutes – over forty times the number of people who are murdered. Scores of thousands of uninsured motorists each year come to light only because they are involved in accidents. American studies suggest that nineteen out of twenty traffic offences at present escape detection.

New Zealand has formed a separate force of 300 traffic policemen. It would not be difficult to recruit drivers for a similar body here. Other people support the idea on the grounds that it would hive off a great deal of public resentment from the rest of the police. The idea of special motor-patrols by the police, whose object was to give advice rather than to prosecute, was tried out by the Home Office in 1938. In the districts where they were used, they resulted in a decrease of 6.7 per cent in fatalities during the trial period, compared with an increase of 3.4 per cent in the districts not operating the scheme; during the same period they prosecuted 12 per cent fewer people, compared with the other areas where prosecutions increased by 5 per cent.

But police officers say that it would be a wasteful duplication of manpower to have a completely segregated traffic police force looking for only one type of offender. The man on traffic patrol deals with crime as much as with traffic: not only are well over 70,000 cars stolen every year, but vehicles are estimated to be employed in between 25 per cent and 50 per cent of serious crimes. Moreover, as an influential study by Terence Willett showed, the anti-social motorist and the criminal overlap to a surprising degree. Of the people convicted of serious driving offences in one area 23 per cent also had a record of having committed other crimes, and a further 9 per cent were 'known to the police'. Four out of five of those charged with causing death by dangerous driving, and 78 per cent of those caught driving while disqualified, had criminal records.

Although there is a clear case for more police patrol cars on the roads, their segregation into an entirely separate force is on balance not desirable. A lifetime spent only in this unpopular work would have a doubtful effect on a man's morale, and there is also a danger that the force might develop into a 'sub-police' which possessed inferior authority and respect.

Regional forces

As an alternative to such specialized departments being coordinated vertically, the existing police forces could regroup themselves regionally. There are many signs that the inevitable pressures towards unification are already having results in this direction. Experiments have been made in combined units to patrol motorways, and crime squads on the pattern of the London Flying Squad have been started in Newcastle,

Manchester, Liverpool, Bristol, Nottingham and Birmingham. In addition, occasional *ad hoc* crime units are formed to deal, for example, with a particular gang which operates in two or more areas. It is likely that regional crime units (the word 'squad' has perhaps unfortunate connotations) will increasingly be extended all over the country by police forces anxious to demonstrate that they can liaise, as the price of their continuing independence.

During the Second World War the emergency conditions showed the creakiness of the local system and brought about a form of regional organization. Twenty-one amalgamations took place, and the remaining police forces were reassembled in eleven Civil Defence regions. Today, a greater degree of coordination would in particular be welcomed by those who are the victims of 'commercial crime'; security officers of companies would like to see movements of valuable consignments automatically planned at regional levels. One firm, which has had £1 million worth of its goods hi-jacked in five years, said that cooperation between some police forces is nominal and that only lip-service is as yet paid to regional crime units. Part of the trouble is that the knowledge that the police possess is often so fragmented that it loses its value. One ex-inspector said, 'The average copper is most reluctant to give away to his superiors and lazy comrades what he has, by years of practice studded with complaints to answer, learned the hard way for himself.' This applies *pro tanto* between different forces, who are all striving to improve their clear-up rate in relation to those of their neighbours.

England and Wales are already divided into nine police districts, and there are regional forensic laboratories in London, Birmingham, Bristol, Cardiff, Harrogate, Nottingham, Preston, and Newcastle. Local government and planning in Britain has increasingly moved in a regional direction. The UK seems to be developing a three-tier form of government; the police might perhaps best be organized in the middle (regional) tier. In this way it would be possible to retain in the reorganization some of the benefits of local liaison committees, though conscientious members could not be expected to travel long distances to regional meetings without payment.

The Special Branch

Two remaining police operations require particular scrutiny: the first deals with possible internal political threats to the state, the second liaises with foreign police forces. The Special Branch execute the least known and most sensitive of all police activities. Not only do they have to identify in their assumptions with those of the current political government much more than the rest of the police service; but their investigations can – as the deportations in 1977 of Agee and Hosenball evidenced – lead to arbitrary executive decisions as a result of evidence which is rarely made public even to the defendants themselves. They form the nearest to political police or Orwell's 'Thought police' that a democracy tolerates. In post-Nazi West Germany, they were hopefully named the Verfassungsschutz – 'the protectors of the constitution'. The Special Branch was started as the Special Irish Branch in 1883, to deal with Fenian extremists who were setting off dynamite bombs in London. Its first name, the 'Political Branch' of the CID significantly was abandoned as too contentious. Within five years the word Irish was dropped from its title. But its ancestors lay as far back as the police spies of Walsingham in the sixteenth century. In the last ninety-five years, its members have successively given their principal attention to violent anarchists, suffragettes, Germans, Indian nationalists, Fascists, communists, and currently have come full circle to the IRA again. Individuals as well as political movements can be their concern. Their duty is in the view of Sir Harold Scott, a former Commissioner, 'to keep watch on any body of people, of whatever political complexion, whose activities seem likely sooner or later to result in open acts of sedition or disorder'. Roy Jenkins, when Home Secretary, said their interest was 'only subversion and potential subversion', which in 1975 was defined in this context by Lord Harris, Minister of State at the Home Office, as 'activities which threaten the safety or well being of the state and are intended to undermine or overthrow parliamentary democracy by political, industrial or violent means'. This goes somewhat wider than the definition previously given by Lord Denning in 1963 that subversion is the contemplated overthrowing of government by unlawful means (Cmnd. 2152, HMSO, para 230), and MPs (particularly on the left) are worried that the Special Branch also concern themselves with legitimate political protest, as happened in South Australia. Ironically, their weekly reports to Lloyd George about working-class unrest played a significant part in influencing and frightening him and his colleagues into making reforms in social policy – a comment on the limitations of democratic political leaders' own knowledge of those who elect them.

Special Branch (SB) officers are stationed at every major air and sea-port in the country: the plain-clothed man standing by Passport Control at London Airport, for example is a SB detective. There are members with each local force, but their main strength – 409 officers – is concentrated at New Scotland Yard in London. Their members are recruited directly from ordinary uniformed policemen. In the 1950s they numbered 200 and were limited to London; by the end of the 1960s there were nationally 400 and a dozen women; today they total 1,250 officers in England and Wales; 300 of those outside London are in the CID and work at the ports. In Scotland there are some further 120 SB officers, with 61 in Strathclyde and 21 in the Lothian and Borders force. The majority of SB officers spend much of their time on surveillance and infiltration, but also vet civil servants, aliens, and applicants for naturalization; deal with Official Secrets Act cases; serve as bodyguards for eminent potential targets; and act as the arresting arm of the counter-intelligence Security Service (now known as DI-5), whose members themselves have no legal power to open a safe, enter a house or make an arrest. In London their head is a Deputy Assistant Commissioner who, through the Metropolitan Commissioner, reports directly to the Home Secretary.

The SB – whose own members themselves often describe it as 'a necessary evil' even though they are subject to the ordinary law of the land – will always generate degrees of unease because of the lack of public accountability about its actions and values. Its officers are not answerable to their local police although one third of the nation's SB officers serve in the Metropolitan force, there is no mention of them in the Commissioner's otherwise detailed annual reports. Inevitably, there is controversy over the overlap of the SB's interest in legitimate political dissent.

The SB's supporters contend that it was the abolition of the political police in the Weimar Republic which greatly facilitated the National Socialists' rise to power. But there remains a degree of coolness not only between the SB and its professional rivals in the government intelligence services attached to the Ministry of Defence, but also in the eyes of several other policemen: Inspector Reg Gale, a former chairman of the Police Federation for England and Wales advocated that the SB should be taken away from the police and, if it were needed at all, put under the army. However, the likelihood of detachment from political control is somewhat more favourable within an independent police service than it would be inside the armed services, who serve directly under the command of the government of the day. In an age of terrorist extremism, it is impossible to do without some form of SB. But the FBI's victimization of Martin Luther King and other non-violent politic dissenters shows the danger of such a force unless there are independent checks. In Britain, with one already overworked and powerful party politician (the Home Secretary) alone in control of the SB, and without his being answerable to Parliament on such matters, the safeguards against possible undemocratic abuse is not enough. It would be better to provide an independent monitor through inspection by, and the chance to appeal to, a senior impartial authority such as an eminent judge or the Ombudsman.

SB officers index the names of people who sign many petitions – often innocuous ones. They report on, and photograph demonstrators and political meetings. Closed circuit TV cameras, ostensibly sited for traffic control, can be used for monitoring marches. C. V. Hearn, a police constable in Surrey for 21 years, pointed out the dangers of injustice in secret security vettings.

Interpol

Interpol is the telegraphic address of the International Criminal Police Organization. This, contrary to popular belief, is in no sense an international police force, but simply a voluntary association of the national police forces of 126 countries. It was started in Vienna in 1923 by seven countries (who did not include Britain). Its headquarters is now at St Cloud outside Paris, and of its fifty-five staff, four-fifths are French officers.

The aims of Interpol are:

(1) To ensure and promote the widest possible mutual assistance between all criminal police authorities within the limits of the laws existing in the different countries and in the spirit of the Universal Declaration of Human Rights.
(2) To establish and develop all institutions likely to contribute effectively to the prevention and suppression of ordinary law crimes.
(3) It is strictly forbidden for the organization to undertake any intervention or activities of a political, military, religious or racial character.

In reality Interpol at present amounts to little more than a modest agency for recording and exchanging information. Its headquarters houses two million files on prominent criminals who work internationally, together with details of their methods of operation. All actual resulting police work is done by the police officers of member countries within the limits of their respective laws, including those circumscribing extradition (see Table 9): there are no separate Interpol agents or detectives. More than half its member countries are not even on the Interpol radio network. Even though its total annual budget is less than £1 million, it would collapse without the French support it receives. One clue to the caution several countries show to developing Interpol's powers is the memory of its unfortunate history during the Second World War, when Heydrich made himself its President and seized its files, moving them to Berlin where they were later destroyed. A further clue is provided by the list of its member countries, which embraces for example both Iraq and Israel. (In 1959 its Annual Conference had to be cancelled because the host country refused to issue visas for Israeli delegates.) Although the US, South Africa and the Soviet Union do not belong, the Argentine, Burundi, Chile, Cuba, Haiti, Indonesia, Iran, Romania and Yugoslavia do.

In order to survive, Interpol has always adamantly refused to deal with political offences; M. Jean Nepote, its Secretary-General, continues to resist demands for liaison over political terrorists. Representative Edward Beard, one of the US Congressmen who attack Interpol as a potential 'threat to the privacy and basic human rights of Americans', criticizes it for 'refusing to assist in curbing terrorist activity or keep files on Nazi war criminals because they claim that terrorism, genocide and other crimes are political in nature.' Considering the disparity of its members' politics, police relations within Interpol have in fact remained encouragingly objective. It concentrates on crimes that are agreed to be such by all its members. Its operations – which would be greatly improved were they computerized – are at their most effective against drug-trafficking; with the growth in speed of international travel, its services are increasingly also being called upon for some cases involving forged currency, stolen art-work or large-scale frauds. (Extradition laws are especially anomalous regarding the latter: unlike Scandinavians or Germans, United Kingdom citizens cannot be prosecuted in Britain for frauds committed abroad; nor can a witness living abroad be compelled to come here to give evidence.) Degrees of police cooperation internationally have been developed in particular by experience of drugs-control: agreement has recently been reached that officers should be exchanged between certain Middle Eastern and European police as well as customs authorities – something that has never happened previously. Another impetus towards trans-national liaison, but one that Interpol by its regulations has to ignore, has resulted from the growing internationally-linked activities of political terrorists. In 1978, after the kidnapping and death of Aldo Moro, since certain West German terrorists were known to have close links with Italy, five members of the German criminal office staff moved to Rome with a mobile terminal which was tuned in to the criminal office's computer records. Some West European leaders have advocated much closer regular links between their respective police forces, and the development of a European equivalent of the FBI within Interpol, but M. Nepote sees no realistic prospect of a European detective force while the area includes such widely different legal systems.

TABLE 10: EXTRADITION AGREEMENTS
A list of the extradition treaties to which the United Kingdom is a party

Year of treaty	*Country*	*Year of treaty*	*Country*
1926	Albania	1960	Israel
1889	Argentina	1873	Italy
1970	Austria	1892	Liberia
1901	Belgium	1880	Luxembourg
1892	Bolivia	1886	Mexico
1897	Chile	1891	Monaco
1858	China	1898	Netherlands
1888	Columbia	1905	Nicaragua
1904	Cuba	1873	Norway
1924	Czechoslovakia	1906	Panama
1873	Denmark	1908	Paraguay
1880	Ecuador	1904	Peru
1881	El Salvador	1932	Poland
1924	Finland	1892 & 1921	Portugal
1815 & 1876	France	1893	Romania
1960	Federal Germany	1899	San Marino
1910	Greece	1878	Spain
1885	Guatemala	1966	Sweden
1874	Haiti	1880	Switzerland
1873	Hungary	1883 & 1911	Thailand
1873	Iceland (with Denmark)	1931	United States
1932	Iraq	1884	Uruguay
1965	Irish Republic	1900	Yugoslavia

The future

Ortega y Gasset predicted in *The Revolt of the Masses* the danger that the police will not always be content to preserve order as defined by the government, but will end by themselves deciding the order that they are going to impose. Most senior British police officers fear the advent of a nationally-organized force – even though several of them regard this as one day inevitable – from the opposite standpoint: a typical chief constable's opinion is, 'I am of course an implacable opponent of national control of the police since I think, particularly in these wild times, it is possible that political control of the Special Branch particularly would be most undesirable for obvious reasons.' But Jim Jardine of the Police Federation of England and Wales disagrees: 'I do not believe that a national police force will inevitably lead to a police state . . . This has not happened in other genuinely democratic countries, such as Sweden and Denmark, where national police forces have been established in comparatively recent years.'

Many other policemen are resigned to the fact that the incipient breakdown of local government financing will inevitably lead to greater powers of central government over the police. The national exchequer's share of the soaring bill for the police is likely to rise to 75 per cent and then to 90 per cent. Another influence pulling in the same direction is the work of the Police Federation, with their developing interest in matters ranging from standard national conditions, centrally negotiated, to their increasing requests for intervention by the Home Secretary. At times of shortage of policemen and high wastage, the power of the Federation is all the greater.

In current conditions, it cannot be a sensible allocation of Britain's resources for rural areas to be allowed to increase their establishments whilst the larger urban forces remain undermanned and overworked. Recruitment, at least, should certainly be national; at present the very districts which most need policemen find it hardest to recruit them – thus in turn making the overstretched jobless attractive. A temporary halt should be called to recruiting in rural areas, and greater financial weighting should be given to London and other cities, until the national imbalance is redressed. Several experienced policemen believe that a strengthened central Inspectorate should – unlike at present – also have the power at least to promote talented officers to the top across the country, to allocate resources more equitably on a national basis, and to deal effectively with cross-boundary problems. Meanwhile, the Metropolitan force should come under the national Inspectorate, and its own democratic police authority should be established to counterbalance any possibility of Home Office control. In addition, for many years a great number of officers have been urging that it is archaic for the City of London to have its own force, and that this should be merged with the rest of London. The present force, which is entirely surrounded by the Metropolitan area, owes its origin simply to the historical accident of Peel having to concede it to the City caucus in order to save his projected New Police from an early Parliamentary death (police officers who aspire to be its Commissioner have to appear before the Court of Common Council wearing morning dress to be selected). The usual excuse for preserving the separate force is that the City population floods in during the day and out again at night, so that the position there of only 7,500 permanent residents but a working population of 345,000 is different from the rest of London. But surely this tidal flow would equally help a combined police force? The extra officers who are necessary for traffic control during the rush hours could economically be used at other times wherever they were most needed in any part of the capital.

Anomalies of promotion in particular can lead to grievances under the present fissiparous system. Four-fifths of all police officers remain constables throughout their career; only 8 per cent of them can ever expect to rise above the rank of sergeant. Outside the Metropolitan area, which has a different system of promotion by examination, almost every serving officer can cite instances where the assessment of one superior is felt to have unfairly prejudiced a person's chances of advancement. The last Royal Commission recognized that in smaller forces promotion tends to stagnate, and it is harder there than in a larger force for a chief constable to ignore claims of seniority rather than merit in filling vacancies. Because of the promotion block the majority of junior officers serving in smaller forces are in favour of amalgamation, and point out that the opposition to this comes mainly from those at the top of the hierarchy such as chief constables and local councillors who have a built-in reluctance to forgo their status.

Anthony Armstrong, the chief constable of Bedfordshire, forecasts that most of the present younger police officers will serve in some form of inevitable regionalization, with a national force probable by the year 2000. Divisional identities could remain whether under a national or regional structure. But for Britain, regional reorganization still seems the most likely direction of development. Some boundary problems would remain, but this would be a price willingly paid by those people who have a lingering political fear of one national force. It is not certain that this would necessarily be a halfway stage towards a national force; central control, in some ways, is easier to exercise over weak local forces than over stronger regional ones.

SIX

The Police Officer's Lot

'Since we know so little, it is easy to make the assumption that there is nothing to know anything about.'
Prof. D. R. Cressey

'The imposition of the office of constable is an unsupportable hardship; it takes up so much of a man's time that his own affairs are frequently totally neglected, too often to his ruin.'
Daniel Defoe, 1714

The attitude of many members of the public is summed up by the man who said, 'Policemen, schoolteachers, doctors and dentists: it is difficult for us to remember they are human. In our minds they exist as a social function; they represent authority.' This image finds a mirror in the feeling of police officers themselves, expressed by one constable who observed, 'The uniform makes the policeman aware he is "different", and society's guilt-complex is continually reminding him of his isolation.' Danger inculcates an ingrained self-defensive protectiveness: being regularly exposed to physical and legal jeopardy (and quite often to calumny) can make policemen not only continually suspicious, but at times subjectively feel they form a race apart. Many of them are in danger of developing a mood of frustrated pessimism and paranoia about their work, coupled with an isolated and introspective personal sense of anomie and alienation from the rest of society. The suicide rate among New York police is 50 per cent above that of the rest of the inhabitants of the city.

Some degree of dichotomy if not conflict in police existence is inescapable because, as the Association of Chief Police Officers told the last Royal Commission, a policeman 'must be part of the community, and yet at the same time it is always dangerous to become on too intimate terms with people to whom at any time he may have to apply the due process of law.' Socially, not only his hours of work and his housing frequently segregate him; in addition he is constrained from talking to ordinary people about most of the things which concern him and justify his existence. The Royal Commission's survey concluded that two-thirds of police officers found it difficult to make friends outside the force. One in four said their children were bullied at school because of their job. A life spent suspecting takes its toll. Some officers are prone to stereotype the people they encounter in terms of the various categories of problems they have to deal with professionally. In time, a policeman can come to view even his geographical environment differently: the public park for him is translated into a venue for perverts; the river or cliff-top becomes a likely place for suicides. A number of recent studies have found that many policemen make less objective witnesses of events than civilians do, because they tend to see and recall sinister things that have not actually happened. In one American test, when civilians and police were shown a film of a man who was carrying a metal can, the civilians deduced he had run out of petrol, but most of the policemen assumed he must be an arsonist. Accumulation of prolonged psychological stress can come to affect the judgement of all but the most mature: 'If you're sensitive, this job can drive you round the twist.' In 1978 the chief constable of Merseyside asked that at least all Senior officers should have an annual medical check, because of the strain of their work. Recent research has demonstrated that police life is one of the most stress-filled occupations, high in the statistical tables for heart disease, suicide, and diabetes. US findings by Stotland and Canon in 1972 showed that people with higher self-esteem are relatively better equipped to cope with stress, and to react constructively to derogation or frustration. For policemen, self-esteem would be increased if they were given more feed back about the outcome of both the criminal and welfare cases they encounter. It is especially important to improve the self-concept of constables – the only police officer the majority of the public ever see, and whose status is lowest at the bottom of a quasi-military organization. The more the police can be made conscious of self- and others' appreciation, the more positively they are likely to act.

The wearer of a police uniform incurs additional pressure because his life is cast as a role of super-human example. Since all civilians tend to watch closely how a policeman behaves, he generally can only let himself go, drinking or acting uninhibitedly, when with other police officers. Unlike most of the rest of us, he has few outlets for any feelings of protest. Yet he certainly disapproves of a great deal of what he observes around him in society: he sees himself – to some extent rightly – as a highly traditional island in a fast-flowing tide. His work impels him to be for order and against change *prima facie*. There is evidence that many US policemen combine Victorian views of morality with active dislike of political and racial minorities, but are theoretically forbidden to express this. One English police officer complained, 'We're in daily, actual contact with crime, the criminal and all the other oddities and dregs of humanity – they're not something we just see on television or read about in the papers.' Habitually, a high proportion of the police's encounters are with inadequate, frightened or uncared-for people. It is understandable how a number of them – particularly those who patrol urban areas – come to feel they are 'an army holding the city down', though Maureen Cain found that rural policemen were more inclined to see the world in much the same terms as those they policed did, often being born and brought up where they work.

At the same time, police officers increasingly feel far from secure or confident in their task. Joseph Wamburgh, who spent fourteen years in the Los Angeles police, states:

> You get young men being exposed to the most terrible kinds of emotional trauma. They see the worst of people, they see ordinary people at their worst, and they become prematurely cynical – which leads to all sorts of emotional disorders. Because when you're that cynical at that early an age you

lend yourself to the kind of destructive philosophy that says something like 'People are garbage. And I am a person, hence I am garbage.'

Young British recruits find the life involves few results from continual strain, with perhaps their greatest worry that every decision they take must be capable of being retrospectively proved correct. The first day out in uniform on one's own can be a 'really frightening' experience. 'If only,' one said, 'I could sometimes do nothing and fade into the background, like the onlookers.'

Even though the amateur gentleman-detective who patronized lower-class policemen, depicted as ploddingly clod-like, has vanished from fiction in favour of other stereotypes (some of them equally unrealistic), insecurity over status permeates many police attitudes today. In New York City, the Patrolmen's Benevolent Association justified their vehement opposition to the recent bill to outlaw discrimination against homosexuals by arguing that 'this proposal to open the ranks to sexual deviants would constitute yet another blow to the police department's once-bright image.' Part of a number of policemen's marked dislike of students stems from the knowledge that they themselves will have little chance of university, reinforced by their own experience of encountering articulate students on demonstrations. 'Many of the Thames Valley police were longing to have a crack at young people at a pop festival,' one of their colleagues said. 'They wished the one at Windsor had gone ahead so that they could have had a real go.' These feelings are often reciprocated: some youth clubs feel there is a danger that if police officers visit or help in them, the youths they most want to attract will stay away. Such feelings of ostracism are shared by some adults: a member of Laisterdyke Cricket Club was asked to resign when it was discovered that he was a member of the West Yorkshire Constabulary, the club secretary stating that it was the club's policy never to admit policemen. Between the police and sections of the working-class inhabitants in certain areas of Liverpool, traditions of endemic hostility are maintained, with some police officers habitually referring to those they are meant to be protecting as 'animals', and many of the inhabitants physically resisting searches and attempting to protect any person who may be threatened with arrest. 'Grassing' or 'shopping' anyone to the police in such areas is the worst crime in the calendar. Murray Armstrong described the roots of some similar feelings when he served as a constable in Glasgow: 'You're taught to be suspicious. You feel alone, and take comfort from the experiences of other cops. You'll learn the petty prejudice of hating those in poorer working-class areas because that's where most of the petty crime is. And for a cop on the beat that's what the best part of his working hours are taken up by.' The feeling towards the police in a number of the most run-down and poor urban areas can parallel that which a subject people show towards a visiting colonial army. This hostile wariness is reïnforced in those American and British cities where virtually none of the police actually live in the poor districts they patrol; and it can be further exacerbated in black neighbourhoods when the police are conspicuously white and originate from different and more middle-class areas.

Recruiting

Overall public support for the police however remains significantly stronger than they themselves imagine. A British survey carried out in 1974 showed that greater public confidence was felt in the management of the police than of any other institution in the country, and that even unskilled workers had more than twice as much faith in them as they had in Parliament, the press, trade unions, or the civil service.

Against this favourable background the problem of manning the police stems not so much from the difficulty of recruitment, as from the haemorrhage of unnecessary wastage. The most controversial question about recruitment itself centres upon not numbers but quality, and on which characteristics should debar potential recruits. Educational and even physical qualifications for entry are now barely above minimal; though bad teeth is still – unnecessarily – one of the most frequent reasons for rejecting recruits, and as we have seen the City of London insists on a minimum height significantly taller than considered necessary elsewhere. Scarcity of men inevitably further lowers standards in particular areas: New York accepts about 15 per cent of

TABLE 11

Percentage expressing a great deal of confidence in the management of:	*(all respondents)*	*(unskilled)*
Police	71	70
Medicine	67	73
The military	60	67
Law courts	42	41
Education	39	41
Civil service	26	30
The press	24	29
Parliament	19	23
Trade unions	18	27

applicants, whereas Los Angeles only takes 4 per cent. In Britain, some 5 per cent of all inquiries and 20 per cent of firm applications are appointed – with a higher proportion in the Metropolitan force, but a three times smaller proportion of black applicants being accepted. Contrary to general belief, a minor previous conviction does not necessarily debar a candidate, provided he or she has been frank in disclosing it. On the other hand educational 'book learning' and even a degree are too often still suspect as incompatible with the traditional ideal of being a 'practical' policeman; in return, few careers advisers recommend the service to ambitious school-leavers. Lanarkshire is currently offering those who have been rejected on educational grounds a free eight-weeks correspondence course.

Far and away the most frequent reason given by recruits in both Britain and the US for wishing to join is the security of the job, followed by the attraction of the early pension. The pre-war inducement of relatively good pay, and the immediate post-war incentive provided by the housing shortage, are no longer so significant. Instead, recruiting advertisements have lately laid emphasis on the adventurousness and the importance of police work (though much of the copy, such as

TABLE 12: BRITISH POLICE RECRUITMENT SINCE 1960

Year	England and Wales			Northern Ireland			Scotland		
	Male	*Female*	*Total*	*Male*	*Female*	*Total*	*Male*	*Female*	*Total*
1960	4,374	405	4,779	167	11	178	505	60	565
1961	5,683	434	6,117	167	—	167	639	57	696
1962	5,952	456	6,408	158	14	172	818	69	887
1963	5,991	538	6,529	157	—	157	680	82	762
1964	6,004	617	6,621	77	14	91	623	67	690
1965	7,773	707	8,480	114	13	127	792	83	875
1966	6,855	848	7,703	132	—	132	616	106	722
1967	8,000	839	8,839	165	14	179	686	93	779
1968	4,757	658	5,415	106	—	106	737	80	817
1969	5,798	652	6,450	166	12	178	668	72	740
1970	5,873	741	6,614	516	44	560	641	70	711
1971	6,297	780	7,077	443	53	496	764	81	845
1972	6,258	904	7,162	307	55	362	800	106	906
1973	5,825	861	6,686	270	61	331	735	113	848
1974	6,408	1,137	7,545	277	79	356	821	139	960
1975	8,681	1,717	10,398	411	94	505	1,195	221	1,416
1976	7,887	2,155	10,042	463	118	581	930	154	1,084
1977	5,857	2,146	8,003	526	153	679	723	161	884

'Britain's police – doing a great job' seems to be aimed at helping serving men's morale as much as recruiting). Such appeals can attract many types of personality. The fifteen-minute interview given to an applicant in Britain is hardly sufficient to determine his underlying character or what temperament he will reveal under stress in a crisis. United States research concludes that police recruits, while being in general conservative, upwardly mobile and conventional, are no more authoritarian than other people of a similar background, but that many of them later become so through their occupational socialization. In Venezuela, a team of psychologists not only screens potential recruits, but also carries out periodic reassessments of serving policemen in order to determine the causes of any adverse changes in their behavioural pattern. As the last British Royal Commission pointed out, the police service gives more immediate power in its lower echelons than any other occupation. It also offers the shortest way to acquire status in a community, when most comparable jobs are still the prerogative of the middle classes. And as in the armed services, many men and a few women are attracted to the atmosphere of a masculine club that has strong identity, hierarchy and group solidarity. Senior Metropolitan officers say they prefer to select recruits who show they have got 'a natural feeling for tranquillity in society'. Professor A. C. Germann suggests that 'it would be helpful to involve citizens of the community policed in the processes of recruitment, screening, and promotion. In time, this would provide for a variety of police personalities and replace the current police-controlled system that develops mirror-image counterparts of existing police.'

Most recruits, unless they have a relative or friend already serving, probably derive many of their main ideas of police life and work from televised fiction. A policeman on his beat can be among the best possible recruiting agents – provided he is satisfied in his work. At present however few serving men say they would like their children to follow them into the force. And the minimum age limit for joining results in many young people, who do not want to become cadets, being lost to recruiting between the time they leave school and attaining the minimum recruiting age. Although efforts are made to give cadets (who enlist at 16) some experience of civilian work, many serving policemen remain unenthusiastic about the limited horizons resulting from cadet entry, and the Police Federation have argued that not more than one third of recruits should be made up of ex-cadets. More extreme advocates of the same thinking support the idea of national service in the police, on the grounds that this would increase the democratization of the force. 'The police,' as one officer suggested, may be 'deliberately drawn from ordinary people so as to be more acceptable,' but only 9 per cent of new recuits have two A levels, compared with over 12 per cent for school-leavers as a whole; and there are scarcely 930 graduates in a total force of 120,000. Another disturbing trend was pointed out by J. J. Tobias, who showed that the proportion of British male recruits in the 1960s who had been educated at secondary modern schools was growing while that from grammar schools was steadily declining:

TABLE 13

Percentages of recruits from:	*1962*	*1963*	*1964*	*1965*	*1966*	*1967*	*1968*	*1969*	*1970*	*1977**
Secondary modern schools	55.3	59.0	58.2	59.7	59.5	61.8	58.6	62.7	63.5	43.5
Comprehensive schools	—	—	—	0.5	3.6	4.0	4.0	3.6	4.7	27.4
Grammar schools	42.6	38.5	39.3	38.2	34.7	31.7	34.7	31.3	29.4	25.6

* 1977 figures not strictly comparable because of changes in the schools.

In the whole of the period between 1945 and 1965 only twenty-five graduates joined the service. Although there is no inevitable correlation between educational background – whether university or grammar or any other type of school – and becoming a good policeman, the scarcity of readily identifiable future leaders is known to worry many senior police officers. In 1964 only five, and in 1965 six, graduates are known to have joined the police in the whole of England and Wales. Any revival of the privileged officer cadre associated with Trenchard's Hendon College would be bitterly resented; instead a much more urgent effort should be made to meet the crisis by enabling more promising police officers to attend universities. In the longer term, the police service needs to take a long cool look at what it is about itself which is anathema to so many graduates and bright school-leavers even during times of unemployment.

A further question that needs to be considered is why, if recruits are still needed, there are still so few black police officers. In America as late as 1965, no black – and only one Jew – had ever been employed by the FBI. After the 1967 race riots, the recruitment of blacks was given top priority by leaders of the Detroit police, who employed intensive black-orientated advertising and changed the entrance test which was felt to be both culturally and racially biased, with the result that the black intake doubled. New York's police are now about 7 per cent black, compared with 17 per cent of the population. As recently as 1963 there was not a single black police officer in the whole of Britain, and several policemen forecast mass resignations if one were ever appointed. By the start of 1978 there were 199 in England and Wales – but this still represents scarcely one-fifteenth of their equivalent proportion in the national population.

A very few now have the rank of sergeant; none has a higher rank. There are also hardly any Jews in the British police: probably no more than ten in the whole country. What are the reasons for such disparities? A number of men who had previously served with considerable experience in West Indian police forces have been refused admission, only some of them because they hold Commonwealth passports. An excellent and forthright advertising campaign for black recruits launched by Sir Robert Mark for a long time failed to produce a single successful applicant. But it will need more than one campaign to reverse the suspicion most black people hold towards the police, which is described later in this chapter. Many blacks fear they would be branded as 'Uncle Toms' if they joined the police; able men and women among them believe they will do better outside the police. Some black leaders such as Darcus Howe, the editor of *Race Today*, view the attempt to recruit blacks for the police as part of the same pattern whereby they

TABLE 14: BLACK POLICE OFFICERS, ENGLAND AND WALES

	Metropolitan	*All*
31 December 1966	0	5
1967	1	12
1968	3	16
1969	4	23
1970	8	33
1971	11	57
1972	13	58
1973	19	78
1974	37	109
1975	39	134
1976	71	182
1977	82	199
June 1978	83	205

are sought only for sections of the economy which not enough whites are willing to staff, such as in transport, nursing and catering. Russell Pierre, the managing editor of *West Indian World*, said some blacks saw recruiting as a plot to bring in black police spies. None the less they are crucially needed, to break down 'them and us' attitudes about blacks both outside and inside the police. Paul Stephenson urges black Britons to enrol, arguing that this 'will help dispel the Powellite myth that black people living in this country present a disastrous and dangerous situation which can only be remedied by a policy of mass repatriation.' There is evidence of this, not least in some of the reasons police officers give to explain why there are so few blacks among them: that 'the public are still reluctant to be policed by a black'; and – ingeniously – that black people themselves are better off by not incurring the unpopularity of being police officers. A number candidly admit that quite a few policemen still have little enthusiasm for black colleagues, if only because they are apprehensive that these would lower the status and standing of their job. But prejudice is not reduced by being pandered to. If the southern United States can be policed by black officers, why cannot Britain?

Wastage

Historically, wastage has always been higher in the police service than in many other occupations. Of the first thousand men enrolled in the Metropolitan force 40 per cent left within its first difficult and unpopular four years. Between 1829 and 1837 6,000 London constables resigned in addition to 5,200 who were dismissed. Pressures on police life were even worse then than today: a policeman was himself expected to pay the costs of prosecuting people he arrested; while at the same time rich men were in the habit of urging their coachmen to lash the Peelers with their whips. In the years which followed, turnover in the Metropolitan police continued to average one-third a year; the discontent (commemorated in W. S. Gilbert's words, 'A policeman's lot is not a happy one') erupted in several strikes towards the end of the century. Today about half the losses are due to resignations from causes other than the predictable ones of health, dismissal and normal retirement on pension. Not all such premature departures are a loss in real terms: dissatisfied and disappointed men who remain can be a greater liability than if they leave. Job satisfaction has never been the same as doing a satisfactory job. But police officers are now able to retire on half or two-thirds pay while young enough to get another job, and the private security industry offers tempting competition. The retirement of many long-serving men of all ranks has been accelerated by the decision taken in 1975 which enables them now to count war service as years of service towards a police pension – although civil servants have been allowed to do this since 1949. Between 1976 and 1979, it is estimated that over 15 per cent of all policemen will be seeking retirement. But in 1977 more policemen in England and Wales resigned before qualifying for a pension than in any previous year:

1974 (total)	3,657
1975	2,701
1976	3,287
1977	5,166
1978 (first half)	2,673

The Metropolitan force, which lost some 1,000 of these, ended 1977 with 150 fewer officers than the previous year. The impetus for this included the rigorous drive against corruption as well as the pressure of the cost of living upon police pay. But the most damaging part of avoidable wastage is the departure of the experienced men whose loss can least be afforded. A great deal of police skill can never be learnt from books but has to be accumulated at first-hand over years of trial and error in decision-taking and hard-earned experience. New recruits depend for their confidence on having this lore passed on to them by longer-serving colleagues, but the draining away of experienced men results in this being done less and less. In several parts of Britain well over a fifth of the force is now under twenty-five years old; in Derbyshire by 1977 over a third of uniformed ground-cover was made up of probationary constables.

Just over half the officers who resign do so, as might be predicted, within the probationary period of their first two years. Wastage is so high, according to Sir Robert Mark, partly because the reality of policing differs so much from its fictional image. The impressions and experiences, largely fortuitous, that a new officer receives in his initial few months often play a key part in determining whether or not he will stay. Such influences include the reactions he has from the public to his new role, whether he finds his colleagues congenial and sympathetic, and how his superior officers treat him. What attracts a person to the police – as in any job – may be very different from the actual work in reality; the wastage of ex-cadets is significantly less than among direct entrants because the former's expectations are more in accord with the practice of the job itself. It is also lower in the CID than it is among uniformed men, who complain that their job is becoming increasingly mundane as anything worthwhile is taken out of their hands and given to specialist branches. Among the most frequently expressed complaints of those who resign voluntarily yet prematurely are that they find the life of an individual in the police too isolated and lonely; that the work is complex yet at the same time monotonous; and that the job involves an intolerable degree of dislocation of private and social life, with arrangements and rest-days frequently being cancelled, on top of

TABLE 15: TOTAL POLICE WASTAGE SINCE 1960

Year	England and Wales			Northern Ireland			Scotland		
	Male	*Female*	*Total*	*Male*	*Female*	*Total*	*Male*	*Female*	*Total*
1960	4,559	450	5,009	147	4	151	429	57	486
1961	2,703	366	3,069	89	1	90	305	45	350
1962	3,419	441	3,860	102	6	108	318	53	371
1963	4,245	383	4,628	113	8	121	498	53	551
1964	5,208	465	5,673	128	12	140	508	59	567
1965	4,764	495	5,260	126	7	133	487	68	555
1966	4,769	529	5,296	178	6	184	780	92	872
1967	4,263	503	4,766	115	12	127	650	78	728
1968	4,612	634	5,246	109	9	118	690	78	768
1969	4,754	615	6,369	162	3	165	657	71	728
1970	3,908	664	4,550	122	5	127	487	73	560
1971	3,508	537	4,045	212	7	219	442	51	493
1972	3,854	589	4,443	171	20	191	422	65	487
1973	5,158	653	5,811	176	21	197	548	78	626
1974	5,208	753	5,961	166	16	182	598	95	693
1975	4,676	638	5,314	145	23	168	682	77	759
1976	6,819	931	7,750	201	29	230	1,053	90	1,143
1977	7,936	1,344	9,280	197	43	240	1,028*	127*	1,155*

*Provisional figures

the regular shift-system and compulsory overtime. In 1977 there were over 580 major public events in London (nearly 200 more than in the previous year), many of them at the weekend, which required special police arrangements involving the cancellation of officers' leave.

Above all, there is resentment that many of the older senior ranks are still enforcing discipline in a petty regimental fashion that is wholly out of date in the 1970s. 'Some senior officers treat you like children, though the law expects us to be highly responsible adults.' In contrast to the contemporary movement towards participatory democracy in other occupations, the way in which many areas' policemen are paraded before they go out on the beat is like a legacy of the army of Peel's and Wellington's day. 'Some aspects of our regulations,' says sergeant David Payton of Durham, 'are archaic and almost feudal.' The public's change in attitude towards authority, lamented so often by the police, finds its echo in the ranks of younger policemen too. The restrictions – petty or otherwise – imposed on the off-duty private lives of police men and women are unknown in virtually any other occupation, and often apply even to the spouses of officers. John Higham for example, who for seven years was a constable in Stockport, quit because 'First I had to get permission to get married, then supply complete details of my wife's background. Even the house we chose had to be approved by the chief constable. When I grew a beard while on sick leave, I was told to shave it off. Finally my wife was refused permission to run a chip shop.' Policemen are expected to continue to observe a nineteenth-century moral code, while daily being vividly aware of its rejection by the rest of society. Almost all unmarried men are compelled to live in Section Houses, some of which are still run on the lines of Victorian boarding-houses, with visitors of the opposite sex forbidden. In Portsmouth an unmarried police woman was put on a charge for kissing a married colleague. A considerable amount of dissatisfaction can be traced to difficulties with particular senior officers, to failures to explain policies, or to resentment against what is felt to be impersonally bureaucratic administration or over-rigidly autocratic treatment. As in the armed services, it is virtually a human impossibility for policemen to observe every regulation all the time, and they are therefore vulnerable to disciplinary censure and control at any moment. Some petty restrictions could safely be abolished; others are inevitable if the police are to continue to be seen as impartial, and can only be compensated for by better pay and conditions. The ban against involvement in politics, for instance, is understandable, but it bears particularly irksomely in some industrial areas where the only social clubs are nominally political ones.

Many resignations are finally determined by the positive incentive of an easier or better job elsewhere; others are prompted by disappointment at failure to win promotion; or by the long stretches of inevitable boredom in police life, coupled with resentment at being frequently pilloried as a liar in the witness-box by a sleek barrister cynically deploying a well-worn 'those are my instructions' defence. The problem can become cumulatively circular: resignations necessitate more overtime being worked, and the increased intrusion into family life then results in more wives putting pressure on further men to leave. Many men are reluctant to cite their wife's or girlfriend's views as their reason for resigning, but it is undoubtedly a significant factor in a large number of cases. 'It is not generally realized,' one superintendent pointed out, 'that there is a vast difference between overtime worked by a factory worker and that performed by a police officer. The first generally does his extra work when he wants to; the second is ordered to do his – and wives and girlfriends do not like it.' The latter are the witnesses about police life that the Home Office and the police authorities rarely see or hear. One resignation was understandably provoked by the upset that four moves in eight years caused to a policeman's wife and to his children's schooling. It is high time that most police leaders came to understand that the attitude of police wives and fiancées is crucial to the service's morale and ability to retain experienced men. Police families cannot escape the basic schizophrenia of the lives of serving officers: on the one hand, the theory that he is never off duty; on the other, the practical necessity that the preservation of any social life demands that he hangs up his uniform when he goes home and stops seeing everything through the eyes of a police officer. For many indeed their off-duty cultural values – of not interfering, not sneaking on their

TABLE 10: POLICE MANPOWER 1960–1977 (authorized establishments given in brackets)

Year	England and Wales			Northern Ireland			Scotland		
	Male	Female	Total	Male	Female	Total	Male	Female	Total
1960	69,972 (77,056)	2,280 (2,910)	72,252 (79,966)	2,865 (2,899)	56 (58)	2,977 (2,977)	8,557 (8,980)	273 (286)	8,830 (9,266)
1965	81,072 (94,972)	2,868 (3,529)	83,940 (98,501)	2,980 (3,107)	63 (58)	3,043 (3,165)	9,993 (10,676)	353 (401)	10,346 (11,077)
1970	90,127 (105,096)	3,621 (4,320)	93,748 (109,416)	3,711 (3,369)	98 (131)	3,809 (3,500)	10,077 (10,794)	382 (434)	10,459 (11,228)
1971	92,979 (105,644)	3,865 (4,425	96,844 (110,069)	3,942 (3,625)	144 (175)	4,086 (3,800)	10,399 (10,950)	412 (453)	10,811 (11,403)
1972	95,494 (106,713)	4,187 (4,521)	99,681 (111,234)	4,048 (3,800)	179 (300)	4,257 (4,100)	10,777 (11,480)	453 (525)	11,230 (12,005)
1973	96,172 (108,448)	4,394 (4,730)	100,566 (113,178)	4,172 (4,100)	219 (300)	4,391 (4,400)	10,964 (11,734)	488 (543)	11,452 (12,277)
1974	97,319 (110,609)	4,767 (5,197)	102,086 (115,806)	4,283 (5,750)	282 (750)	4,565 (6,500)	11,187 (12,444)	532 (577)	11,719 (13,021)
1975	101,298 (117,176)	5,840	107,138	4,549 (5,750)	353 (750)	4,902 (6,500)	11,700 (12,564)	676 (581)	12,376 (13,145)
1976	102,410 (118,101)	7,066	109,476	4,811 (5,750)	442 (750)	5,253 (6,500)	11,577 13,163)	740	12,317
1977	100,335 (118,279)	7,866	108,201	5,140 (6,500)	552	5,692	11,275 (13,146)	771	12,046

neighbours – are in direct conflict with the norms of their work when on duty. Overall this can lead to doubt as to where in reality they stand in society. In the US, more policemen commit suicide than are murdered.

Pay

The wastage rate is smaller in rural than in city areas, partly because competing wage rates there are in general less attractive. For all police officers, accommodation is free in addition to their basic pay, and there are a number of additional allowances – though the maximum rent allowance can vary geographically, from £12.22 weekly in North Wales to £22.25 in Kent. It is true to say that more policemen evaluate their job in terms of its job-satisfaction and interest than its economic rewards. Two officers said: 'No one does it just to earn a living. You could earn twice as much outside,' and 'You won't find a wealthy policeman unless he's thieving, but the job's enjoyable.' Nevertheless, as the Home Office state, 'We have little doubt that it is easier to recruit and retain police officers when the economic and employment situation generally is difficult.'

BADGES OF RANK

CADET | CONSTABLE (T 330) | SERGEANT | INSPECTOR | CHIEF INSPECTOR — ALL FORCES

SUPERINTENDENT | CHIEF SUPERINTENDENT | COMMANDER | DEPUTY ASSISTANT COMMISSIONER | ASSISTANT COMMISSIONER | COMMISSIONER — METROPOLITAN AND CITY OF LONDON POLICE

HM INSPECTORS OF CONSTABULARY WEAR CHIEF CONSTABLE'S BADGES & HM CHIEF INSPECTORS WEARS COMMISSIONER'S BADGES. BOTH WEAR THIS MONOGRAM ABOVE THE BATONS AND LAURELS

(The letter and number on a constable or sergeant's shoulders are their individual personal identification: the letter denotes which division they come from. Special Patrol Group members have the letters CO (Commissioner's Office) on their shoulders.)

The basic annual rates of pay, with effect from 1 September 1978, are:

Constables:	£3,189–£4,809
Sergeants:	£4,683–£5,406
Station sergeant (London only):	£5,700
Inspectors:	£5,406–£6,489
Chief Inspectors:	£6,198–£7,260
Superintendents:	£8,436–£9,333
Chief Superintendents:	£9,426–£10,326
Commanders:	£8,985–£9,471
Dep. Asst. Commissioners:	£10,029–£11,136
Asst. Commissioners:	£13,542
Chief Constables	£8,731–£14,410
Deputy Commissioner	£14,898
Commissioner:	£18,883

But a number of police officers today still earn less than the dustman or the unlicensed street-trader they meet on the beat. Certainly there must also be financial inducements for unpleasant jobs like refuse-collecting, but a good deal of police work is more skilled, demanding and hazardous than most salaried jobs paid four times as much.

TABLE 17

	Weekly wage rate of Metropolitan police constable (excluding overtime and rent allowance)			*Average weekly earnings in manufacturing industry (including overtime and bonus payments)*		
	£	s	d	£	s	d
1938	4	0	0	3	10	11
1948	5	17	0	7	3	4
1958	12	15	0	13	5	5
1969	23	15	0	25	10	10

Opportunities for overtime are much rarer outside London. By 1977, a constable's pay had fallen to 20 per cent below the average male earnings in industry, though the Willink Royal Commission had said it should stand 4 per cent above. Whereas until recently a prison officer with five years service received £2,800 annually, a fireman after fifteen years £3,036, and a staff nurse £2,646, a police constable after seventeen years service was only paid £2,562. (Though, anomalously, with overtime and other allowances, some London police inspectors and even constables earned more than their superintendents, who cannot claim for overtime. As a result, a number of chief inspectors did not want to be promoted.)

In the US, two policemen in every five have a second job. The low quality of many US policemen is not surprising when it is seen that their average earning is only three-quarters of the sum the US government estimates to be necessary to raise a family of four at a minimum standard of living. The remedy, to double the US police budget, would cost only one-thirtieth of that nation's defence expenditure. Inadequate police pay not only discourages able people from joining or staying, but also has an effect upon morale because, as Professor James Wilson of Harvard says, it 'is interpreted by policemen as palpable evidence of the contempt in which the police are held by the public and politicians.' In America, despite the litany reiterated towards law and order, a policeman is today paid less in comparative terms than he was in the 1930s, and consequently recruits tend to be drawn from a diminishing pool of undereducated people.

British policemen, unlike their American counterparts, are rarely allowed to take any outside job when they are off duty, though a number of men moonlight as barmen, gardeners or window-cleaners, and some patrol-car drivers give driving lessons. Police pay should compensate for the social sacrifices policemen inevitably undergo and (as in the case of judges) as far as possible inoculate them against corruption. It is hard to resist the suspicion that snobbery about the police's historical working-class origins – prior to the Edmund Davies committee's recommendations – played some part in keeping their pay low. Professor Nevin of Swansea University deduces that 'the question "What should the policeman be paid?" is unanswerable,' and the only possible approach is 'how much do we need to pay to get the policemen we require?'

More encouragingly for policemen, on average they draw their pension about ten years earlier than most other occupations. They can opt for half-pay after twenty-five years service or for two-thirds pay after thirty years – though a New York police officer is able to retire on half-pay after fifteen years service.

Training

A policeman's training, like a soldier's, is intended to sever many of his ties with his previous civilian life. During this time, the recruit who commits himself to the service gradually acquires the basis of a permanent feeling of solidarity with his colleagues, which results in a mutual sense that in virtually any situation it is 'us against them' and that it is up to them to help each other even against the public. This closing of ranks, which is intensified by the unusual stresses under which the police are working, runs directly counter to what is taught to a policeman about the kernel of his office being its individual responsibility.

Since the character of a police recruit is more crucial a matter than his physique or previous education, it would be preferable if not all of his initial training were cloistered in a Police Training Centre, but included some periods of practical duty in contact with the public, when his reactions to crises would soon reveal the real quality of his personality and judgement. And in place of attempts to commit slabs of obscure law to memory – which causes some potentially effective police officers to resign in bored despair during training – it would be preferable to have more teaching and discussion about the role of the police in society, their discretion in enforcing the law, their relations with the public, and the social problems they are likely to encounter in their work. Although some improvements in the syllabus have recently been made, one chief constable's opinion is that 'Basic training should be revolutionized in my view. The concentration on legal and procedural matters is too marked, and not enough of the study of society and people is done.' More than half of police recruits have no O level, and nearly 90 per cent no A level: there are arguments for making their training more interesting in human terms – both in order to explain to them the implications police work has for civilian people, and in order to win their commitment to a career which inevitably will involve many frustrations. Policemen above all need training as diagnosticians: they cannot expect omnipotently to fulfil every service role in society, but they can be trained to identify for example when and which specialist medical, scientific, psychiatric or welfare agencies need to be contacted. Knowledge of the social sciences can help police work as well as criminology and penology; and psychology can give a recruit not only insight into the nature of some of the problems he will encounter, but also – perhaps even more importantly – some understanding of his own reactions to those situations. Taking part in role-reversal sessions can be particularly useful experience in both these respects.

It is no use confining such wider perspectives to a few, mainly more senior, ranks at Bramshill Police College. Bramshill is a fine Jacobean house, standing in beautiful grounds near Hartney Wintney in Hampshire, which acts as a police university for England and Wales; the Scottish equivalent is at Tulliallan Castle, Kincardine Bridge. Here, each year courses with a strong liberal component are held for policemen of special promise, including 560 inspectors and 180 superintendents, besides police officers from mainly Commonwealth countries overseas. The police colleges give a valuable opportunity for officers to compare police problems outside the limited focus of their own local force. But 90 per cent of policemen never see inside the police colleges; yet the British service is based not on an élite, but on the authority and responsibility of each police officer. As inspector Graham Marsden perceptively points out, 'The human problems of prejudice, sensitivity and social awareness arise at the point where the police meet the public. They occur at constable and sergeant level. The West Indian immigrant does not have a problem with the superintendent in his office – his problem is with the policeman on the High Street; and the policeman on the High Street will not have been to the police college.' A chief constable agreed about the same difficulty: 'One of the great problems of changing policemen's attitudes is breaking down the prejudices and subjectivity of the middle service and older police officer. It is quite possible to introduce training programmes, but if they are negated at police station level then clearly something has to be done at police station level.' Down at this level, those who go to Bramshill are sardonically spoken of as 'plastic men – ones who know all about how to hold a knife and fork but nothing about how to catch villains'.

Most of the courses at Bramshill are admirable (even though, for instance, 'Attitudes and Beliefs' have to be covered in one morning, compared with forty hours at the Open University), and they could be used to fertilize more of the rest of police training. The Home Office Research Unit, together with an international research liaison unit, could also be moved there, and police graduates and overseas secondments debriefed on their experience. This could serve to build up a national police research centre, which is needed because individual forces have little time or resources for any but *ad hoc* research. The police college itself should be expanded, to make up the backlog prior to its existence and also, as Tony Judge suggests, because police suspicion about it can best be broken down if more of the service were allowed to see it for themselves. For the first 110 years of its existence, the British police imported its leaders from outside the service. Now it trains its own; but at present good recruits often 'have to be chased' to Bramshill, because chief constables are not anxious to spare able men, and officers themselves are reluctant to be separated from their families and homes as well as having a fear that they might lose from being 'out of sight, out of mind' for promotion.

Police training can never be finished: as with other occupations, such as teaching, medicine or law, it must continue with regular periods of not so much 'refreshing' as retraining. One day a fortnight or a week each year is preferable to a month every decade. Too often senior officers' views reflect their experience when they were last on the beat, which can be seriously obsolete. As John Alderson says, in the future, leaders will be in a 'world of permanent reorganization. This is already happening and many are finding it difficult to comprehend. The leader therefore must no longer regard the service of a long apprenticeship and a comforting mastery of the *status quo* as a qualification; rather it will be a disqualification since he will require great flexibility of mind to adapt to constant change. And as he will be responsible for creating improvement without increasing resources he will need to innovate.' A number of the older officers need courses on social questions such as drug problems much more than recruits do. Some teaching about race and community relations is necessary for all ranks and ages. It needs to be supplemented with additional special knowledge about the background and customs of local groups: for example, Irish or Cypriot culture, religion, family habits and history to help the understanding of tensions in particular areas. Six officers in Sheffield enterprisingly have recently learnt Urdu as volunteers so as to be able to talk to the city's 6,000 Pakistanis; it will also be necessary to teach policemen, for example, that many Asian women will traditionally never answer the door if any strange man (including a policeman) calls.

For all this increase needed in training, civilian teaching facilities (including polytechnics and the Open University) will have to be used, which – since police training at present suffers from being too exclusively police-run – will bring other benefits for both police and public in ending 'us against them' attitudes. Shift work makes the organization of courses far from simple, but the Police Federation needs to remember that better qualified and trained policemen will lead to better paid ones performing a job that has higher status. In areas of the United States, the minimum basic training period for a policeman was recently a mere 200 hours (compared with for example 11,000 hours for a physician, 5,000 for an embalmer, and 1,200 for a beautician). Most American patrolmen buckle on their guns and start enforcing law and order after less than five weeks training of any kind – and their pay and position in society reflect this. But Chicago is now trying a training period of seven months (compared with the basic ten weeks in Britain), which incorporates new techniques to teach what it is like to be at the receiving end of police work. The British chief constable of a Midlands force recently commented: 'I read an article by an American police chief who sent out his men as layabouts and bums to get themselves arrested, so that they would know what it is like to be in a police cell. If it were possible, I would like to see my men go out like that. I ask them often if they ever think what it is like to be locked up. I am only sorry that I cannot make my policemen black for a time.'

In the United States, there are now at least 234 university courses designed for policemen. Most of the courses are part-time and in the evening; an increasing number of policemen there feel that a university degree is necessary for promotion to senior ranks.

Promotion

In Britain, 80 per cent of the police force have the rank of constable; 12 per cent are sergeants and 8 per cent have the higher rank of inspector or above. 'Too many chiefs, not enough Indians' is a common view amongst constables. There are still archaic class differentials between the ranks: inspectors and positions senior to that can be recommended for the MBE; the remainder can only aspire to the BEM. Suspicion of graduates in the British service ('with such qualifications, what's he doing wanting to join the police?') is only slowly diminishing as more graduates throughout the country are unemployed. But policemen are unanimous in their opposition to any privileged entry and stick to the principle that the only road to higher promotion must be through the ranks, because police officers have to deal with and understand 'all manner of peoples'.

The qualifications necessary for being promoted have moved on somewhat from the day in 1878 when Captain John W. Nott-Bower candidly described how he came to be appointed chief constable of Leeds:

> A pretty strenuous canvass was necessary, and I succeeded in my efforts mainly owing to the strong and friendly support of Sir E. H. Garbutt, then Mayor of Leeds, of Mr. M. W. Thompson (an old friend of my father's, a director of the Midland Railway and formerly MP for Bradford), and of Colonel Gunter of Wetherby (my old militia commanding officer) who had one or two tenants who were members of the Leeds Town Council . . .

A. E. Wilcox, a recent chief constable of Hertfordshire, lists the qualities he looked for in making promotions: 'sound judgement, knowledge of the world, strength of mind to resist partisan pressure, respect for individual freedom, and an understanding of human frailty.' Today promotion increasingly tends to be based on ability and future potential, rather than – as it used to be – experience and length of service. There is still however an evergreen suspicion among the public and some policemen themselves that promotion is assisted by the number of arrests or convictions a candidate has to his name. This is denied by authorities, who claim that an over-zealous arrester would in fact lose thereby rather than gain; but there have been cases where men with no or few arrests to their name have been told to 'get the figures up', and at least in the CID where competition for promotion is more intense, detectives with a string of successes obviously have a headstart claim to being noticed.

Police relations with immigrants and black people

Outside the Republican areas in Northern Ireland, the most widespread hostility felt in Britain towards the police is among young blacks from West Indian families. They are the section of the population who suffer the highest unemployment and disaffection, and when concentrated in deprived inner city areas, often see policemen as personifying the unfair white majority in the society they resent. James Baldwin wrote of the Harlem police in *Nobody Knows My Name*: 'None of the Police Commissioner's men, even with the best will in the world, have any way of understanding the lives led by the people they swagger about in twos and threes controlling. Their very presence is an insult, and it would be, even if they spent their entire day feeding gumdrops to children. They represent the force of the white world ...' Sir Robert Mark's perception is not very different:

> Race is, with public order, probably the most important problem we have to face. The police bear more than anyone the brunt of it. The immigrant or indigent coloured youth, living in under-privileged and unfamiliar circumstances, has little knowledge of the lofty sentiments voiced in Whitehall and Westminster. His dissatisfaction with reality is expressed in his own locality and the policeman is for him a target for the sense of injustice from which he understandably suffers.

The current insecurity felt as well by many policemen can result in hardening tension from a damagingly reciprocated spiral of stereotyping and mutual distrust.

Alienation among blacks towards the police is if anything even greater in the US: the Presidential Commission in 1967 found that whereas 63 per cent of whites there thought the police 'almost all honest', only 30 per cent of non-whites did. Some blacks are alleged to have ironically insisted on being arrested only by white police officers, describing black police officers as a second-class service. Whereas in Britain opinion is unanimous that black policemen should be posted to any area irrespective of colour, views in the US are more divided. Sergeant Samuel Dacus of California finds confronting a white citizen can often be less difficult than confronting his fellow blacks: 'There's this feeling that because we're of the same race, I owe him something' – but others report increased support for the idea that black officers can best control black crime. There is evidence that some black officers take a harder line in black communities than their white colleagues: 'I never felt like I was spying on my own people,' said sergeant Theron Jackson, who worked under cover in Los Angeles. 'I know my people and I'd rather be in a position to determine what's a crime than somebody else, say a white officer who doesn't know the culture.' Black consciousness is on the increase within the American police service itself. Henry Nelson, a New York detective who is president of the all-black National Council of Police Societies, believes that 'the establishment enforces law and order in this country to the benefit of whites, not for the benefit of blacks, and we can't live with that.' At a black police convention, James Russell from Pittsburg said: 'I think the military aspect of police departments should change, and I think black officers are going to lead this. It comes down to the very simple thing that when they get home at night and take off their uniform they are black. They are not blue.'

At the start of this century, police misconduct towards immigrants was a major political issue in the US. In every nation, many immigrants – not only blacks – bring with them suspicious memories of the police in their home countries, either through the latter being in general of a lower standard, or having in a particular case contributed towards the migrant leaving home. Both sides in black–white confrontations are often victims of the psychological conditioning of the past. In the West Indies there is a historical resentment of the police because of traditional memories of the function of the latter in a slave-owning society. In Britain, on the other hand, a number of black families today wish the police to intervene in their domestic and landlord/tenant disputes and become disillusioned when they refuse. Others frequently make the converse complaint: that the police unduly harass blacks and West Indian youths in particular. Black critics of the police allege that some officers are indulgent towards the attacks of the belligerent Right on non-whites; that some of them have made pro-National Front remarks; and that others show more interest in pressing blacks for proof of their right of residence than in investigating their complaints. On the police side, several officers resent their inability to obtain statements from immigrants whose English is poor, and are surprised that not all minority groups have organized leaders who can control or speak on their behalf. Anthony Armstrong, the chief constable of Bedfordshire, caused some surprise to the House of Commons Select Committee on Race Relations with some sweeping assertions about coloured witnesses, whom he said frequently changed their evidence, failed to attend court and were unreliable as witnesses. None the less, he declared, he never appointed any full-time community relations officers because such methods only generated complaints. Other officers resent that they 'have to bend over backwards to be nice to blacks', accusing blacks of not wishing for impartial treatment, and of using their colour as a weapon. They frequently blame trouble on unrepresentative political demagogues. Yet, *pace* Mr Armstrong's assertion, research by Dr Michael Billig and Dr David Milner at Bristol University has found that white police officers – including many with experience of policing black communities – made more than twice as many mistakes in trying to identify black faces as they did white ones. They commented that this may evidence a problem more disturbing than overt racism: 'even if the police think they are being scrupulously fair, they may be working under difficulties without realizing it.'

The French police are markedly even less polite towards

boignoliles ('niggers') or *ratons* (Arabs) than they are to *ritals* ('wops') or *espingouins* ('dagoes'). When a higher proportion of innocent black people are regularly liable to be stopped by the police for questioning or arrested, the result can obviously affect race relations. One single bad incident can have a chain or ripple effect. A superintendent working in Brixton said it is now difficult to arrest a black person publicly without causing a scuffle, so that the police try to do so discreetly. But some of the contributions on the problem are like a dialogue of the deaf. A commander at Scotland Yard stated that he could not understand the tension in the Notting Hill area. 'The police stations that have been critized employ canteen staffs and other workers who are nearly all coloured, and this surely answers the criticisms.' During the same week, a meeting of local black leaders passed a proposal that police pay should be doubled to attract better-qualified recruits and to exclude 'those with the kind of hang-ups that need scapegoats or victims for their own inadequacies or phobias.'

It is too simple a summary but still not unfair to remember that the police often attract intolerance, in the same way that blacks do, as easily identifiable objects of group prejudice and as scapegoats for resentment at social conditions. Only one conclusion is certain: that the police alone cannot solve a country's racial problems, nor the conditions in which they ferment. As Peter Marshall (now Commissioner of the City of London) said, 'It is not the relationship between the police and minority groups which is the central issue but the social factors underlying the position. We have no power to solve the problems – poor housing, unemployment, discrimination – but we have to bear the brunt in containing trouble.' If more policemen, however, lived in the neighbourhoods they patrol, they would appear less often like alien invaders. Most police officers sincerely believe they are impartial; prejudices generally show at times of emotion and under the exceptional stress inescapable in overstretched policing of urban areas. Not only police training but all school curricula should include the study of prejudice to help people to recognize and discount their own biases. One northern chief constable gave as his opinion that there is broadly the same amount of racial prejudice in the police force as there is among the public. The service certainly inevitably includes a cross-section of white attitudes; yet the police – by selection or training – must aspire higher than those because, in the nature of their job, the slightest overt prejudice or discrimination can do grossly disproportionate damage, including, not least, to the task of the police themselves, for as William Lunt a Salisbury magistrate pointed out in 1978 'any discrimination carries with it the virus of disobedience'.

For a long time, the police's attitude to the whole issue was first, that there was no problem; and second, that it might go away if no one mentioned such distasteful and sensitive things. But in 1971 a Home Office working party on police training in race relations recommended *inter alia* that:

> Training should help members of police forces to develop an insight into their own role and to be aware of the difficulties which racial tension can create for the police ... There should be a frank recognition that the police service, like the community at large, contains some members who are prejudiced; that in most circumstances this will not prevent their acting correctly; but that there will be other times when their supervisors must be prepared to intervene. Training should emphasize that law enforcement is a public service.

Racial complaints against the police centre mainly on a few stations. John Lambert believes that much of the trouble originates in instances where young black Britons are being policed by older white officers who include in their number men with obsolete preconceptions about blacks, some of whose origins are traceable to the slave-trade. Senior officers in turn find scapegoats in younger colleagues' inexperience and insecurity. The community liaison officers which many forces have appointed – often full-time chief inspectors – have most difficulties with, and least influence on, hardened CID men. But both Sir Kenneth Newman (now head of the Northern Irish force) and Peter Marshall worked hard and earned considerable respect when, as commanders, they headed Scotland Yard's A7 Community Relations department. Mark Bonham Carter's verdict was that 'the police force in London has done much more than, say, employers or trade unions, schools and social security departments in creating a framework of community relations (including twenty-two community liaison officers), but little has been done to make sure that proper training in the implications of a multiracial society reaches the policemen on the beat.'

Sir Kenneth Newman believes that racial problems are a necessary catalyst, and in fact can have a positive social value. He recognizes that relations between police and all the public are changing; that the tacit acceptance of the policeman's authority is no longer universal, and that wearing the uniform is now not enough. 'In many ways the police have to thank the West Indians for doing us a favour in making us think again about our authority.' Race, as it has markedly done in the United States, often highlights shortcomings in society and its justice. The content of a number of complaints by black people that have been recorded by Derek Humphry and others – about the unfairness of judges' *obiter dicta* against which there is no appeal, about policemen colluding when writing their notebooks, and about the necessity for anyone alleging rough treatment immediately to have an impartial medical examination – demonstrate the need for reforms of such issues for the benefit of people of every race.

Police families' problems

'A police constable does not merely take a job; he embarks on a new way of life . . . the convenience of his wife and family must be a secondary consideration,' the Association of Chief Police Officers pointed out to the Willink Royal Commission. Like the spouse of an MP, parson or diplomat, the wife or husband of a police officer cannot escape being tied – unpaid – to the job. Higher than normal standards in many respects are expected of her or him by her neighbours. A police family's life literally has to be exemplary: inevitably their personal existence becomes public property. Consumer durables that a police officer purchases will be scrutinized by his neighbours to see if they are compatible with his pay. The behaviour of not only his children, but his dog, will be carefully watched and commented upon. The *Daily Express* once scrupulously designated a man who was sent to prison as 'the great, great grandson of a police inspector'. A policeman's wife, like a doctor's, must be reconciled to answering the telephone twenty-four hours a day, and can never truly be off-duty and refuse to open the door. Few members of the public, once they learn of a police person's occupation, can resist talking to him or her about some police matter. Several police wives say they sometimes get the feeling that they are regarded as a potential spy by their neighbours. People have been known to apply for a reduction in rates because policemen live near them. Mrs B. Kingston, an area beat officer's wife, said that when she and her family were first posted to a council estate, they were met 'with a blank wall of hostility'. Shop assistants were reluctant to serve them, refuse was thrown into their garden; it took six years of hard work by herself, as well as her husband, before the estate gradually came to accept him as a reliable social worker.

As Dr Cain describes, the life of a country policeman, lacking the support an urban one receives from his colleagues, can be socially isolated. Constable Kevin Fowler of Lancashire states, from his own experience in a small rural community, that 'the difficulties facing the individual policeman produce much more of a problem and strain on his family than that facing a large body of policemen in the larger conurbations where law enforcement is a little less of a personal family involvement.' A survey for the 1960 Royal Commission found that 66.8 per cent of British policemen said that The Job – as policemen call their lot – adversely affected their outside friendships. Many American policemen try to conceal their occupation when they are off duty both because of its low status and because of the effect such knowledge produces. Because of antagonism towards the police in some urban areas in the US, patrolmen decline to wear their uniforms when going to and from work. A London superintendent stated: 'I take extreme care in forming relationships with people, and it probably means that I have nobody whom I regard as anything more than an acquaintance outside my immediate family circle.' But a black officer said, 'When you join the force, you keep your friends and lose your acquaintances.' Frequent compulsory reposting can however forfeit even the friendships, as well as causing disruption to children's schooling. In Scotland, an officer and his family can be ordered at a few weeks' notice to transfer their lives to a Highland village or Hebridean island, and, unlike a teacher or local government employee, he receives no allowance for serving in an isolated area.

But internal family relationships can suffer strain too: the police officer in Scotland who was aghast to find himself questioning his wife in the same way as he treated suspects was not unique: the wife of one detective-sergeant said, 'Sometimes I feel he treats me as if I'm on the other side, as if I'm a criminal.' Police families worry more than others when their officer is unexpectedly overdue and very late home – as his work frequently compels him to be – even though statistics show that the occupation is less dangerous than others such as that of building workers. Nonetheless, in London the number of assaults on police officers rose from 1,411 (1 in 14 officers) in 1966 to 4,030 (1 in 6) in 1977. During that period the number of man days lost through assaults on Metropolitan police officers doubled. Between 1969 and mid-1978, 82 members of the Royal Ulster Constabulary were killed and over 3,000 were injured, out of a total strength of about 5,700. Policemen often have to sleep in the daytime when they get home to catch up for night shifts, which means their family has to keep unnaturally quiet. Increasing trouble at football matches has taken its toll of Saturdays: the number of people arrested at football grounds has risen from 460 in 1972/3 to 1,363 in 1976/7. Any police wife finds it difficult to take a job, because – besides the official power of veto – she can never be certain when her husband will ever be free to look after the children. The police officers who took part in 'Operation Julie', were not only separated from their families for several months on end, but also were unable to tell them the reason for their absences, which caused much domestic strain and misunderstanding. The curious code of police restrictions will continue to pursue a wife even after her husband dies: police widows are liable to lose their pension if they cohabit with a man.

A survey in Seattle's police force found that 60 per cent of married officers were divorced during their first three years as a policeman. In theory an officer works a night shift every third month, but court appearances can cut additional swaths in his off-duty hours; for example, if he makes an arrest just before his leave starts he will have to attend court, no matter what holiday arrangements he and his family may have made. 'After a twelve-hour day you don't feel much like talking about what you've been doing.' And every evening and weekend social plans are always at risk. Constable Jim Jardine described how some of the London policemen on duty at the violent demonstration in Red Lion Square in 1974 had already done eight hours duty at the Trooping of the Colour:

> They had to be on Horse Guards Parade at 8 a.m. That probably meant reporting to their own station at 6 a.m. Then after standing all morning they had to handle a difficult demonstration ... The Metropolitan police force is very tired. Officers are going for months without a weekend off. I know they volunteer for weekend duty, but it's volunteer or else! – or else you'll be detailed ... In fact, as a Federation we think there are men on duty today, in every branch of the police force, who should be classified as unfit for duty through tension or emotional strain.

The uncertain and uncongenial working-hours of the police, together with the effect these have on their families, probably cause as many resignations as any other factor. The crux of the problem is that police responsibility never stops: a service has to continue for twenty-four hours a day 365 days a year. Evenings and early hours of the morning, when the rest of the population is resting, are two of the most key periods requiring police vigilance. Obviously not all the officers with families can take their annual leave during the school holiday periods, though a leave when the children are still at school will probably mean that the whole family cannot go away together. There is no simple solution to the problems caused by police hours, other than by recruiting more men to spread the load, and by giving compensation by other means such as higher pay.

Housing however is a factor affecting police morale whose problems are easier to alleviate. Less than one officer in five prefers to live in a colony with other policemen. Inhospitable, single-sex blocks which are segregated from the community are not psychologically good for unmarried officers. Maureen Cain points out that policemen's wives as well object to living in too close proximity with other police wives. 'There are problems of rank, embarrassments when friends get promoted

... The men bring their work problems home, and the atmosphere can deteriorate into one of unkind gossip and antagonisms.' A senior officer in Scotland described the change in men's attitude to accommodation. 'Some years ago the provision of a police house was an important factor in attracting and retaining men in the service. Now, with the increased popularity of house ownership, many officers regard the need to live in police houses as an undesirable restriction on their life and their means of providing for the future.' In a test case recently brought by a constable against Lancashire Police Authority, Mr Justice Caulfield decided that police officers do not have the right to live in their own homes rather than in police houses. A constable in Weymouth who had bought his own house and moved out of a police one without permission was indeed dismissed by the chief constable of Dorset, though the sentence was quashed by the Home Secretary. But in fact the dispersal of segregated police housing could be a major factor in ending the police's internal and external isolation from the public.

'The Job'

What are the overall effects of police life? One wife's view was that the work made men harder characters; an officer conceded that he found the most difficult part was not to get personally involved in cases. 'Unfortunately you've got to be a bit of a cynic, and basically disbelieve everything you hear first time round,' said one CID man. 'Being a policeman is a job that shouldn't be asked of any human being. You live in an enclosed world where it's easier to do your job if you're totally without feeling.' Inspector Jennifer Hilton, who has a degree in psychology, suggests there is often too much pressure on policemen to act toughly and instantaneously in stereotypes of masculine behaviour. The profound pessimism of many officers is generally somehow reconciled with a faith that society is worth saving. But by their role policemen are temperamentally conditioned towards being conservative, and incline to find what is conventional reassuring and anything unusual or eccentric disturbing and suspicious. 'We become increasingly conformist through a life that never questions the structure of society,' said one inspector. The common police dislike of gipsies stems partly from the latter not being part of settled society with its familiar ideas. A man's work can be the most important part of his social identity: authoritarian tendencies are inculcated more by the role which policemen have to assume than by any psychology of the people likely to be recruited into the service. 'Police officers must remember that there is no law against making a policeman angry and that he cannot charge a man with offending him,' O. W. Wilson reminded his men when he was head of the Chicago police.

In Britain Judge Gill, quashing a conviction not long ago, ruled that not only is a policeman not protected from being sworn at and having the door slammed in his face, but in fact it is every Briton's right to do this. 'You have to be emotionally committed or you can't stand the life.' Sir David McNee, the Metropolitan Commissioner, concludes, 'This isn't just a job, it's a cause.' But ex-inspector Reg Gale said that an officer also has to conform to the prejudices of his police station in order to survive. The influence and example of experienced officers are seminally formative, but Simon Holdaway – a former police officer now teaching at Sheffield University – points out how the rough traditional methods of older sergeants and constables can often be at variance with the attempts to adopt new policies of managerial professionalism suggested by the Home Office and taught at Bramshill. There is thus a built-in resistance to change or modern ideas. One of the few holds lower ranks have over senior is that the latter depend on the former for information. The British police service, like British society, remains much more hierarchical and formally disciplined than the US equivalent. For years the Police Federation have unavailingly tried to have saluting abolished. By tradition, ranks of inspector and above, but not sergeants or constables, are addressed as 'Mr' like commissioned service officers. Federated rank officers, as these two lower ranks are called, have very little say in matters of police policy: few have any access at all to their police authority or chief constable. Policemen work in an undemocratic organization which is basically antithetical to the democratic society it is their job to protect. Superintendents still maintain 'the flummery of mess-jackets' – 'the Hendon mentality aping the armed services,' in the words of one of them. Conditions have improved since the days remembered by the older policemen when 'the tyranny was awful. The force was riddled with nepotism, and the best way to get promotion was cutting the chief inspector's lawn.' But there are a surprising number of freemasons in some forces, particularly the Metropolitan CID. Many officers allege that joining the freemasonry is 'a sure way to promotion', while B. M. Watt of the Thames Valley police states:

> I speak from personal experience of no less than three occasions on which I have been approached, and even threatened, by more senior officers who sought to influence my dealing with their fellow-freemasons and relatives of fellow-freemasons, with regard to offences committed by them. ... In my humble opinion, which is shared by many of my colleagues, it ought to be a disciplinary offence – and in certain circumstances a criminal offence – to be a member of any secret society while serving as a police officer.

Power in the New York police, by contrast, has always been in the hands of Irish Catholics.

'Some chief constables are still living in the last century,' is a common view in all ranks. Policemen remain outside the protection of recent new legislation such as the Employment Protection Act 1975, the Redundancy Payments Act 1965, the Contract of Employment Act 1972, and the Trade Union and Labour Relations Acts 1974 and 1976. Senior officers can still exercise forms of despotism, some of it distinctly less benevolent than others. A charge of 'discreditable conduct' can – like notorious offences such as 'dumb insolence' in the army – be based on virtually anything; the first offence of the Police (Discipline) (Amendment) Regulations 1967 reads:

> which offence is committed where a member of a police force acts in a disorderly manner or in any manner prejudicial to discipline or reasonably likely to bring discredit on the reputation of the force or of the police service.

A policeman can, in the first two years of his career, be dismissed solely because the chief constable does not consider he is likely to make the grade, and no further reason – or appeal – need be offered. One woman sergeant had to give up her job because her husband ran an off-license. Another policeman in a county force was carpeted at a full-dress disciplinary hearing because his dog attacked another in a park, despite the fact that the animal at the time of the fight was being exercised by his wife while the policeman himself was working miles away. Certainly in a number of forces up until recently men were required to resign if it was discovered that they were having an extramarital affair. Whereas Swedish officers are allowed to join political parties and have been elected to parliament, in 1970 a chief inspector in Scotland was threatened with disciplinary proceedings if his wife stood for the local council. One East Midlands officer believes it would be preferable if the public knew the political prejudices of the service, which he estimates to be 30 per cent strong Tory, 40 per cent soft Tory, 25 per cent traditional Labour and 5 per cent libertarian. But every station still has its tales of bureaucratic lunacy: of, for example, the superintendent who ordered that all files more than five years old must be destroyed – but that copies must be kept of them.

Police officers' loyalty to the Police Federation – which four out of five of them consider effective – is principally based on the help it gives men facing disciplinary charges. The respective Federations for England with Wales and for Scotland form the police equivalents of quasi-trade unions for all ranks below chief officers and superintendents, who each have their own separate association. They have formed a *de facto* closed shop for sixty years: fewer than one per cent of officers default on their voluntary subscriptions. The Federation is by law forbidden to affiliate to the TUC, and had an understandable grievance that it often appeared to be bound by TUC decisions about pay policy which it was not a party to nor had even been consulted about. As a trade union, the Federation is hamstrung by law: unlike the much more independent police unions of Scandinavia, the British Federations are not even allowed to ban overtime working, on penalty of two years in jail. Only a minority of members as yet wish the Federation to affiliate, but almost every officer wants the rights that other employees now take for granted: safeguards against wrongful dismissal and access to the Arbitration and Conciliation Advisory Service. At present the Federation's income is small – the NUR has seven times as much with a membership only 50 per cent higher – and it does not pay its own officers. In the US, there is no police union, but Patrolmen's Benevolent and even Police Wives Associations have been formed as fronts, and, through their knowledge of and influence in their precincts, exercise political clout – almost invariably of a reactionary hue – out of all proportion to their numbers.

Half the British police are now aged under thirty. There are increasing signs that a generational gap in attitudes is opening up between the older disciplinarians and the younger officers who surprisingly often now have nonconforming appearances. Officers can be socially less confident than the members of the public they are reprimanding; but one of the things policemen frequently say they like about their job is its egalitarianism – unlike in most other occupations, they are rarely patronized by social superiors they encounter. Nevertheless all policemen feel relief on holiday at being able to drop their role. A few other professions such as tax inspectors are treated with equal reserve by the public, but their members are able to disappear into anonymity when off-duty more easily than policemen can; hence the wish of many police officers to spend their off-duty time in a place where they are not known. Seventy-two per cent of policemen said they did not like their occupation to be known when on holiday. Some of the younger ones have a reputation for letting themselves go with drinking and horseplay on outings when they can temporarily escape their exemplary role.

A uniform man's life is much more routine than that of a CID officer who works on his own initiative and exercises considerable freedom over his hours. The worst experiences policemen recall in their work are usually incidents involving fatal accidents or vomiting drunks; stationary guard duty outside places like embassies is also disliked as being work which men say is both boring and makes them feel they are a sitting target. The best civilian allies of the police tend to be taxi-drivers, publicans and newsvendors – all of whom depend on the police's goodwill. Symbiotically, few policemen can help admiring good criminals – as long as they are not violent; finding it necessary to know criminal slang, they absorb much of it into their own speech. As every television-watcher now knows, a good detective will learn where a criminal drinks, his habits and whom his friends and enemies – male and female – are. Detectives are on first-name terms with their quarry, and share with them – besides a fascination with crime – similar archetypal prejudices against social deviants and dissidents. Some criminals and policemen's careers run in parallel throughout their lives, encountering each other at successive stages as they age together; indeed an enterprising criminal will follow news about a key detective's whereabouts, postings, characteristics and methods as much as vice versa.

'A practical copper' is the highest commendation a policeman can give a colleague; intellectuality on the whole is as suspect as other non-conformity. Deeper contempt is reserved for those liberals and do-gooders who theorize about criminals and deviants but who – unlike policemen – rarely meet them in practice. Although it is less homogeneous in its spectrum of attitudes than some of the public suppose, the police's propensity to conventionality is reinforced because those officers who do not instinctively identify with the traditional values of the *status quo* are sooner or later likely to resign, out of discomfort from work involving such conflicting feelings. A few officers are influenced by new TV images of the police, but traditional outlooks are continuously recycled because many skills of the craft of policing can only be absorbed from older low-ranking officers. The fact that their job or their uniform often acts as a cue for prejudice to be shown against them, makes police officers increasingly sensitive and unable as a consequence to admit any need for internal change.

The police service has developed many of the characteristics of a secret society. It is a defensive and introverted, but also a self-consciously masculine, world; together with the fire service, it is perhaps the last profession likely to be headed by a woman. In the US, junior female police officers have been accepted much more easily than their male colleagues predicted, though a few still share the resistance to women maintained by the firemen described by a lieutenant in Queens: 'What men are afraid of is that something will be taken away from them that has been theirs for years. They love the department, they protect it for their egos, for the money. A male prerogative will be taken away and women will come into their community.' The New York police and firemen have long and emotionally resisted employing homosexuals, in order to maintain 'their virile image'.

Cohesiveness is buttressed by the considerable number of police officers with relatives who have also been or are in the police. Their solidarity is underpinned by the feeling that in a crisis no policeman can count on the help of anyone who is not a policeman; ultimately, they are alone, and stand or fall together. Arthur Niederhoffer, an American police officer, describes their view as 'Hobbesian – the world becomes a jungle in which crime, corruption and brutality are normal features of the terrain.' The strength of the police lies in loyalty: to be off-duty from sickness – other than injury – is extremely rare. But unfortunately reciprocal dependence can extend, as we shall see in the next chapter, not just to mutual physical assistance but to help over illegalities in court.

Norman Mailer's summing up is that 'when you get a good cop he is a work of art. He has got to be brave, to have high standards: it is the hardest kind of working-class life a man can have.'

SEVEN

Quis Custodiet? Policing the Police

'The conscientious bobby who works his beat is honest: you always know where he is, and if you get in his way that's your own fault. It's the man who neglects his duty to go courting the servant, or nips up the entry to get a surreptitious drink, who causes all the trouble. You never know where you may meet with him.'
Charlie Peace, nineteenth-century criminal

'All professions are a conspiracy against the laity.'
George Bernard Shaw

'When the law breaks the law, there is no law.'
Ramsey Clark

Complaints against the police
In police work it is often only a narrow though not unimportant divide that separates punishment for excess zeal from commendation for meritorious work. A policeman expressed the view about one of his colleagues that 'he was the greatest villain that ever walked, but he was a good copper.' Unfortunately such villainy is frequently infectious. Detective-sergeant Challenor is still regarded by many Metropolitan officers as a hero who sacrificed his sanity working overtime to protect the public. A large number of police officers, certainly

the majority of detectives, feel they are fighting a holy war against crime. Authority can have a dangerous effect on some personalities: entrusted with certain powers on a lease, they come to think they hold them freehold by intrinsic or even divine right, and start to confuse the public interest with their own dignity and prerogative. The responsibility and power that are given to a young officer after only a few weeks training are enormous; and it is only surprising that not more are corrupted. A policeman needs an exceptional degree of tolerant detachment if he is to retain an overall faith in human nature. The late Commissioner Simpson once said, when he was asked why he looked so gloomy, 'So would you if you saw what I see daily of human behaviour'. But too many of his colleagues at Scotland Yard succumbed to copying cynically what they saw. More recently, a squeeze on expenditure coupled with rising crime figures has meant increasing pressure on senior officers for visible results. A policeman gets credit for successful arrests and convictions; merely sticking to the rules is less obviously likely to attract praise. At its worst, a vicious circle is formed when – as in France – policemen who feel beleaguered and endangered, as crime and disturbances increase, draw closer to each other and become more defensive and hostile towards the public; this is felt and returned by the public – which in turn causes reciprocally increased secrecy and violence on the part of the police.

The number of complaints against police officers in England and Wales more than doubled between 1968 and 1977. Research should have been undertaken a long time ago into the aetiology of complaints against the police. Although it is difficult for the individual policeman not to feel personally aggrieved when his career is threatened, some complainants, like some criminals, are attacking the police only as symbols of the society which they think has treated them badly. Other criminals have been known to plant complaints so as to cause a particular detective officer who is following them too closely to be suspended from duty. A few allegations originate from neurotic people who develop a deluded fixation that they are being persecuted by the police as being the most accessible personifications of Fate. Others come from touchy people whose *amour propre* is hurt if they are spoken to unobsequiously or indeed by anyone in authority. And some – whose exact number we shall never know – of course are justified. The police, like most human beings, often reciprocate the attitudes and behaviour – real or perceived – of the people they are dealing with. Inspector Jennifer Hilton suggests for instance that 'a police officer may feel less constrained by normal patterns of behaviour against outcasts such as hippies, criminals, drunks and drug-addicts.' In addition, they succumb to other pressures: the need to improve figures in a battle they always feel they are losing; a sense of loyalty or friendship to a colleague; or perhaps a *post facto* attempt to justify some wrong procedure adopted in the confusion of an arrest.

Most of us are hungrily eager to enjoy the simple satisfaction of hearing complaints against those set in authority over us. A ready audience can always be found for allegations against schoolmasters, clergy, royalty, civil servants, Members of Parliament, and – above all – the police. But whereas when a leading politician is defamed under protection of court privilege there is often a furore, policemen are traduced daily without sympathy. A London judge said that, whereas each jury was likely to hear only one attack on the police, listening himself to a succession of them day after day sickened him. Deputy Assistant Commissioner David Powis also pointed out that whereas lawyers and social workers are often over-credulous of professional criminals because they only meet them after they are caught and harmless, policemen – like the victims of crime – often enounter them when they are very different: greedy, ruthless, and sometimes violent. One result can be a curious reversal of normal liberal values. Otherwise fair-minded people have an indefensible tendency to assume the guilt of the police until they are proved innocent, and sometimes even after. Some comments that are made about the police call to mind the frontier judge's policy of 'I'll give you a fair trial and then hang you.' For the press, there is no news value in patient, unspectacular virtue in the police service or anywhere else. Some of those who were loudest in condemning Senator McCarthy for his technique of guilt-by-association are often the same people who habitually smear 'the police' with the failings of a minority of officers. In incidents which involve allegations against policemen, some people seem all too ready to be carried by their emotions into unfairness that they would denounce on other occasions, and the exoneration of an innocent policeman rarely seems to give comparable pleasure. The total number of complaints has risen disturbingly each year; but the actual number of allegations that are proved are by comparison amazingly few.

TABLE 18: COMPLAINTS IN ENGLAND AND WALES

Year	*Complaints against the police*	*Metropolitan London*	*Substantiated*	*Resulting criminal charges*	*Disciplinary charges*
1970	12,044	4,669	1,077	152	222
1971	12,271	4,332	1,062	90	209
1972	15,543	5,671	1,334	127	258
1973	16,155	5,566	1,144	110	186
1974	17,454	6,173	1,141	105	189
1975	19,205	6,233	1,254	128	247
1976	22,738	7,432	1,334	124	182
1977	27,450	8,679	1,107	156	205

What is less widely known is that the police got 23,020 letters of appreciation, referring to 33,652 officers, in 1977. Two letters at random will serve as undramatic examples of police behaviour which rarely makes the headlines. In the first, Constable John Thompson of Manchester went to tell a couple that relatives of theirs had died in a gassing accident at Blackpool and that their six-year-old daughter was critically ill. Before breaking the news he arranged for close relatives and the family doctor to be present. The man and his wife were shocked, and were given sedatives, but wanted to go at once to Blackpool to be at their daughter's bedside. Constable Thompson saw that they were unfit to travel alone and drove them to Blackpool in his own time. He returned to Salford at 2.30 a.m. the following morning and told nobody about it when he went back on duty only five and a half hours later. His action only came to light when a letter of thanks from the family was received at police headquarters. In the second case, during the heat of the troubles in Northern Ireland, three policemen and a military policeman who rushed a seriously ill little girl to the Mater hospital were told by letter from her grateful grandparents that but for the prompt action of the crew they thought she would have died. 'They even took the trouble to come back and let me know she was out of danger and also offered to go back to the hospital to bring my daughter and my neighbour back again.'

The award given for bravery, £20, has not been increased for forty years. But because any attempt to cover up a bad incident will destroy the public's faith in the police, and because one defaulting policeman who is unchecked can lose goodwill for the whole force, it is vital for the police themselves that every allegation is cleared up thoroughly. It is because the present arrangements for handling complaints do not satisfy the public that many have to be investigated by, for example, the National Council for Civil Liberties (186 Kings Cross Road, London, WC1) or by Justice (2 Clements Inn, London, WC2). The overworked volunteers at the NCCL – who also take up cases on behalf of individual policemen – are doing work which should really be done by an Ombudsman. It is regrettable that some senior police officers show a hostile attitude to the NCCL: they refused, for example, on one occasion to show the Council a specimen police warrant-card, although it is in the public interest that people should be able to identify bogus policemen. Police officers are wrong to sneer at the NCCL, who are performing a valuable function: in Athens, some people once grew tired of Socrates. The NCCL and the police are at heart pursuing identical objects: they should form a permanent joint committee and work together.

A senior officer in A10, the department at Scotland Yard which investigates complaints, estimated that of every 100 complaints he dealt with, some 6 were justified (mainly involving rudeness to the public); 20 were later withdrawn (sometimes consisting of exaggerations told to a wife or friend which the complainant is reluctant to admit – even to himself – as being wrong); 10 were criminal calculations; another 10 were also malicious; 5 resulted from mental illness (although allegations such as of rape by electronic rays are not recorded); and a disturbingly high 25 remain a mystery. Whatever their origin or foundation, it is almost as essential for the police themselves that complaints against them should be investigated as speedily as possible as it is that they should be thoroughly pursued. When, for example, it was once widely reported by newspapers that a prisoner in Edinburgh alleged that he had had both his arms broken by police taking his fingerprints, irreparable damage was caused by the seven days' delay before it was announced that doctors said he had had no recent fracture to either arm. In case after case, Lord Trenchard's maxim for police public relations, 'Tell the truth – immediately,' appears to have been forgotten. No policeman can give the excuse, if he has broken the law, that he was ordered to do so by a senior officer. But equally, in other cases where their support is justified, police authorities should act much more quickly in giving it: considerable damage to morale in the past has resulted from delay in, for example, refunding damages or costs inadvertently incurred by an officer in his duties. The CID of one city force went so far as unofficially to work to rule because they felt they were not getting backing-up from their chief constable against the public, when he disciplined two of their number. One chief constable said, 'Perhaps the real trouble lies in some chief constables being unable to admit mistakes by their men gracefully.' A determined member of the public described how he had to spend £200 before he was able to wring even an apology out of the Metropolitan police.

But, in a more important way, the crucial value of speedy rectification will never be illustrated more clearly than by the disturbing series of cases that involved Detective-sergeant Challenor in 1962–3. His illegality was unmasked only when he 'planted' a half-brick on an educated man who happened to be resourceful enough to be able to prove that he was inescapably innocent. Other less articulate victims who had evidence planted on them had regularly been convicted: twenty-four were later pardoned, but had already served a total of over thirteen years' wrongful imprisonment. Responsibility for these appalling events over so long a period cannot be sidetracked onto Challenor's paranoid schizophrenia: not only Challenor's colleagues – men trained to suspect misconduct – but the whole vaunted process of criminal justice in Britain stands condemned. Half-bricks are not dangerous without men of straw. Challenor's earlier victims had all been working-class people, often black, whose rights the police, the legal profession and the courts had totally failed to safeguard: but for the accident of his picking on one person who was able to exonerate himself by his own efforts, Challenor's methods might be continuing to this day. A system of justice that cannot work without good luck and a campaign by voluntary organizations like the NCCL must be capable of improvement. Andrew Cunningham, while he was chairman of Durham police authority and before he was himself imprisoned, said that the police sometimes have to break the law in fighting crime, but that 'the point is they have not got to be found out breaking the law.' But contrary to what many policemen think, it is not the instances of police misconduct themselves which most worry the public. The social survey taken soon after the Brighton, Worcester, and Thurso cases, showed that the great majority of the public had strong faith in the police and must have been aware that these cases were the actions of individual human beings who happened to be policemen. The prosecution of a guilty policeman in fact renews the public's confidence and thankfulness that they live in one of the countries where this happens – instead of in a country where those who protest about police misconduct are liable to be charged with military rebellion. The focus of attention on defaults, although it irks the police, is in reality a compliment; elsewhere their abuses are often taken for granted. In New York, for example, police corruption has been recurrent. What was even more serious than the unacceptable police violence at Sheffield in 1963 was the disclosure, in the subsequent inquiry's report, of wholesale covering-up and even fabrication of evidence by several police officers. The violence was unanimously condemned by the police themselves ('absolutely disgraceful and disgusting', said the Secretary of the Police Federation at the time); but the glimpse the inquiry gave of the police's investigation of that case made independent inquiries thereafter inevitable, although they took twelve years to arrive. Most chief constables investigate scrupulously – and not by means of the very officers involved, as happened at Sheffield – but this incident marked a turning point, after which the public could be satisfied only by the involvement of someone from outside the police in the inquiries. The past system not only bred rumours, but also weakened the value of police evidence on other questions – which is a serious matter, particularly in a legal system which is dependent on juries and magistrates.

The other grave revelation made by the incident at Sheffield was that, although – as at Brighton between 1951 and 1958 – many officers must have known the truth, not one member of either of these forces had the integrity to come forward and speak out. The trouble is that the wrong loyalties are, at times, uppermost and strongest in the police today: comrades and the service come first, with justice and the public a poor second. (How can such men be surprised that the public do not help them more?) As they feel their authority decline, internal solidarity seems to have become increasingly important to the police. Despite the individual responsibility of each police officer to pursue justice, too often there is a tendency to close ranks and to form a square when they themselves are concerned. The majority of policemen, however, concede that an attempt to whitewash invariably does more harm than good in the long run by devaluing the coinage of police denials. Most of them, including some chief constables, now realize that independent inquiries will be to their own advantage.

The police make it harder for people to appreciate the true incidence of misconduct by not publishing full details of complaints. The allegations received by Justice fall broadly under eight headings:

(i) *Actions that annoy the public or arouse resentment, but may cause no actual harm,* including:

(a) Incivility and unnecessary aggressiveness, including threats;
(b) Failure to take action and make proper inquiries when information is laid: this can occur frequently in disputes between neighbours or landlord and tenant.

(ii) *Actions causing anxiety or mental worry which may have harmful results,* including:
(a) Failure to advise relatives of the detention of a man in custody or, more seriously, of a juvenile;

(b) Frustrating efforts of relatives to see an arrested person;
(c) Refusing requests from a detained person to communicate with a solicitor;
(d) Making inquiries at places of work or in full sight of neighbours;
(e) Unauthorized and oppressive searches;
(f) Harassing men with records by periodic questioning and putting them on identification parades for offences in the locality.

(iii) *Corruption which influences the course of justice,* including:
(a) Requesting or accepting bribes for not opposing bail, or for not bringing charges;
(b) Making arrangements with known criminals, or protecting them, for personal gain.

(iv) *Criminal dishonesty,* including:
(a) Theft from premises under police surveillance;
(b) Appropriation of part of proceeds of theft;
(c) Appropriation of or carelessness with prisoners' property.

(v) *Unnecessary violence or brutality in course of arrest or detention.*

(vi) *Violence or intimidation to secure an admission or confession.*

(vii) *Unfair practices in the course of investigations and interrogation and evidence gathering,* including:
(a) Refusal to listen to or to investigate a suspect's explanations;
(b) Unfair pressure on a suspect to make admissions or plead guilty by threats to charge a relative or girlfriend;
(c) Unfair pressure to plead guilty by a threat to bring a more serious charge or by a promise that the penalty will be light or that there will be no publicity;
(d) Refusal of identity parades;
(e) Irregularities in holding identity parades that prejudice a suspect:

(f) Neglect or refusal to make scientific tests which might help to clear an accused (e.g. not testing for fingerprints on an article he is alleged to have used or a car he is alleged to have driven);
(g) Discouraging or threatening defence witnesses;
(h) Some cases of plea bargaining.

(viii) *Fabrication of evidence to ensure conviction.* This includes:
(a) Falsification of verbal admissions;
(b) Planting of evidence on the person suspected;
(c) Alleged finding of evidence in house or car;
(d) Falsification of scientific evidence.

In middle-class suburban areas, where most of the public have some idea of their rights and many of the complaints concern comparatively trivial allegations of discourtesy, the police concede that one-fifth have some substance; in rougher inner-city slum areas where the allegations are usually more serious but the complainants less respectable, the proportion admitted to be true is less than half as many as that. In London, the percentage of allegations substantiated ranges by categories from 12.7 (neglect of duty) and 7.7 (mistaken arrest) down to 0.8 (bribery), 0.6 (false evidence) and 0.1 (assault). The standard of police conduct is usually set by the senior officer at each police station, in the same way as a governor or chief officer does in each prison. (In January 1978, the head of Tokyo's police had his salary cut by one-tenth for a month, because unknown to him crimes had been committed by some of his subordinate officers. This is not the custom at Scotland Yard.) Lawyers find that allegations are almost invariably made against the same minority of police officers, who frequently come from the same few stations. Some solicitors have built up their own record files of descriptions of these detectives; they form not more than 5 per cent of the CID, but are among its most active officers. (The bulk of complaints have always been made against the CID: this may be because, whether or not the uniformed branch are citizens in uniform, CID officers are policemen out of uniform.) Ethnic minority members, proportionately, are the most frequent complainants: in Philadelphia in the US for example, whites who form 73 per cent of the population laid only 37 per cent of the complaints.

Serious complaints against the police come within three main types: corruption, perjury, and violence. The incidents recounted in this chapter in order to illustrate the problems and points of friction with the public have been either described by police officers themselves or are well substantiated. The reader should bear in mind that the incidents refer to only a small proportion of a large number of human beings – probably no greater a proportion than might be found among lawyers, MPs, writers, journalists, and the other most frequent critics of the police.

Corruption

Second Watchman: *If we know him to be a thief, shall we not lay hands on him?*
Dogberry [a constable]: *Truly, by our office, you may; but I think they that touch pitch will be defiled.*
(Shakespeare, *Much Ado About Nothing*, Act III, Scene 3.)

If society had a totally honest police force, it probably would not need any police. Temptation is probably more frequently offered to an active CID officer than to anybody else in society. In his work he has to mix a great deal with the criminal world, sharing its thoughts, its language, its haunts, and many of its views on politics, while often seeing more dirty money being made tax-free by those who offer it to him than he himself earns. We require a good detective to be adept at bribing and blackmailing informers on our behalf, but never on his own. 'Chummy' implies the warm-cold relationship that links police and villains, compared with the universal contempt in which criminals hold their victims. Not all criminals' talk of the mutual acceptance they and policemen have for each other should be believed: it can add to their status, as well as be dangerous, if they boast that they have a working relationship with a detective. But rapid transfers of officers to a new area have to be balanced against the social dislocation and the loss of information and contacts which this causes. The majority of arrests result, not from any inspired deduction, but from the police being told something. A CID officer has a unique freelance relationship of mutual trust with his circle of informers. They are his private personal sources, jealously guarded and cultivated and not shared with other officers. Historically, the role of informer antedates that of the British policeman. These are the men who are responsible for the link of 'information received' which is never disclosed at trials. Many are ex-criminals who have reached the criminal menopause. Others are still active themselves, and open the corners of their mouths either because the criminal world – like the legal one – can rarely resist talking shop, or else from motives of envy or revenge, or in order to escape their own deserts. They have their own code: long-established police informants in the East End of London staged a silent mutiny in order to show support for George Davis's innocence. Payments made to them are small: often just the price of a drink or two, rarely £30 or at most £100, and always paid after the information is proved correct. But now that insurance assessors are giving 10 per cent of the value of stolen goods for their recovery even without an arrest, informers have a more profitable trade and sometimes are able to earn over £5,000 a year. It is not unknown for such rewards to be split with the detective in the case. The protection given to informers, unless it is carefully watched, can become a vested interest which causes a net loss to the community. There have been cases when, for example, dealers in drugs were permitted to continue operating in return for information about some of their clients – thus in effect being licensed by the police, who on occasions even returned seized drugs to the dealers to be recycled as a reward. Since the recent scandals, Scotland Yard detectives have been warned not to speak to underworld contacts without the permission of senior officers.

Any accurate estimate of the actual, as distinct from the detected, incidence of corruption must be elusive. A police experiment made in New York three years ago found that of 51 patrolmen who were handed 'lost' wallets containing $20 or more by strangers, 15 kept the money themselves. In Metropolitan London some 2 per cent of complaints relate to alleged bribery. All the available evidence tends to show that police corruption is almost exclusively a monopoly of the CID, and in general is confined to inner urban areas, with its most heavy concentration – where the rewards and temptations are greatest – in particular parts of the West End of London. It is localized – there has never been evidence of corruption in, for example, the Fraud Squad; and its incidence is much less common among uniformed men. The experience common to all countries is that the bulk of police dishonesty occurs in connection with offences that are 'victimless' and which substantial parts of police as well as public opinion do not really regard as morally reprehensible, such as gambling, drug-usage, the sale of pornography, contraventions of licensing laws, and – formerly – Prohibition, street-betting, smuggling, homosexuality and prostitution. Significantly, these are all areas where the police have wide discretion about deciding to prosecute. As a Home Office civil servant observed, 'Young policemen are not so different from their friends of the same age. If their friends smoke cannabis we should not be surprised if the law against possessing it operates somewhat erratically.' The playwright Troy Kennedy Martin gives an unconventional view of the police's corrupt involvement in pornography: 'The police have been running the business very well: they've licensed it out, they've kept gangsters and violence out, they've run it the way the state should run it. Where do you draw the line? At allowing people to trade guns.'

But a London police officer disagreed. 'We're so shot at, we're shell-shocked.' In a service where group loyalty is as strong as in the police, it is hard to find an officer who is not painfully embarrassed by the recent conviction of so many London policemen for corruption, including the former commanders of both the Flying Squad and the C1 department at the Yard (London's longest-serving CID officer, in charge of ten specialist detective squads, although his conviction was later quashed by the Court of Appeal) and even the detective chief superintendent who himself had headed the investigation into the cases of corruption revealed by *The Times*. On 29 November 1969 that paper recounted how a Scotland Yard detective inspector had tricked a man into placing his fingerprints on a piece of gelignite, and used this as blackmail to suggest that he plant stolen goods on a victim whom the police would then raid in order to extort money from him. A detective sergeant who was independently extorting money from the same small-time criminal told him, 'We've got more villains in our game than you've got in yours.' None the less, unlike the situation existing in several major American cities or Hong Kong, corruption almost certainly touches only a small minority of the police in Britain. Recently, two London airport police officers were offered, but refused, £5,000 a day (more than they were paid annually), plus numerous girls, by heroin smugglers. Attempts at bribery are only rarely prosecuted, which is regrettable because they would vastly outnumber the total number of policemen who succumb. Whereas few people are even surprised if journalists or businessmen fiddle their tax or expenses, if a policeman follows suit he faces ruin – a point the sanctimonious view of police dishonesty forgets.

Nevertheless, what worries thoughtful policemen is the number of Metropolitan CID officers who, at the least, must have connived at the corruption which existed unchecked under previous Commissioners, and have since then been promoted and may become future senior leaders. In addition, some of the police officers who resigned under a cloud during Mark's purge, but who never faced prosecution, are now holding top security jobs outside the force. Mark's predecessors had feared to expose the extent of the CID's corruption because of the effect this would have on public confidence as well as on police morale: juries were already with increasing frequency acquitting in cases where police evidence was disputed. But what was even more disturbing than the recent series of cases was their revelation that a regular system of police corruption had succeeded in flourishing unchecked at least from 1953 to 1972 in the centre of London. It is doubtful if the extent of corruption among parts of the Metropolitan CID would ever have been believed without the press doing the police's own job for them; in particular *The Times*'s own exposé in 1969 secured the conviction of some corrupt London detectives by using hidden taperecorders. The most disturbing feature of *The Times* case was that the paper itself felt it had to investigate and provide the evidence because, as counsel told the court, at that time 'the police could not be trusted to inquire into the dirty laundry in their own house.' As one of the corrupt detectives in that case explained, 'I'm in a little firm in a firm.'

The smallest suspicion which must fall on many of the convicted police officers' colleagues is that they are very poor detectives. It was stated during one of the trials that up to £50,000 a year was being paid in bribes to certain Scotland Yard officers, on a *pro rata* basis by rank: £150 per week for a chief inspector; £100 for an inspector; £60 for a sergeant. The Obscene Publications Squad itself used to grant licences for new pornography shops in the West End, charging £1,000 for protection against close police attention or attack by competitors' strong-arm gangs. The corrupt officers, in return for their pay-offs, warned clients when they were about to be raided, ensured that there was insufficient evidence for the Director of Public Prosecutions to decide to bring a charge, or else arranged that the prosecution's case collapsed in court. Some of the officers met their corrupters at Masonic functions. CID officers themselves actually used to sell hard pornography from the basement of Holborn police station, recycling seized material to vendors. After he was posted to be head of the CID at Kingston in Surrey, one detective chief inspector continued to provide a consultative service, in return for £200 a month, by vetting the proofs of pornographic magazines.

Sir Robert Mark's comment was, 'Having had CID experience, it was not difficult for me to diagnose the illness. The problem was to cut out the cancer without killing the patient.' When Roy Jenkins appointed Mark as Assistant Commissioner in 1967, he had never previously served in London. He is a Mancunian who had nearly joined the Rhodesian police, but instead spent ten years in the Special Branch. At Leicester as the youngest chief constable in the country, Mark had once withdrawn his order for a suit from a tailor who had offered him a special discount. Initially at Scotland Yard he was ostracized, by what he calls the Edgar Wallace generation, as an outsider who had not been to Hendon. There had previously been only one provincial policeman in the whole 138 years of the Metropolitan force at the rank of Assistant Commissioner, and he had only lasted for three years. James Callaghan had wanted to make Mark Commissioner in succession to Simpson: two years later a Conservative Home Secretary, Reginald Maudling, appointed him as the successor to Waldron. Mark says that from his years as a police officer he knows what it is like 'to be attacked one day and patronized the next.' When he took over in April 1972, Mark faced the problem that numbers of his detectives, besides acting with the private solidarity of an exclusive élite, were also, in the police's own words, a 'sea of villainy'. In under five years, at a time when the force was very undermanned, Mark with his deputy Colin Woods got rid of over 450 officers by shot-gun resignations and dismissal – a rate more than ten times that of his predecessors. There were protests and opposition: Mark was accused of destroying the CID. One typical London detective, who watched Mark with bewilderment but grudging admiration, asked, 'He's clever, yes, but is he a policeman?' Peter Brodie, the former head of the CID who had not been pleased by the preferment of Mark, said he was sad to see so many experienced officers going before they qualified for their pensions. For the first time, while the crime figures increased, more men left the Metropolitan force than came into it. Some detectives threatened to stop making arrests: Mark retaliated by warning that he was prepared if necessary to put all the 3,200 CID men back into uniform. One man however, Frank Williamson, a former chief constable of Cumbria and a friend of Mark's with a passion for justice (who had been brought into the Yard to investigate corruption in 1971) thought Mark moved too slowly and circumspectly. A man of cast-iron integrity from a religious background and, like Mark and Woods, a sea-green incorruptible, Williamson gave pessimistic warnings of the extent of the Metropolitan CID corruption and finally resigned in frustration.

How had it come about that, to accept the assessment of the Yard's own most senior officers, the Metropolitan CID was 'the most routinely corrupt organization in London', 'a sink of iniquity' and 'bent as a corkscrew'? One major problem had been that, uniquely in the country, in the Metropolitan area the CID has sole control of dealing with the allegations against them. The CID freemasonry was so daunting that a former Commissioner once confided that he had been half afraid to take the job. Mark says, 'A great mistake was made in 1878 when the CID was established as an autonomous body.' He integrated it with the rest of the force by placing most detectives under uniformed divisional commanders, and made interchange between the two branches necessary for those who wanted promotion. Mark instituted a rule that no detective was to remain at one station for more than two years. He removed obscene publications duties from the CID altogether, and planned to change the members of the Flying Squad every three years. At a cost of £1 million a year, A10 was established at the Yard as a new specialist department to investigate complaints (known to policemen as 'Mark's suspenders') – and it was put under uniformed, not CID, control. Mark's skill at press and public relations, and his attack on corrupt lawyers, gradually revived police morale.

Mark believes that his cleaning-up, of which the results are still coming before the courts, was not only necessary in itself but also a prerequisite for the criminal law reforms which he dearly wants. He attributes part of the blame for the corruption in the CID to frustration at the present methods of trial and investigation:

> The idea that there is some moral justification for getting around the rules, if it increases the likelihood of getting men convicted whom they believe to be guilty, is not a far cry from bending the rules for other rather nastier reasons, in particular for the share of the profit from crime ... A detective who finds general acceptance of a system which protects the wrongdoer can come to think that if crime seems to pay for everyone else, why not for him? The next step may be to demand money for not opposing bail, for not preferring charges, for omitting serious charges, for a share in the stolen property, and so on.

The 1929 Royal Commission reported: 'The fact that the sentence may be varied as a consequence of statements made by the police in effect puts into their hands a power which it is undesirable they should possess.' Forms of corruption can range from accepting sweeteners in order to put in a good word for a client during a trial, not to oppose bail or to overlook a crucial piece of evidence such as a weapon found during a robbery; influencing the granting of licences or the choice of doctors, garages or break-down vehicles; allowing access to confidential records or agreeing to alter them; claiming payments for non-existent informers; leaking the exclusive advance news of an arrest or a breathalyser-test to the press; tolerating certain street-traders more than their competitors; helping oneself to goods at the scene of a breaking-in; down to petty 'mumping' ('mooching' in the US) – accepting free meals and drinks or goods and services at a discount (many all-night cafes, for example, give police officers on duty a free meal, or at least cups of tea, generally in the kitchen). Donors of the last kind think of themselves as paying merely an extra voluntary tax or insurance, and often expect nothing in return or nothing more anti-social than extra police protection. However, all policemen know that once they accept anything they render themselves hostages – even if, as not infrequently, they are certain that the briber has no moral right whatsoever to the 'bung' he is offering. A police officer is not allowed to accept any farewell present when he moves – not even a presentation watch from a village where he has worked for a decade.

A bribe is tax-free and therefore worth at least one third more than its nominal value. Even though 'organized crime' offers three- and four-figure sums, much police corruption remains surprisingly petty and has hardly kept pace with inflation. 'It used to be a pound note in a driving licence when I was on the beat, now it might be a fiver,' said a chief superintendent. (Bribes are fairly frequently offered or hinted at in breathalyser cases.) A different technique is practised in Germany, where some motorists carry a policeman's hat which they place on the front seat of their car when they park illegally, since policemen there rarely prosecute their colleagues. One motivation for bent 'grass-eaters' as distinct from the more serious 'meat-eaters' is a sense of loyalty to their fellow officers: the Knapp Commission in New York found that 'accepting pay-off money is one way for an officer to prove that he is one of the boys and' – ironically – 'that he can be trusted.' Most policemen know cases of respected citizens falsifying their insurance or tax claims, and can develop a cynical view that in our society the only crime is to be caught. But once a policeman eats even a little grass, he often becomes addicted: he raises his life-style and comes to depend on the additional income for hire-purchase payment if not for gambling. Frank Williamson says, 'Corruption so often starts from the smallest beginnings. Criminals make constant efforts to place detectives under obligations, and once they have succeeded, they keep the pressure well and truly on. Detectives, like anyone else, can become greedy.'

Newcomers and younger policemen find that the pressures to conform and join in on a 'pad' are very strong. 'It is a system which,' Tony Judge of the Police Federation explains,

> has its own rules, based on a curious code of ethics. The man who takes the money is expected to be scrupulous in his division of the spoils; another who finds himself transferred from a precinct can expect a lump sum by way of 'severance pay'. The police officer with the personal courage to refuse to take part is shunned by colleagues. Any officer who exposes the system is marked as a traitor.

When corruption becomes a finely organized system, extending right up to commander level as it recently did at Scotland Yard, younger honest police officers are not sure which of their superiors to trust. When one CID officer became so nauseated by the corruption that he decided to get out, he was forced to pay a bribe to obtain his transfer. In a recent trial, a detective inspector confessed he had not reported corruption in his squad because (shades of the Soviet Union) he was told he would be thrown out of the force as medically unfit if he did. An officer needs a good relationship with his colleagues for his work, if not for social contact. This case was one of the few where police officers gave evidence against their colleagues, which was a key factor in the jury's verdict; one major impediment to securing corruption convictions is the difficulty of proving guilt: most allegations involve criminals who may have more than one interest in discrediting particular officers.

Bent policemen are nothing new, particularly in London, whose underworld is estimated to contain 80 per cent of Britain's major criminals. In 1877, three out of the CID's total of four chief inspectors were convicted of corruption at the Old Bailey; in the 1920s sergeant Goddard made several thousand pounds from West End night-clubs. A QC says that he once advised a bookmaker to claim £24,000 payments to the police against his tax and that (surprisingly) this was allowed. Dishonest policemen also have the great advantage of being able to move unchallenged at night-time. But few British – slow capitalists as always – can compete with the business efficiency of Hong Kong or the New York City police, where the Knapp Commission reported in 1971 that corruption was 'indulged in to some degree by a sizeable majority of those on the force.' Police pay-offs were estimated to total $75 million a year; 5 per cent of New York contractors' building costs were going to the police so that building code regulations could be violated. Corruption in the force was an institution with a highly sophisticated structure, complete with apprenticeships, the purchase of lucrative posts and evidence, its own severance pay and retirement benefits. It was discovered that 179 pounds of seized heroin, including 81 pounds seized in the French Connection case, had been re-sold by the police on the black market, where its price was £90,000 a pound.

The police in Britain's colony of Hong Kong recently gained the reputation of being 'the best force that money can buy'. Ernest Hunt made £500,000 tax-free in bribes in eighteen years there in the course of rising to be superintendent in the Homicide Squad. Deputy district commander Godber was found in 1973 to have saved HK $4 million, nearly six times his total net salary during his entire twenty-one years in the Royal Hong Kong police. In secret evidence, Hunt alleged that 90 per cent of the Chinese and between 30 and 60 per cent of the European officers in the force were bent. 'The CID,' he claimed, 'run all the gambling, prostitution and vice and to a certain extent drugs. The uniform branch . . . take the share from licensed premises.' Fairly junior officers used to buy profitable posts for HK$250,000 (£30,000), which they recovered in pay-offs within three months. Some of the more senior officers who have sought immunity in Taiwan are reliably reported to have absconded with HK$60 million (£7 million) each. When the Independent Commission against Corruption probed the remaining policemen in Hong Kong too deeply they mutinied, in October 1977. The Commission's office was stormed by angry policemen, and the 17,000-strong force refused to enforce the law, coordinating resistance to their leaders on their two-way radios. The Governor, faced by a police force out of control, was compelled to concede a broad amnesty for past corruption, which was greeted by the police with shouts of 'We have won' and 'Police power'.

'In CID work when you capture robbers you all go out and have a few beers. But there's no celebration when you capture a bent police officer,' a British policeman said. 'I worked on a case where I'd known the man for twenty years. I knew his wife and his kids.' But no policeman will defend bribery because, unlike other police malpractices, it is not committed on behalf of society – however much it may reflect that society. The new Commissioner, Sir David McNee, a man of religious rectitude and that quietness which comes from great strength, is maintaining his predecessor's onslaught against dishonesty in the force. Even though most police corruption is petty compared with the scale of commercial frauds, the maximum penalty of two years jail under the Police Corruption Act 1906 is overdue for an increase. The public's prurient pleasure at authority's feet of clay and any proof that policemen are human disguises its unease at the frightening danger of dishonesty in the hands of the powerful. 'Organized' crime can only really flourish when the police are corrupt. 'Dishonest, perjured officers are,' in the words of Lord Justice Lawton, 'like an infernal machine ticking away to the destruction of us all.' Corruption, inside or outside the police, is a cancer which spreads unless it is dealt with early. The example of Hong Kong shows what can happen to a police force once it is allowed to take hold.

Evidence

Dogberry: *One word, sir: our watch, sir, hath indeed comprehended two aspicious persons, and we would have them this morning examined before your worship.*
Leonato: *Take their examination yourself, and bring it me.*
(*Much Ado About Nothing*, Act III, Scene 5.)

There is a natural temptation for policemen to feel that they, rather than lawyers or juries, are the best judges of guilt. In the great majority of cases it is true that they are; in this country probably at least eight out of ten people who appear in court are guilty, and the only issue at the trial is whether the guilt can be proved. People are inclined to forget that the police have not only to discover the criminal, but also to produce quickly enough the evidence upon which to convict him: few of the inspired guesses of fiction's detectives would be provable in court. It is highly frustrating for policemen to see their careful work ruined in court by a naive jury or an incompetent prosecution; it is even more galling for them to listen passively while the defendant and his witnesses lie freely. There are far too few prosecutions for perjury in our courts, despite the difficulties involved. If some of the witnesses who concoct false alibis were prosecuted the police might feel less handicapped and frustrated. Many police officers naturally resent the licence which is given the defendant in court to perjure himself, and thus to jeopardize their own careers by inventing malicious allegations. They are also accustomed to having to listen to untruths from the friends of an accused man giving evidence in mitigation of sentence, when it is too late for them to be disproved.

A completely fabricated case from a policeman is almost unknown, but there is a strong temptation for him to embellish his evidence. The 1960 Royal Commission reported:

> There was a body of evidence, too substantial to disregard, which in effect accused the police of stooping to the use of undesirable means of obtaining statements and of occasionally giving perjured evidence in a court of law. Thus the Law Society suggested that occasionally police officers colour, exaggerate, or even fabricate the evidence against an accused person. These criticisms applied, in their view, only to isolated cases.

The 1929 Commission had said:

> Responsible witnesses, with experience on the Bench, have stated that there is occasionally a tendency on the part of the police, when they genuinely believe a prisoner to be guilty, to strain the evidence against him to secure a conviction. This danger is greatest in charges of a vague character, such as 'loitering with intent to commit a felony' or indecent behaviour.

Lord Reid, a Lord of Appeal and formerly a criminal law officer in Scotland, said in addition that the impression he had formed was that the police virtually never harassed a man who had no record. But if he had, and the police were convinced that he was guilty of an offence, they sometimes used very undesirable methods in questioning him.

A policeman rationalized the moral, if not the legal, justification of bolstering prosecution evidence in this way: 'The public are demanding crime be suppressed. If we know X is guilty, and he's too crafty to give us the evidence we need, is it so important that our evidence conforms to strict reality?' 'All right, guv, it's a fair cop', once monotonously stated to be a part of defendants' statements, is dying out, though the equally improbable 'Fair enough' or 'Who shopped me?' are having a vogue in what criminals call 'Yardese'. It is even easier to be selective when recounting the defendant's statement, and to disregard what does not fit in with certainty of his guilt, than it is inventively 'to put on the verbals'. One retired police inspector, who has now become a solicitor, said in this connection that 'it took three or four years out of the force for me to realize what closed minds we had.' A serving Midlands officer said that a 'good copper' was defined by some of his colleagues as a corner-cutter who was not tied down by bureaucratic safeguards. Some detectives will – as a senior officer described – 'invent a couple of verbals because it's easier than interrogating a prisoner when it's time to go home.' A key opportunity for *suppressio veri* can occur when sending evidence for forensic analysis, and when the officer in charge of a case decides how meticulous he should be in reporting negative findings to the court or the defendant's lawyers. Not all police officers are as particular as others when they attribute 'crimes to be taken into consideration' to the correct defendant: some have been known to agree to put in a good word in return for help in clearing up their books.

The police sometimes feel bitter towards lawyers who attack them in court; one solicitor who threw doubt on a policeman's statement about the 'rear door of a Mini-car' was told that 'he was not performing a public service'. A number of barristers and solicitors allege that the police have vetoed their doing any more prosecution work, as a result of their cross-examination of police witnesses. These are distinct from the small number of crooked solicitors who pay policemen for recommending clients to them, or those criminal lawyers attacked by Sir Robert Mark for their 'forensic trickery' in fabricating alibis or defences beyond the intellectual capacity of the accused. Scotland Yard is believed to maintain a 'black list' of lawyers whom the CID deter arrested people from contacting. The Bench is much less rarely complained about: 78 per cent of police officers said they thought that judges and magistrates were fair to them, compared with less than 49 per cent who felt the same about lawyers. Indeed some policemen said that they thought that magistrates were sometimes over-helpful, by, for example, invariably granting adjournments in order to allow the police to reprepare their evidence. An ex-chief inspector said, 'There is no surer way to ruin the police than by supporting them against the weight of the evidence'; one QC who sits as a Recorder commented, 'Nothing can do more good than for the judge to come down hard on police lying in the witness-box.' But not everybody subscribes to this view: some non-policemen criticize police malpractices – in the same way as they criticize the Suez operation – not for being immoral but for being inefficient and failing. They want confessions extracted from criminals, provided they do not hear about the methods. Their reasoning is that they do not wish to undermine confidence in the police; unlike most intelligent policemen, they fail to realize that it is the attempts to gloss over which have this effect. The counter-productive consequences were observed by Neville Braybrook when he served on a jury: 'After the first day of my fortnight's jury service, I found that most of my fellow jurors believed in the general integrity of the police. Yet after three days I did not find a single juryman in my own court whose faith in the police had not been shaken. We had seen them blush under oath, and the law turned into an ass; in the witness-box they were sometimes as much tied into knots by the prosecuting as the defending counsel. In a straight issue between their word and the accused's we invariably gave the benefit of the doubt to the latter. Daily we grew more suspicious of their evidence, and often the verdicts that we returned were based on considerations which, strictly speaking, were nothing to do with what we heard.'

Superintendent Robert Robinson of the Metropolitan police said that juries' increasing tendency to distrust police evidence had resulted in a rising rate of acquittals, and this had led detectives in several recent cases to use a 'supergrass' as the key witness. (One, Bertie Smalls, caused the conviction of twenty-seven active violent robbers in London.) But policemen should not feel that it is necessarily a personal slight on them for costs to be awarded to a defendant. The expression 'costs against the police' should be dropped: the police's supreme duty is to obtain justice, not a conviction. Any verbal evidence even at best is a tenuous account of a past event, by the time it has been subconsciously edited by the mind of a witness and the ears of jurymen. C. H. Rolph's opinion is, 'I've never known a criminal or civil case where there wasn't perjury on both sides.' One police officer said, 'Everything reported, even by truthful witnesses, is wrong,' and a chief constable commented, 'If every person who lied on oath in court were prosecuted, finality would never be reached.' The police are, if anything, more likely to make honest mistakes than the average witness; research by Brian Clifford, a psychology lecturer at the N.E. London Polytechnic, has shown that while policemen are no better than the general public at perceiving and remembering events and people, they are more likely to misinterpret impressions becase of their past experience. It is doubtful how much police notebooks fulfil any useful probative purpose (especially since Mr Justice Byrne allowed two or more policemen to synthesize their entries), unless the defendant has read and signed the entry at the earliest opportunity; a record made an hour or two later by anybody is rarely accurate. Yet it is disturbingly rare for a policeman, once he has grown accustomed to taking the oath and to giving evidence, ever to admit any human uncertainty in the witness-box. Many lie in order to protect the identity of their informants, and many more because they know that the Judges' Rules are more honoured in the breach than the observance. A police officer is in a terrible dilemma when called upon to verify a lying colleague: though one Special said he knew an officer who acted as an 'understudy' in the witness-box for a colleague who had gone on holiday. 'It's a poor job if you can't help a colleague' remains part of most policemen's unwritten code.

Part of justice is the conviction of the guilty, and it is essential for juries to be satisfied about the truth of statements and witnesses. Under the present system, a premium in a prosecution is put upon the integrity of the police. Some forces have a reputation for being conspicuously fair towards the defence. The majority of policemen are worthy of their responsibility; years of undermanning and overwork in a losing battle have affected some of the few who are not. But people who break as well as those who observe the law have their rights, and their problems have been highlighted recently through the prosecution of many reliable citizens who are motorists or political demonstrators. The tenacity, finances, and previous good character of some of these defendants have enabled them to make exposures in a way denied to the usual criminal. In one case, only expensive analyses enabled a man to prove that some spittle on a jacket, which was the main prosecution evidence, could not originate from himself. In California, a victim had to spend more than £12,000 in legal fees before he successfully proved that his fingerprints had been falsified by a policeman who was waging a lone vendetta against crime. But between 1956 and 1971 it has now been revealed that the famed FBI itself mounted 2,300 'dirty tricks' operations against black and radical groups, including the planting of disruptive and damaging evidence. There have also recently been startling disclosures that some similarly illegal tactics have been used by a number of Canadian police agents, and that some RCMP Security Service officers had burned a barn and stolen dynamite to discredit Quebec separatists.

Even the most minor instance of falsification is a grave matter, because of the frightening power the police have to cause injustice to any individual if they are so minded. Police officers too can be among the victims: in 1978 a sergeant was awarded £37,000 damages for being framed. One CID sergeant recently voluntarily confessed, because of his Pentecostal conscience, that he had planted evidence on four innocent men in order to get his promotion.

A disturbing comment about his own unorthodox methods was made at his trial at the Old Bailey by another constable, who had set up a divisional record of sixty-seven arrests in a week in an attempt to become a permanent member of the CID. 'They get results. While everything is going all right nobody complains. But when it goes wrong you're left standing alone.'

Violence

Lear: *Thou rascal beadle, hold thy bloody hand!*
Why dost thou lash that whore? Strip thine own back:
Thou hotly lust'st to use her in that kind
For which thou whipp'st her. The usurer hangs the cozener.
Through tatter'd clothes small vices do appear;
Robes and furr'd gowns hide all. Plate sin with gold.
And the strong lance of justice hurtless breaks;
Arm it in rags, a pigmy's straw doth pierce it.
None doth offend, none, I say none . . .
(Shakespeare, *King Lear*, Act IV, Scene 6.)

Ramsey Clark, the former US Attorney General, suggests that of all violence that of the police is the most dangerous, 'for who will protect the public when the police violate the law?' Policemen are frequently the victims of violence in their job, but when police officers, as in Brazil's 'Death Squad', become a law unto themselves, there is no one to check them.

Police officers and criminals in both Britain and the US agree that violence by the police is diminishing faster than corruption or perjury. Policemen and criminals both accept that they run occupational risks, and complain in court of violence less frequently than they might. Nobody can expect an unarmed policeman to tackle an armed criminal without using force, and a police officer who fails to make an arrest or allows an escape is liable to find himself on a serious disciplinary charge. The police's opponents are bound by no Queensberry rules, and recently in America officers have rightly begun to win punitive damages in the courts against those who have injured them. Some criminals like to exaggerate an injury to give themselves a heroic aura instead of the ignominious one of being caught. Although people are often sceptical when they hear 'he became violent and had to be restrained', a high proportion of police violence is the result of some verbal or physical provocation. But this can be reciprocal, as one policeman described: 'Provoke him until he can't help hitting out and then do him for assault and resisting arrest while hitting him back.' Reports of the conduct of some plain-clothed *agents provocateurs* and of police smashing cameras on occasions are especially sinister. The crowd in Downing Street at the time of Suez was perfectly good-tempered until it began to be squeezed by mounted police. (Policemen like their horses so strongly that they react violently when they fear attacks upon them. Mounted police are now an anachronism, and often can do more harm than good in the delicate relationship with crowds.)

Police violence, when it does occur, cannot be viewed outside the context of the climate of our society, and in particular the masculine *mores* of the world which many policemen share with prison officers and criminals. In the US, political corruption in some courts used to impel the police to inflict their own physical punishment on suspects, and also made the public less inclined to blame them. Some policemen are as emotionally involved against crime as religious crusaders. An ex-detective superintendent wrote, 'I love the thrill of the chase. There's a warm satisfaction which rises inside of me when I sit in a courtroom and hear the judge pronounce sentence.' In some other memoirs, an ex-inspector has written, 'I enjoyed every arrest I made, from simple drunks to life-sentence felons ... but I seldom loved the prisoners.' Indignation and strain on occasions cause policemen's repressed tension to break out in aggression. Some of them frankly enjoy fighting, in the same way as many schoolboys or soldiers do: photographs of policemen hitting students with clubs in the US show that they are smiling as they do so. A neighbourhood beat officer explained to a woman friend of mine that his personal obsession was against 'flashers', and guffawed as he described how he and his colleagues roughed up such characters and kicked them down the stairs at the police station. Many policemen are opposed to violence but have aggressive feelings within themselves which are brought to the surface by frustration. Dissatisfaction resulting from a feeling of low status sometimes gives rise to violence, verbal or physical, against prisoners as an outlet, which in turn gives further backing to the negative stereotype. A police 'backlash' alienates society and reduces the likelihood of its helping the police. In part this accounts for the greater incidence of violence in city areas, where the public expectations are less favourable. One very senior retired CID chief seriously offered as his solution to the crime problem that '45,000 decent Englishmen should march on the prisons and string up the inmates.' Psychiatrists say that we wish to destroy in our enemies what we are unable to stomach in ourselves.

The US police killed 2,941 civilians in the decade ending in 1970. Aggression has never lacked rationalization. A policeman, in particular, needs to excuse his anti-social conduct if his life is not to be meaningless. The sadistic outrage at Sheffield in 1963, analysed below, was a manifestation of the pathological conviction in some CID officers that they are the last defenders of 'the essential decencies' against not only criminals but the purblind courts and public. One of the main police participants in the Sheffield affair said that he felt that beating such as that was certainly justified – 'the hardened type of criminal will not respond to the normal methods of detection and therefore probably a good hiding or a beating is the only solution.' Although generally policemen say that it is no concern of theirs what sentence a criminal receives, others consider it should be part of their function to add a 'rough time' to the court's sentence when, for example, they know extra information about an offender from their informers. Their victims are often, but not always, violent men themselves: criminals who have shown particular disrespect for the police, or whom the police have either been unable to convict and decide to punish themselves, or whom they have beaten in an exasperated attempt to solve a crime they feel they cannot solve by any other means. Some prisoners give as their reason for not complaining that 'the police can make a lot of difference to your life when you're out.' A punch-up in the cells is less easily concealed than the electrical assaults of the Chilean or South African police, because the former leaves marks except in a very few places which have to be expertly chosen. Men sometimes allege that they have been hit in the small of their back or on the back of their neck so as to leave no traces. The most uncontrolled occasions are when a colleague policeman has previously been injured. As with corruption, the Hong Kong police can excel in this. Ernest Hunt, a former officer there, alleges that interrogation methods included putting suspects in refrigerators, and that he witnessed a firework being lighted that had been inserted in a suspect's anus.

Violence in any circumstances is unhesitatingly condemned by the majority of policemen: 'There is no excuse for a policeman ever assaulting a prisoner, however tempted,' said a recent Secretary of the Police Federation. Fortunately in Britain force and threats generally result in acquittal; the law insists that confessions must be entirely free and voluntary. In the US in 1931, the Wickersham Commission reported that the extraction of confessions through physical brutality was widespread, almost universal, police practice. Subsequently the Supreme Court ruled that such confessions were inadmissible as evidence in court. Not only are such means never justified, but they also often lead to false confessions. In 1973 an Indian youth in Southall who had had his face slapped in the police station, 'confessed' to a crime of which not only he was innocent, but which in fact had never occurred. In 1977 free pardons were given to three boys, whom a detective sergeant had beaten and forced to clean up his mother's home which he suspected them of having broken into, when two different boys confessed to the crime. In the words of one senior CID officer: 'Hitting's not the slightest use; it only makes men tell you what they think you want to hear; what you need is subterfuge to get at the truth.'

Physical violence is easy to define and exclude; it is more difficult to draw the borderline where mental pressure becomes oppressive. Some police officers regard alcohol as a justifiable ally to help loosen tongues. One constable recounted to me with pride how he and some colleagues once extorted a confession from two West Indians by staging a mock trial at the police station, sentencing them to death, and leading them to an adjoining room where they were told they would be hanged immediately. 'Frightening people is basic if the police are going to get results,' a gentle chief superintendent explained. Dr William Sargant describes how the technique of obtaining a 'voluntary' confession in police interrogation is exactly the same as that used in persuading a beseiged criminal to surrender:

> ... trapped and kept under controlled tension and

> progressive nervous fatigue until two states of brain activity occur, inevitably, in any normal person. When the brain finally switches under induced fatigue and stress, it becomes first of all very 'suggestible'. People can be made to sign statements they would never have given when mentally normal ... A second stage of brain activity may also finally supervene when the brain goes into 'reverse', as does a rabbit's when it suddenly turns to run into the mouth of a pursuing stoat ... Stress must be gently applied, be varied, but basically persistent. Too much stress leads to violence, hence the cups of tea and other comforts given to an increasingly tense victim. Also, he must be talked to as much as possible to maintain brain-washing contact ... After all, ordinary police get the most extraordinary confessions by this method, if given the time, without any need to beat up the suspect. The only big joke to all, except lawyers, is that these skilled techniques of brain-washing produce what are termed 'voluntary' actions by the 'hypnotized' suspect or kidnapper. That is why there is such a demand for solicitors to be present to prevent this.

A few examples of the instances, however exceptional, when a minority of British police have resorted to degrees of physical violence, remind us that they can still occur. Violence takes place daily in society; what shocks us about police violence is that it is committed by those employed to protect us from it. Allegations are almost invariably concentrated in certain localities: Liverpool 8, the north, and especially the north-east, Glasgow and parts of London have a reputation for tough police methods. At a disarmament demonstration in Trafalgar Square on 17 September 1961, Lord Kilbracken witnessed policemen carry two women demonstrators and throw them into the fountains. Adam Roberts, a respected lecturer at the LSE, describes his treatment at Bow Street station then: 'A policeman said: "All right, take him where there aren't any witnesses." Six policemen dragged me with roughness down a corridor. At first two held my arms in a Chinese twist while the other four kicked. A well-built policewoman said, "Kick him harder; kick him harder".'

Generally during strikes, commonsense arrangements are

worked out between the police and the trade unions, but in 1969 £2,280 damages were awarded in an uncontested civil case against the Cheshire police for physical injury they had caused to workers striking at the Roberts Arundel factory at Stockport. Three men with fractured noses alleged they were beaten at Stockport police headquarters until they obeyed demands to shout 'Mercy, mercy'. No policeman was prosecuted, suspended or even brought before a disciplinary hearing as a result. After a more recent assault on a picket line at Fine Tubes in Plymouth, policemen were asked to attend an identification parade for an inquiry into injuries and complaints by the strikers. They refused point blank, and their superior officers did not compel them to do so. In the November following the Stockport case 236 complaints were officially investigated as a result of violence at Swansea rugby ground when there were demonstrations against a South African team; yet no report was ever published, other than a bald statement – that there were 'no grounds' for criminal or disciplinary proceedings – which satisfied nobody. Again in the same year, an inquiry by Detective chief superintendent Drury (later himself imprisoned for eight years) failed to discover which RUC officers had killed Samuel Devenney and caused Sir Arthur Young, the chief constable, to accuse that 'among those officers who possess this guilty knowledge there is a conspiracy of silence motivated by a misconceived and improper sense of loyalty to their guilty comrades.'

In one of the most brutal recent cases, a Leeds detective sergeant and former detective inspector were imprisoned in 1971 for assaulting David Oluwale, a harmless Nigerian vagrant who had been subjected to a prolonged campaign of police harassment during which officers had beaten and kicked and urinated on him and taken him miles into the countryside before abandoning him. It took eighteen months before the offences for which the two policemen were convicted came to light. To cover up, police notebooks and other station records had been doctored, for which the complicity of several officers was necessary; indeed, during trial several other policemen said they had seen Oluwale assaulted but had failed to report anything. All sixteen policemen accused of disciplinary offences in connection with the case remained in the Leeds force. But standards are contagious: in two years, eleven members of the Leeds force were convicted of criminal offences. (Less surprisingly, during the past two years, 455 men have been retained in the South African police force after being convicted of crimes of violence, ranging from assault to attempted murder: seventy-five of these had previous convictions. The South African police shot dead 149 people and wounded 403 during 1977.) Another deeply disturbing outrage occurred in Yorkshire at Sheffield in 1963. It is worth while examining in some detail the genesis and lessons of this episode. The Sheffield force had not increased its establishment since 1947, and its CID was in fact actually reduced in size between 1953 and 1958, while crime rose by 25 per cent. As a result, its fifty detectives in 1962 worked more than 16,000 hours of unpaid overtime, for which they could not be compensated by time off in lieu. The next year a drop in the detection rate caused a special crime squad to be instituted. After five whole days the squad had not made a single arrest; so in desperation six suspects were taken out of a pub and a rhinoceros whip used on two of them as a 'lie detector'. The report of the subsequent inquiry (Cmnd. 2176) says that:

> The minds of the appellants were already conditioned by the dangerous notion they had formed that a Crime Squad was a *corps d'élite* which could use tough methods to deal with tough criminals and take risks to achieve speedy results ... Mr Streets (the chief police officer inculpated) ... told us that he held views that criminals are treated far too softly by the courts, that because criminals break rules, police may and must do so to be a jump ahead.

The report stated that the mitigation for the two detective constables who carried out 'deliberate, unprovoked, brutal, and sustained assaults, with weapons in the nature of a truncheon and a short flexible piece of gut-like material, upon prisoners who were defenceless and did not retaliate, for the purpose of inducing confessions of crime' was: (a) they had been working long hours and were overtired and hungry; (b) they were, and felt, under pressure to obtain results; (c) their use of violence had been encouraged by hints beforehand, and it had been instituted and witnessed with approval by senior officers; (d) that these senior officers and another detective constable who joined in the violence were wholly inadequately dealt with by the chief constable; and (e) that they had been told to give a false account in court by a senior officer, who concocted it.

The 'gut-like material' to which the report referred was a rhinoceros whip that one of the detective constables had appropriated from the offensive weapons which had been handed in to the police, and which he said he carried 'in case of conflicts between coloured informants'. With it, together with an old-type truncheon, and several fists, four men were beaten in relays, one of them sustaining some seventy blows in five separate beatings. The detective inspector who watched and 'displayed callous amusement' told the inquiry, 'these things go on fairly frequently, don't they'. The report concluded that he had thought an assaulted man 'would be unlikely to complain or to be believed if he did.' When the victims did complain in court, the inquiry recorded that nobody in the Sheffield force took any action for at least five days, with the result that the officers involved were able to burn the two weapons. The victims' solicitor was thereupon told misleading statements; the Crime Squad concocted lying stories and even fabricated evidence; the detective chief inspector who was deputed to investigate the culprits 'commiserated with them'. The chief constable who, the inquiry found, was 'over-obsessed with the bogey of publicity' and 'shut his eyes to the evidence', when he purported to reprimand the officers shook them by the hand.

From the inquiry's report, which should be required reading for all police officers, magistrates, and members of police authorities, there are still some lessons to be learnt. It is clear that the tragedy had its roots in overwork and the lack of standards set by the senior CID officers then at Sheffield. But there was no evidence to suggest that any of the offending officers was abnormal. Most disturbing of all in its implications is the fact that not one man in the force reported the incident, although a number of officers certainly knew about it. The true facts only became known because of the coincidence of a determined lawyer, an outspoken local newspaper, and a case by two officers which led to their superiors being exposed. And it is unlikely that such open assaults would ever have taken place unless the junior officers felt confident that they were safe from disciplinary proceedings.

In the most serious recent case Liddle Towers, a thirty-nine-year-old electrician, died in 1976 from injuries allegedly received from policemen at Gateshead. His doctor, Alan Towney, said, 'I've never seen injuries like them. He has been pulped. He had about forty bruises and seven large abrasions.' The dying man told his doctor, 'They've killed me Doc. . . . They shouldn't do this to a dog.' The police version is that one officer accidentally fell on top of Mr Towers, but eye-witnesses saw three officers kicking him as he lay handcuffed on the ground. The first inquest returned a verdict of 'justifiable homicide' and a second inquest resulted in an equally unsatisfactory verdict of 'misadventure; but the Home Secretary has unfortunately and astonishingly to date declined to set up an inquiry under section 32 of the Police Act 1964.

Inquiries

'For all its imperfections, the criminal law is designed not merely as a buttress for the privileges of the powerful but as a shield for the elemental human liberties of the poor and the weak against the assaults of the strong and the treacherous.'
Sir Leon Radzinowicz.

In virtually every one of these cases it was covering-up by the police that was at least as disturbing as the illegality itself – yet it took many years of argument before a system of independent inquiries was instituted. Time after time, senior officers persisted in denying anything was wrong until there was a sustained public outcry. And in almost every instance numerous policemen, while not themselves primarily guilty, knew what the truth was but kept quiet. Covering-up for colleagues' minor habits of 'easing' (relaxing, chatting, drinking or even sleeping on duty) can build up an interdependent loyalty when more serious police malpractice appears. In a survey among 1,000 Metropolitan officers carried out by Dr Belson, some 25 per cent of them admitted that the police are too ready to protect each other. To replace the recent haemorrhage in the leadership of London's CID, more outside officers of the calibre and integrity of Frank Williamson and David McNee should be drafted into the Metropolitan force. For the corruption networks recently unearthed in the Metropolitan force to have survived for so long, covering-up for colleagues must have been almost as common in parts of that force's CID as it was in Hong Kong. A keen senior officer could – and should – have arrived unannounced at any time to check what was happening. In 1973 the New York Commissioner, Patrick Murphy, ordered that every police commander would in future have to prove he did everything possible to prevent any case of corruption that was found within his own precinct.

Lord Gardiner, the former Lord Chancellor, recently described the British police as 'the most powerful and least accountable of any in western Europe. Nowhere else do they have the power to prosecute without any independent evaluation; and in other countries forces are accountable through a minister.' Yet on the other hand all officers, even up to the highest rank, are liable in British courts to private or public prosecution as well as civil claims. Tom Sargant, the experienced secretary of Justice who himself sits as a magistrate, believes that 'judges and magistrates could do far more to stop police malpractice by following up suspicious facts that emerge in court.' The same applies to prosecuting solicitors. As a *quid pro quo* for the reforms in police powers proposed in Chapter 4, there should be a special department, perhaps under the Ombudsman, reinvestigating strongly disputed convictions with an open mind; neither the NCCL, Justice nor MPs have the necessary resources to make proper inquiries. This might also serve to separate the question of a prisoner's innocence from the issue of whether police misconduct has taken place; at present in some cases reluctance to admit the possibility of the latter inhibits an objective or speedy decision about the former. In the past, an allegation against an individual police officer has too often been resented by the service – and regarded by some of the press and the public – as an attack on the police as a whole. An apparent lack of criticism within the service has only served to fuel criticism outside it.

The reasons why inquiries into major allegations against the police must contain an independent element are unassailable.

They parallel those which led to the establishment of an Ombudsman:

(i) *No authority should be the judge in its own cause.* A chief constable, who held inquiries under the previous system, was in the invidious position of being at the same time judge, jury and of having initiated the charge, as well as being a quasi-defendant because he held ultimate responsibility for the state of his force. Some police officers themselves also favour inquiries having independent chairmen because of the personal prior views chief constables often have about their men.

(ii) *A complainant has a natural sense of frustration if he has his complaint rejected without being given the opportunity of putting his evidence before an impartial tribunal, or without knowing why it was refuted.* Thus the previous system caused some members of the public unnecessary resentment towards the police, even in cases where complaints were justifiably rejected. In addition other people with a grievance used to refuse to lodge an official complaint with the police because they lacked faith that this would do any good, but nevertheless continued to criticize them, to the benefit of neither the police nor the public.

(iii) *The independent element can also help innocent policemen.* If complaints are able to be impartially sifted, both the service and individual officers are able to clear themselves convincingly of bogus or malicious charges made against them, with the result that greater confidence and mutual respect develops between the service and the public. As a protection for police officers who are impugned, their names should not be published unless and until they are proved guilty; and they should remain on full pay whilst suspended from duty – not as up till recently on two-thirds – since they are innocent until judged otherwise.

In the face of such considerations, why were independent inquiries delayed for so many years? Those in the Police Federation who argued that such a system would place officers in double jeopardy forget that members of some other professions – such as doctors, dentists, lawyers and journalists – already face complaints before similar tribunals, sometimes headed by a layman, at the risk of their careers. The same principle should certainly be extended to all professions and the trade unions, and to cover all cases – for example in prisons – where the complainant is at a disadvantage against a body that is all-powerful. Perhaps the greatest value of independent inquiries is preventive as much as curative: the establishment of such a system is a strong deterrent to misconduct or covering it up. But it is also essential for such inquiries to have the power to subpoena and hear evidence on oath; the tribunal which investigated the Thurso case went out of its way to point out that it had been able to determine the truth only because it had had the power to call the police as witnesses, and that in an inquiry where the police could decline to be cross-examined their word would probably have been preferred to the boy complainant's. As John Alderson, the chief constable of Devon and Cornwall, makes clear, 'A policeman is very skilled in covering his tracks. He knows all the tricks of the trade and he's likely to make it as difficult as possible for the investigation branch.' It was deplorable that when after long delays the Police Act 1976 was finally passed, some Federation leaders urged their members not to cooperate with its new system for investigating complaints; the spectacle of policemen declaring that they would refuse to comply with democratically enacted law was not attractive.

A wholly different objection to the system of inquiries set up by the Police Act 1976 (described in Appendix B) was taken by Sir Robert Mark; and this was one factor which contributed to his early retirement (on 13 March 1977) from being Metropolitan Commissioner. Together with other chief constables, Mark feared that the new system would inhibit rather than strengthen the fight against police corruption. They objected to civilians being involved, before the police's own inquiry had been completed, on the grounds that the new Police Complaints Board would judge guilt according to the higher standards of a criminal court. The balance of proof in disciplinary hearings has never been laid down, but is often closer to a civil court's 'balance of probabilities' than to a criminal one's standard of proof 'beyond a reasonable doubt'. Of the first seventy-two police officers who were prosecuted in court after Mark became Commissioner, thirty-six were acquitted by juries, although Mark believes that not more than two or three could conceivably have been not guilty. But 80 per cent of officers acquitted by courts have later been dealt with for breaches of the Disciplinary Code. 'Few juries will believe a criminal in preference to a criminal police officer,' Mark explained. 'But internal police discipline is more effective. An officer who is acquitted of committing burglary on duty can be done for leaving his beat while on duty.' Police officers none the less are entitled as much as civilians are to justice and the benefit of a doubt. Other critics of the new system maintain it is flawed because it still depends so heavily upon investigation by the police. In addition Mark, who always agreed that the police should be more accountable to the public in their handling of complaints, and accepted the need for an *ex post facto* civilian review, feared there was a threat to democracy from the possibility that a future Home Secretary might pack the Complaints Board with extremist political placemen. The initial appointments certainly gave no grounds at all for such a fear. But a similar system for Scotland is still awaited.

In the United States, the Supreme Court sometimes intervenes drastically in criminal trials against the police partly because there is no other proper independent watchdog of police conduct; the New York Patrolmen's Benevolent Association spent $500,000 in the 1960s in a successful campaign against a civilian review board. Yet many people have no wish to risk an expensive court action or to get damages against a police officer, but only desire to pursue their complaints from a sense of injustice, whether justified or not. Lord Devlin has said, 'It is the general habit of the police never to admit to the slightest departure from correctness.' They are not the only people to share this characteristic. It would be better if both civil servants and policemen felt that they were allowed to admit that they are human, and that to do so would not necessarily prejudice their job. As Sir Robert Mark advised recruits at Hendon, 'Don't be afraid of making mistakes. One policeman who never made a mistake probably never made a decision. But if you make a mistake or do wrong, tell the truth about it.' Some police discipline at the moment is too drum-head; an independent inquiry should make every allowance for mistakes committed in the public interest. In addition, maliciously false letters of allegation should be made available to the victims, so that police officers could pursue their right to sue for libel in the same way as anybody else.

In some individual cases in the past, senior officers have been reluctant and slow to investigate thoroughly because of fear of publicity and an illusion that to do so would sap public confidence in the police generally. Since the Second World War, Home Secretaries have set up independent inquiries into a police matter on few occasions, and not at all in several recent cases – such as those of George Ince, the Luton murder, and Liddle Towers – where there were strong *prima facie* grounds for doing so. But many other more minor disputes call for conciliation rather than adversary proceedings. It is also worth noting, as Mervyn Jones points out, that the police system is designed to deal with complaints against individual members of the force. But the complainant may prefer not to single any policeman out, feeling that superior orders were to blame for what happened; he may be concerned over the conduct of large numbers of policemen: or it may be that he cannot make an identification. In any event, many inarticulate and working-class people remain at a disadvantage in using any complaints procedure, and require patience and time if – in the police's interest as well as their own – their sense of grievance is to be dispelled. At present a middle-class person's prospects of having his complaint upheld is 3.5 times as great as someone who is working-class. And virtually no complaint originating from a person who was arrested and subsequently found guilty, or from anyone who has a criminal record, has been upheld.

Dealing properly with complaints is a heavy investment of police resources and manpower. Currently nearly 2,000 complaints are being investigated every day in Metropolitan London alone – often meticulously; when a visiting American professor recently wrote a spontaneous letter of commendation because a policeman drove him home after his car crashed, he was astonished to receive in reply a visit from the officer's superior, concerned lest there had been a pay-off. And John Cheney, a former chief constable of Buckinghamshire, once set a famous example by successfully prosecuting himself after a traffic collision which he had anonymously referred to the county's clerk of the peace. Even a trivial complaint activates the same cumbersome machinery: yet the resentment a trivial incident may engender can, if not dealt with, cause wholly disproportionate damage to relations with the public. Often there are constructive lessons to be learnt from some complaints, even where no police misconduct is proved. Frequently the communication of the outcome of an investigation could be greatly improved: a senior officer should offer to discuss the result with genuine complainants. Such efforts are valuable for the police as well as necessary for society. The virtue of its policemen is one key criterion of any nation. Any sweeping under the carpet of criminal misconduct by those who are in authority can lead only to greater damage and further danger.

EIGHT

The Cost of Freedom: The Police's Future

'Beyond the many faces of crime, the police confront the leading edge of attempts to cause change outside the system of law. . . . The policeman is the man in the middle. It is imperative that he stay in the middle. . . . A government can endure only if those who enforce its laws have the confidence and support of the public they serve.'
Ramsey Clark

'How do you equate a belief in freedom with a police force? The old answer is by putting them in a psychological ghetto. No wonder they don't like us much.'
George Melly

Democratic policing in theory acts as a balance between the rights and needs of the citizen as an individual and his responsibilities as a member of the community. But to perform his role the modern police officer needs to be not only a lawyer and a social worker, but also something of a scientist, marriage counsellor, mediator, criminologist, sex, race and community relations psychologist and youth worker, together with having some skill as an athlete, accountant and marksman, and in dealing with drug and mental problems. In addition it is necessary for him in his job to be knowledgeable about politics and current events, although he is never allowed to participate in them. Few people advocate either the police's abolition, or that they should be run by private enterprise. Only the purest anarchist can envisage society without any police – and in practice he might well need to look to some service which would safeguard an anarchist state from being abrogated. Only the most optimistic foresee the situation portrayed in Mrozek's satirical play *The Police*, where the police have been so successful that they have made themselves redundant, and are attacked by the public among whom they try to provoke some crime or subversion in an effort to justify their existence. In the absence of 'those dressed in a little brief authority', the strongest will inevitably oppress and the crooked exploit the weakest in society. That there is too much avoidable human suffering and fear as a result of crime, no one can deny.

Yet the actuality is that a country's policing inevitably reflects its internal politics. Sir Robert Mark believes that 'in the long run it is the social contest in which they work which will always determine both the acceptability and effectiveness of the police, and the broad similarity of the police function in different countries obscures fundamental differences.' The nineteenth-century writer Alexander Herzen said that whereas seeing a policeman in Russia has an effect like a tile falling on one's head, in England the same sight surprisingly increased one's sense of security. In democracies, we prefer that our police should be too weak rather than too strong. As demands and pressure on the police increase annually, the alternative to improving the police service is the more threatening option of an even more powerful private security industry plus the growth of local vigilantes. Those voices which are most active in demanding greater law and order are often just the same ones which are most vociferous in calling for cuts in public expenditure. Ever-increasing legislation and overdue improvements in the police's hours and pay are likely to erode any savings from the use of computers and other new technology; if the police are not provided with new resources and strength, they will be driven to re-examining their traditional work priorities. In the United States, Professor Richard Farmer already sees a situation where, since many people decline to obey laws, the costs of enforcement

> may be so high as to make controls impossible. While new laws are being added all the time, governments and taxpayers are not willing to spend the money to make them stick. ... If 1 per cent of the tax returns that are seriously wrong were to be taken to court, then we would have to find room in our crowded courts for 900,000 new cases. Nobody talks much about this, but already huge parts of the American economy are operating illegally. Perhaps a third to a half of all trucking is illegal but the trucks still run, because the laws would need perhaps 30 million policemen to enforce properly.

In Britain, different but equally important questions of social principle are raised by, for example, the police's recent inability to safeguard the right of public political procession because of shortage of manpower, and the new threats from violent terrorism and thc techniques developed by the police to counter it. The police are currently going through a difficult and transitional stage in their existence, and their relationship with society around them is no longer either as readily definable or as secure as it used to be. The challenge they are faced with is whether they can assume a broader role – of being more social workers and less authoritarian symbols – in a society from which their new impersonal technology and specialized squads have largely isolated them.

Most policemen stand so close to their work, and have so little time for detached reflection about it, that they find it difficult to consider their response to such problems. The role of a police service is delicate, crucial, complicated and conspicuous. The police will always (as was seen in the last chapter) have to resign themselves to suffering more complaints than any other profession or service; uniquely, in their case, assiduity is often as little welcomed as inefficiency. In addition to being exposed in the same way as doctors or lawyers to allegations that they have in some way fallen short of their duty, the police receive nearly twice as many complaints that they have exceeded their duty. In 1977, complaints were made against 11,978 Metropolitan police officers out of a total strength in the force of 22,174. A considerable number of the allegations made by motorists and criminals may be conscious or subconscious attempts to justify misconduct on their own part. It is not surprising that some policemen become stoically immune to criticism, for the demands that the public make are often conflicting and incompatible; officers are told by councillors or the press to 'clean up all vice' and at the same time to 'make allowances for human nature'. And the client of a brothel or street-walker may be the very same man who is most vocal in complaining about the toleration of an abortionist.

A car driver who is angry with other motorists who exceed the speed limit while he himself is not doing so is often equally indignant when the positions are reversed. Many complaints against the police arise out of their duties in connection with traffic. Motoring is most often blamed by members of the public who feel that relations with the police have deteriorated; yet people who consider themselves law-abiding can reveal unexpected characteristics when behind the wheel of a car. In 1976 there were over two million prosecutions for traffic offences in Britain, compared with one million in 1960 – more than one for every nine vehicles on the road. The police themselves regret and are apprehensive about this trend as much as anybody. More experiments should be tried like that of the Southend-on-Sea police who dealt with 300 traffic offenders by explaining their faults to them and, in some cases, giving them advanced driving lessons instead of taking them to court.

There is a steady rise in other categories of offences among people who do not normally regard themselves as enemies of the police, including cases of drunkenness and tax-evasion. Recent demonstrations have also involved other and highly articulate sections of the population, some of them holding strong principles, and many of whom are at a young and formative age. In addition, racial prejudice has augmented the numbers of minority groups who find most difficulty in integrating into the community.

'Of course nowadays we tend to get a better class of villain on the job,' said a detective sergeant. But even law-abiding people have always had a curiously ambivalent attitude towards policemen and criminals. Almost universal hostility greeted the earliest police officers when they first appeared; today many people still seem reluctant to take sides in what they tend to regard as a private war between police and criminals. A fear of getting involved may often be due to unwillingness to become a witness, but it can also go deeper. People sometimes think that an offence does not constitute a sufficient threat to society; they may have a sneaking envy of the criminal, like admiration for the rebel and Robin Hood throughout history. Most fiction-writers and a number of journalists find it easier to sympathize with a criminal than with a police officer. Smugglers have always been more popular than customs officers. We associate crimes with forbidden pleasures, and also feel a lack of identification with, for example, a massively wealthy bank, hotel or factory that has been robbed. People are attracted by the 'sporting' element in crime, particularly if no violence is used; some boast with pride at their skill at diddling the tax-inspector or the storekeeper at their works. Many modern business practices can be hardly distinguished from 'white-collar crime' – delinquent activity that is generally socially accepted.

The police's inability to strike or publicly protest means we take them too much for granted. Ironically, the more professional the police become, the less communal responsibility much of society feels for helping with law enforcement. Acting as neighbourhood politicians who interpret the state to their constituents, the leaders of our police have always recognized that their ability to fulfil their functions depends on public approval. But today, as the late Colin MacInnes – no apologist for the police – said, 'They are doing the difficult and dangerous job society demands without any understanding by society of what their moral and professional problems are.' The public use the police as a scapegoat for their neurotic attitude towards crime and own lack of social responsibility, as well as for resentment that should more properly be aimed at the government. Schizophrenically Janus-like, we have always turned at least two different faces towards a policeman, as we do towards any symbolic hero-figure our age lacks. We expect him to be human and yet at the same time para-human. We welcome official protection, yet resent official interference. We employ him to administer the law, and yet will ask him to waive it. We resent him when he enforces a law in our own case, yet demand his dismissal when he does not elsewhere. We offer him bribes, yet denounce his corruption. We expect him to be a member of society, yet not to share its prejudices and values. We admire violence, even against society itself, but condemn force by the police on our behalf. We tell a policeman that he is entitled to information from the public, though we ostracize informers; we ask for crime to be eradicated, but only by the use of 'sporting' methods. Yet we also expect him to cut corners to fight crime, without being willing to share responsibility for this with him. We criticize, fail to support, and deceive him; yet we cannot escape depending on him.

The paradoxes of policing are reciprocated. The police were created, and derive the necessity for their continued existence, from the human failings they dislike and try to eliminate. Even in his judicial detachment, a policeman still needs and is anxious for public support. He is uneasy about how little he is esteemed; but he often arouses antagonism in those he is meant to be protecting. Disliked as well as admired, his role is to cause fear at the same time as it is to reassure. Despite this, and the constant pessimism of policemen themselves, their general relations with the public on the whole remain very good. Clive Davies of Liverpool University found in a Merseyside survey that even among slum-dwellers 70 per cent of people thought of the police as 'friends', compared with only 3 per cent who considered them 'enemies'; and that 86 per cent of the poorest inhabitants wanted more police in their area, compared with 2 per cent who wanted fewer.

In the face of such and similar findings, it is interesting to ask why there is such gloomy alarm among the police themselves concerning their work and their relations with the public. Roy Jenkins publicly advised the Police Federation in 1976 to 'be more self-confident and less self-pitying'. Their blackening of criminals and the crime situation is to be expected, as self-justification and reinforcement for their own identity and self-respect (even though crime is only one part of their work); and it is true that they alone see the whole of reported crime, including the two-thirds which is not cleared up. But regarding their relationship with the public, even after the reassurance of the last Royal Commission's surveys, 58 per cent of British policemen who were asked by the author in 1963 how they thought relations between the police and the public were then, compared with before the Second World War, replied that they were worse, compared with 10 per cent who said they were better and 12 per cent who said they were the same. The Social Survey for the Royal Commission suggested one reason for this:

> There is a further not inconsiderable disadvantage in police work, and this is the burden of social isolation that the police feel their position carries. This isolation is experienced not only by the police themselves but to some extent by their wives and children as well. In these respects police work is probably unique. It follows that the police are continually in a defensive position and any real or imagined criticism from individuals or sections of the general public, the press, or authorities such as the courts or Members of Parliament is liable to produce in the police mind a distorted impression of what the public in general feel about them. There is no way in which the police can assess changes of opinion in their favour, as praise is less likely to be expressed than criticism.

An officer serving in a Scottish country force wrote to me,

> That I am becoming embittered and disillusioned by much that I have seen in three short years is not in doubt. This concerns me deeply as an individual who has what could be described as a 'social conscience'. ... It has been said that we only get the police force we deserve. How true this is, and how distressing to those of us in the service who care very deeply about the quality of service we provide, when we get the feeling that however hard we work for the protection and safety of our neighbours, they don't really give a damn what happens to their police service.

This feeling of isolation is even greater in urban areas. Such feelings can be carried to extraordinary degrees. One inspector, who had served for twenty years in the Metropolitan force, wrote when he retired: 'Few people other than dear old ladies and foreigners really liked the London policeman. The vast majority longed to score off him. Many feared and hated him as much as he feared and hated them.' Serving policemen describe themselves as 'the third pigmentation – white, black, and blue'; and as 'the country's untouchables – doing all the jobs that other people don't want.' They say that 'the public dislike us until they need our help,' and that 'the public stand by and leave it all to a policeman, and are then delighted when he goes wrong so that they can complain.' Some officers speak very bitterly of the public's lack of loyalty, and even more so of journalists and lawyers who often make them feel that it is the police who are on trial instead of the criminal. (Under cross-examination in the witness-box, a police officer's whole justification and self-value is liable to be challenged; hence their warm expressions of fondness for defending barristers.) Other policemen wondered if they themselves were not affected by thinking of the public only in terms of perverts, nuisances or complainants. A sizeable proportion of police work is concerned with drunks, addicts, the mentally disturbed, sick, or dead people. When a policeman deals with other men or women, many are in a shocked or degraded state; it is very much less often that he gets the opportunity to see any of the good in people. One young officer in London said that when the public always appeared to be dependent on him for elementary information about directions or the time, it was easy for him to feel that the public were fools and the police superior; however, in some US cities, overseas visitors who inquire the route from a cop may receive the reply 'Go buy a map!' If the police's losing battle against crime is coupled with social isolation, there is a danger that they will increasingly see the public as 'them' – a nuisance, if not an enemy – and hence will lose touch with the public's views as well as their help.

The police, rightly, claim they must be allowed discretion in their work; consequently they cannot object to public scrutiny or accountability as to how they exercise this discretion. But the most frequent complaint made by a policeman against members of the public is that the latter forget they have any responsibilities or duty to help the police, though the same people are never slow to remember their rights. In the Social Survey for the Royal Commission, 87 per cent of the police considered that the public did not do enough to help them (and 75 per cent of the public who were questioned agreed). Increased wealth has caused more people to insure their property and not to worry unduly about its loss. Many stores today do little or nothing to discourage shoplifting; a few even say they are pleased when it occurs because it proves the attractiveness of self-service from their open-shelf display. Witnesses are deterred from coming forward by the delays and adjournments of many criminal processes. Unless they themselves or their personal friends are threatened, people are reluctant to interfere and report suspicious circumstances; the civic responsibility of many people in peacetime often extends only to people they know, and stops short of the full community. This is a problem which any democratic government should tackle urgently. Not only might those who show courage by going to the help of the police figure more often in the Honours List and receive more generous compensation when they are injured, but civics and discussions of the causes of crime should (as in Japan) be part of every school curriculum. Few European university departments are doing research on police problems. Senior officers should also hold regular conferences at police headquarters in order to exchange views on issues of policing. Particularly in racially or socially mixed areas, local inhabitants should be invited regularly to meet the police to work out solutions to local problems of tension and crime. It would also pay the police to follow up and personally thank people who did help them; one man who has given them assistance on six occasions during his life complained that he had never heard the outcome of any of the cases.

For the individual police officer, morale – based on his and the public's view of his work – is the most pressing problem of all. Relations between the police and the public have not necessarily worsened in recent years, but they have altered. Both bodies have become more distant and less human to each other as each has become increasingly urbanized and motorized. Even if he is not a motorist himself, the man in the street is cut off from direct contact with a policeman who is in a patrol car. The trend is carried to an even further degree in the United States. Studies there have shown that public attitudes towards the police result primarily from personal interaction between individual citizens and police officers, and the evidence in this country is that both are suffering from increasing isolation from each other. Police relations still tend to be better in rural communities and small towns, and at their worst in large cities, because in the village the policeman is still known by his name as 'Mr —', whereas in the city he is an anonymous figure in uniform. Police officers say that the most difficult districts of all are the new housing estates – 'no community spirit and no informers,' one detective constable complained in a voice of despair. Chicago has recently experimented with the policy of allowing journalists and other observers to ride almost at random in its squad cars, perhaps on the assumption that anyone who shares their dangers and frustrations will change his attitude to the police. As the danger grows of the police becoming a defensive and introverted in-group, their links with the community weaken through their inability to control the latter informally by personal influence and authority. Self-respect is crucial to a policeman; inspector Jennifer Hilton has pointed out the relevance of self-fulfilling prophecies, and that bad stereotypes often produce bad behaviour.

Communication

The key to successful democratic policing lies to a considerable extent in the problems of communication. Is it inevitable that 'sheep never like their sheepdog', as one chief constable has said? Most policemen disagree, but too often only in a negative and defensive way. It is a disciplinary offence for a police officer to be uncivil to a member of the public: but the Police Federation say that 'the police service has not yet recognized that there is a public image of the police.' 'It's the public who need to learn about good relatons, not us,' one senior officer stated significantly. 'Too many chief constables,' a younger colleague remarked, 'just believe in shutting up and saying nothing.' Until recently, police relations with the press were limited to generally defensive contacts with a few crime reporters, and seldom risked initiatives explaining police problems and actions. Sir Robert Mark changed that in London, but in many other forces 'public relations' are still regarded as dirty words; if they are to have any effect they must be tackled with positive initiatives and not defensive passivity. There is much more to public relations than issuing an occasional success story to the press. Policemen, outnumbered by 500 to one, can never hope to be omnipotent without communual consent. 'Even the most powerful and arbitrary police state, in a simple rural environment,' Ramsey Clark says 'will be unable to frustrate the deep desires and secret acts of people.' In influencing the public's attitude towards them, the way the police do their job is almost as important as what they do. Relations with the community should be a major priority for all ranks, and not be concentrated merely in a special unit, which can lead to the idea that since community relations are the responsibility of the specialized team, the ordinary officer need not concern himself with them. Various government departments in the last few years have gradually come to realize that they must take the initiative in order to gain public understanding and goodwill: the British police are almost alone now in lacking a national department able to do this and also to reply to criticism. Much more could still be done by the police in explaining to the public reasons for their policies whenever possible, and in building a partnership by asking for cooperation. The potential causes for bad relations between the public and the police are so many, that good relations have to be worked at continually – even if most of the faults may be those of the public. Contact on a personal level will always, however, remain the most important factor. Wearing personal name badges would both emphasize officers' individual responsibility and make them appear more human than numbers do. In Detroit and some other police stations, officers also have their names on their desks and members of the public feel they are being treated as well as they would be in a well-run shop: whereas in many other American and British police stations witnesses feel as intimidated as if they were criminals. Too often the stations also are brutally designed and badly-kept buildings, depressing to work in and unwelcoming to the neighbourhood's inhabitants. It is wrong that some witnesses fear to talk to the police more than to press reporters.

Policemen should take every opportunity of exchanging views with the public in clubs, universities, schools, and on the radio and television. The Special Constables, who have a foot in each camp, could play a particularly important part in explaining to both sides the problems and points of friction. The Northern Ireland and Derby forces issue graphic well-designed annual reports, but many others miss opportunities by conveying little or nothing to their public. To most police officers, public speaking does not come as easily as it does to a Robert Mark or a John Alderson; but they have nevertheless a fund of knowledge about social problems. It is in the public's interest that policemen should be encouraged to speak their views; even if the listeners do not always agree with or like what they hear – such as some chief constables' reiterated calls for a return to Christian tenets, in a country where a great many people are no longer Christians – partiality is better known about than not realised. Public interest in police matters is enormous, as the insatiable audience figures for police programmes on television show. The public in fact have a right to know more about the actual police whom they pay for. At present it is largely left to novelists and script-writers to supply impressions and knowledge about the police to the public; many forces still have a detrimental cult of unnecessary secretiveness. In some cases this is due to fear in the police that crime might be helped by knowledge about themselves. The whole force is also proud of its tradition that they 'hear all, see all, and say nothing'. It is greatly to their credit that their immense knowledge concerning the private details of so many lives is never made public.

The media and the police

But the tradition of sealed lips has other, less fortunate, repercussions: it means that people rarely hear anything other than criticism concerning policemen. Their many instances of kindness and humanity are not reported; people never know when a policeman dips into his own pocket to help the family of a man in prison, or finds a job for a recidivist after his release. Most policemen are outstandingly helpful when breaking news of a death to relatives or friends. But such items have little news-value for newspapers. In addition they are sometimes illegal: one officer I know who allowed a prisoner on a very grave charge to visit his relative in hospital could have been in serious trouble. The absence of independent inquiries for many years led to a continuous ventilation of complaints about the police in Parliament and the newspapers. The obdurate incredulity shown by the police towards some complainants caused the latter to feel that the police would only take seriously a writ or an MP's question. Policemen intensely dislike politicians who try to make capital out of incidents concerning their work, and many officers have become very sensitive and even hostile towards the press as a result of reading only denigration of themselves. Of police officers questioned by the author in 1963, 72 per cent said that they thought reporters were unfair towards the police, together with another 8 per cent who said they were 'sometimes', compared with 14 per cent who said that in the main they were not. Complaints by policemen ranged from exaggerations and twisting of stories to the general charge that untrue allegations are rarely corrected when they are proved to be false. The Press Council might consider some rule whereby, after an allegation against anybody (police or otherwise) has been made and reported, a newspaper should be obliged to report the eventual determination of its outcome with equal prominence. Reporters are inclined to forget that individual policemen are unable to reply to allegations: even when a case is not *sub judice*, it is an offence in the police Disciplinary Code for a police officer to communicate to the public or the press without proper authority. Policemen also complain that their superiors 'do not back them up' sufficiently by challenging allegations or by putting these into their correct perspective before they are blown up into huge proportions. They also blame reporters for not ringing up the authorized police spokesman to hear his version before they rush into print and cause damage that no later denial – even if made – is ever able to repair.

Part of this ill-feeling between the police and the press is caused by a lack of understanding about each other's function and difficulties. In 1978 Scotland Yard asked the BBC for the right to view its documentary programmes about the police in advance, and to cut out anything it found offensive. The main aim of a newspaper (although often the last reason it gives) is to sell copies. News – and the police are always news – must be printed quickly or not at all. When the police are asked for their verion of some story, it is frequently not forthcoming for several days, either because the matter is *sub judice* or because it takes time to make a thorough investigation. By the time a refutation or explanation is available newspapers feel it has little interest for readers. With certain crime reporters whom they know and trust, the police have working relationships in an informal lobby system: sometimes they feed them exclusive news in exchange for information (reporters can, and do, give witnesses money to speak, when the police cannot). Each side tries to make use of the other through their personal contacts. Robert Mark was the first to grasp the fact that the press in general was a potential ally, not a rival – and could also be used as a weapon to try to get the changes in the law which he wanted. In 1978 (unlike Scotland Yard), Kenneth Oxford, Merseyside's chief constable, allowed the BBC freely to film the reality of police work. Policemen's main complaints about the press are often directed against sub-editors, whom they feel are frequently only interested in building up a sensation, and irresponsibly tend to ignore any wider implications of how they present news about the police or a criminal. The media have been made the scapegoats for the police's belief that the public are incomprehensibly and irredeemably ungrateful. Many senior police officers believe that crime is encouraged by newspapers glamourizing it and describing successful methods: others feel that a few papers are actually malicious towards the police and report them only in such a way as to give the impression 'that they are never able to put a boot right'. Both sides are resentful because of each other's lack of cooperation in the past, though on occasions when the police have taken the press into their confidence, it has helped by withholding a story, or by keeping the search for somebody in the public attention. With their local newspapers police forces on the other hand generally have a good relationship, because each depends on and has learnt to live with the other. The actual degree of liaison is set by the individual chief constable; some have appointed a public relations and a press officer; others remain deeply suspicious of either. It is essential in order to do the job successfully that a police press officer should know the workings of both the service and the press, and also should enjoy the full confidence of his chief constable.

Relations with the press as well as the public should be part of all ranks' training. A central bureau is also needed which could speak on behalf of the police nationally; at present the service suffers because forces and ranks are fragmented and each is unable to speak for all. (The Home Office has always been reluctant to arouse suspicions of central interference: the Police Federation do not possess all the facts: chief constables and superintendents meet only occasionally: local police authorities are too slow.) The more open and accountable the police are, the more likely they are to be supported and their problems and work appreciated.

At present not only the best, but virtually the only, attempt to increase public understanding about the police is being done by television programmes. Certainly for the urban population in Britain and the US, television has now replaced personal contact as the main source of the public's superficial impression of the police. (Is it possible that people's failure to intervene in cases like the Genovese one is because they feel the detachment of spectators of a film?) Views about the police – like those about other minority groups – easily become stereotyped. People forget that inside police uniforms are individual human characters, perhaps young and inexperienced or tired and worried. One of the virtues of series like *Z Cars*, *Softly, Softly* and *Kojak* (although the episodes are too well written to convey the monotony of much police life, and there is more swearing in a real squad car than there is on the screen) is that without patronizing them it shows policemen as individuals with problems in relationships among themselves as well as towards the outside world. Many serving police officers think such programmes give 'as accurate a picture of police life as you are likely to get', and often they watch them compulsively. *Dixon of Dock Green* on the other hand they used to describe as 'an overgrown Boy Scout looking for his good deed' ('It's a good image, but it doesn't fool anyone nowadays', said one serving PC). But – significantly – some senior police officers have attacked instead the realism of *Z Cars*. 'I hate it,' said one deputy chief constable, 'it shows no respect for the police.' '*Z Cars* is a typical bad example whereas *Dixon* is a good example,' said the chief constable of another force. It is true that the programmes have begun to affect the police: some policemen feel a danger that they have begun copying the image of them portrayed in these 'urbanized Westerns' on the screen. But in fact most of these programmes and films, by showing the human problems and tensions of the police, can do them nothing but good: realism is just what public thinking about both the police and crime so badly needs. (What the effect is on the average American child of having viewed some 11,000 fictitious murders by the time he or she is fourteen years old is another question.)

The public's fascination with law enforcement television programmes, and films such as *The French Connection* or *Serpico* which portray the ambivalence of police life, seems insatiable. They mine deep traditional seams, particularly in masculine preoccupations: vengeance, violence, ends and means. In the US as many as twenty-nine different police series occupy a third of prime network time and have ousted Westerns as the most popular viewing on television. More than one in every three American policemen themselves watch them regularly, and the majority do so occasionally. But, despite the rule on American television that the police always get their man, only 12 per cent of policemen there who were questioned thought that such programmes increased respect for the police, compared with 76 per cent who thought that they lessened it – mainly by rousing expectations that could not possibly be fulfilled. Sir Colin Woods remarked that to be really true to life, the majority of police dramas should end with a mystified look on the detective officer's face, instead of every case being solved in fifty minutes – perhaps to reassure viewers worried that the real crime situation may be getting out of control. Other officers criticize, 'They're all so deadly serious – they don't show the zany side of police life.' And it is conspicuous that no television policeman ever expresses racist views, because of fears of weakening the standing of the police: all the series' writers are basically sympathetic to the police, though the best are credible about their faults.

Self-policing

Since the public are part of the police, as much as vice versa, it is obviously logical to encourage society's involvement in good policing as much as possible in order to create a symbiotic common interest. Strategically, this would counter the danger that problems of crime, social order and peace-keeping are felt to be concerns of the police alone, instead of all society. It also makes tactical sense, because it would be shortsighted in the extreme to skimp on housing or education to pay for a greatly strengthened police – and therefore the community itself must help.

Self-policing on a basis of social obligation and mutual responsibility is an ideal for the future, yet even that can have its risks, and professional police might be needed for example to protect unpopular minorities from vigilantes. But one corrective to a more centrally-assisted police service would be to give each neighbourhood more say in its local policemen's work. Some centralized professional policing will always remain necessary to combat corruption and favouritism as well as professional crime, and to operate in those areas where community norms are weakest. But without ceding control, neighbourhood police officers should at least meet the people of their community regularly to exchange and discuss local problems and their solution. The bulk of police work is concerned not with dramatic crimes, but with everyday public order and service. If the community's responsibility and interest in preventing and reducing less serious infractions of the law, such as vandalism, were encouraged, the professional police service would be freed to concentrate more of its time and resources on dealing with serious and dangerous crimes. Even though attempts at local control have not been encouraging either in Northern Ireland or the southern United States, neighbourhood links – as distinct from political groups – could play a role in humanizing police forces: and community policing, when successful, has the virtue of being continuous and positively preventive rather than always reacting tardily *post facto*. At present, modern police techniques based on patrol cars have separated the public from its police. Strong community ties – from schools to the shop floor – are not only the best hope but the traditional foundation for all successful police work, including the containment and reduction of crime. The basis for such ties can only be mutual confidence and respect: if the police should ever lose these, there is no way a force of 100,000 men can police a country of 50 million people. As the last Royal Commission emphasized, the areas where at present confidence and respect are weakest are between the police and the poor, the young, and minorities, if only because this is where much of the police's activity is concentrated – and will continue to be until society corrects its injustices.

With authority no longer receiving automatic deference, Michael Banton prescribes that in today's circumstances new methods are needed to inculcate social norms: there will have to be greater reliance upon internal controls deriving from early socialization and schooling, rather than upon external sanctions such as punishments. Whenever possible, vandals and other criminals should be made to make restitution for the damage they have caused. In any event, stronger community involvement has the best chance of taking root in small-sized neighbourhoods: in such areas, where people know each other better, the clear-up rate is three times as high as in anonymous cities. Despite other appalling social problems, there is a surprisingly low crime rate in some African shanty towns, because of a sense of community feeling in them which is absent in London or New York. As John Alderson explains,

> You can go through various stages in the development of the police. First of all, it's a community responsibility without a police force. Then you set up a sort of police force and part-pay it, and then the whole thing becomes too complicated. You have to reform the police, highly professionalize it, push in lots of resources, higher training, equipment, technology and so forth. And you can then reach a stage – a frame of mind in society where you think crime is only the business of the police. You pay a police force, you pay it well, you equip it well, and you expect them to do the job and it's no concern of yours as a member of the community. Now we've to get out of that frame of mind and turn back to first principles and say to the community: here we are, we're a professional police force, we're limited in expansion by economic restraints, so now we're turning to you to help us. ... Parents, teachers, social workers, probation officers, police and innumerable voluntary organizations all have a part to play.

As resources to combat crime fail to measure up to the demands the only way to slow down or halt the present rise in crime lies in community policing, promoting an active communal response to the problem without in any way invoking the vigilante. Alderson has pioneered a 'community policing consultative group' in Exeter. In New York, policemen are using bicycles instead of panda cars in an attempt to gain closer ties with the public: but in several other areas police stations have been made to resemble forbidding fortresses through fear of possible terrorist attack.

The most law-abiding capital city in the non-communist world at present is Tokyo. In Japan, alone of developed countries, the statistics for most categories of crime have in recent years gone down: Tokyo now has only two-thirds of the crime that London has, despite its population of 11.6 million being considerably larger; criminal violence has been reduced over the past decade to half the rate prevalent in Britain. (There were 1.1 crimes per 100 people in Japan in 1975, down from 1.7 twenty years earlier. In Britain in 1977 there were 5 indictable crimes per 100 people, four times the rate twenty years ago.) Since every other capital faces a seemingly inexorable increase in crime, might there be some lessons to be learnt from Tokyo? The basis of the police system there is 1,237 *kobans* or corner police stations, many of them residential, each manned by ten foot-patrol officers working four shifts round the clock and who total 37 per cent of the city's 40,655 police force. Each officer has special responsibility for 300 or so families on his beat, and civilian volunteers are responsible for every thirty households. One result is that relations between the police and the general public are noticeably more friendly and less tensely confrontational than they are in America or Europe.

The future of the police

If it is true that a society gets the police that it deserves, the time has come for more realistic thinking about the police and their problems. Over a period of many years there has been a serious lack of research into these: Royal Commissions have been asked to report virtually in a vacuum. Britain should cease relying – in this as in other contemporary issues – on complacent generalizations about alleged 'national characteristics'. The government should no longer hesitate to spend heavily on research or on gaining people's goodwill for public services: it should recognize that doing so will save immeasurable friction and expenditure in future years. Private commercial companies are far more alive to such necessities than public services are, for which they are infinitely more essential. It is the old story of private waste and public squalor: only public servants who are unable to strike would have had their pay neglected for as long as that of the police. The service has in the past been given too many pious platitudes instead of support from the public or adequate finance from successive governments. The harvest of years of parsimony cannot be reversed overnight; their accumulated effect on police manpower means that entry tests at present are being used more to reject the worst than to select high-calibre new recruits. Physical health is necessary for a policeman, but modern conditions require that more emphasis in the future must be given to intelligence, character and attitude. IQ and temperament tests should be part of a more scientific selection procedure for recruits, which should concentrate on attributes such as common sense, honesty, emotional stability and a sense of fairness and tact, rather than on physical prowess: the police rely more on moral suasion than on physical force in their work. Whereas totalitarian countries only require unthinking public servants such as Eichmann, individual responsibility among public servants remains an essential safeguard in a democracy. The police themselves are endemically apprehensive about the future, and especially about the results of the particularly lean decade of recruiting in the 1950s (when police pay lagged behind industrial earnings throughout the period between demobilization and the Royal Commission). The courses at Bramshill are commendable efforts to plug the future gaps; but many policemen fear that the new approach to training was both introduced too late and reaches too few to change overall mixed attitudes in the service.

Since 1960 the number of reported indictable offences has more than trebled while the actual strength of the British police has increased by about one half. The effective increase in police strength is even less, because of reductions in working hours and the additions of new tasks. Wastage is, and is likely to remain, an even greater problem than recruitment. In 1977 it was higher in Britain than ever before: new police strength fell in that year by 1,200 in England and Wales and by another 270 in Scotland. In Metropolitan London, where the police are already most over-stretched, the force's net decrease of 191 left it 4,389 (over 16 per cent) below its minimal establishment. 'We expect policemen to be Solomons and we pay them as dustmen,' said one superintendent prior to the Edmund Davies committee's increases. 'Society is not entitled to want them to be so perfect.' Overwork could be reduced if we were prepared to spend more money; but it is even more necessary for a policeman to feel that his job is constructive, interesting, and valued by society, if he is going to be resilient to its inevitable frustrations. Work satisfaction, recognition and self-respect are as important as pay to most officers.

The attractive myth of a policeman being only a member of the public in uniform cannot be perpetuated; in fact he increasingly performs a number of professional roles, each of which requires extensive specialized training. The advent of personal radios has changed the individual autonomy of the single law officer on his beat into a function based on specialized and team policing. The changes that psychology, sociology and politics have brought about in general attitudes to criminal behaviour have made the work of policemen much more complicated. Their skills too must therefore develop. For their work of prevention they will increasingly need to become agents of social welfare; to succeed in detection they will have to succeed as scientists. If one lesson appears throughout the chapters of this book, it is that it is not the changes in modern society which affect the morale of the police (as the Royal Commission thought), but the reluctance of the police themselves to adapt to many of those changes. It is true that the roots of many of the problems the police have to contend with – such as political and racial tensions, people's greater mobility and impersonality in urban society, the weakening of traditional institutions such as religion and the family, advertising's emphasis on conspicuous status symbols, ever-increasing traffic, the effects of poor urban environments on young people – lie outside their control; often they can only try to cope with the symptoms. But successive Home Secretaries have, when declining to make a reform, sheltered behind the excuse that police opinion would not at present stand for it – sometimes giving the impression that society exists for the benefit of the police rather than vice versa. The training of a policeman should equip him to adjust to new conditions: a knowledge of psychology, for example, would help him in both his fields of preventive and detective work. Our national cult of the amateur has in the past not always provided policemen with sufficient training to give them the several skills their job requires. The training itself should progress organically and not be restricted to the ideas current when a man was recruited: the more senior an officer becomes, the more important it is for him to be able to learn about and make use of new developments. In order that he can keep in touch with legal, social, and scientific changes, every policeman should be given a refresher course of at least two weeks a year. And the national inspectorate – which must be extended to London – should be both strengthened and used more effectively for disseminating inter-force and international advances in methods and research, incorporating the work done by the Police Foundation and the National Criminal Justice Reference Service in the United States.

The police will in the future inevitably face many difficulties due to being human agents of stability during times of rapid change. As Professor Michael Banton says, 'The police have to bear the brunt of the disorder resulting from the mistakes of previous generations and the country's inability to satisfy the aspirations it encourages.' In the developed countries, as rising unemployment (particularly among younger people in stagnant economies) becomes commonplace, expectations of mass materialist consumption continue to be advertised without being coupled with any offer of legitimate means of satisfying them. A key help for the police would be national policies which unite the society they work in. Instead, increasingly, the police are faced with social problems for which the criminal law manual offers no solution. They are expected to try to shore up and plug the results of society's and governments' weaknesses and deficiencies. Like the 'other ranks' in the services, the police bear the immediate and often unpleasant impact of policies and decisions about which they are not consulted. Their work has not become easier because people today are less credulous of the simple myth of good men versus bad: one officer complained, 'The younger generation who have grown up since the war are no longer certain it is possible to say what is right or wrong.' But at the same time as our society has become more permissive in moral matters, it has also become readier to intervene in other directions – though more uncertain what it should do to the individual when it does intervene. The principle of state interference – in particular in the shape of creating public welfare offences – has been accepted in many fields, yet we remain undecided about the means and ends of such intervention. Both developments have complicated the concept and work of the police. The late Arnold Toynbee predicted that economic deterioration in the developed world will result in 'a severely regimented way of life ... imposed by ruthless authoritarian government.' Anthony Burgess forecasts for the future that 'the police, being powerfully syndicalized, will approach autonomy in its modes of keeping order. It will be the alternative criminal class.' But police leaders like John Alderson are clear that 'the police in a democracy are not an agency to be used in the prevention of change'; rather that the job of the police is to see that change takes place in democratic ways.

Such problems are not unique to Britain and affect a growing number of countries: in time some form of West European, and eventually a UN, police service will probably evolve. The alternative to a good police service however is people taking law into their own hands, whether as vigilantes or terrorists. As Charles Reith argued, in a democratic country the police's dependence on public approval results in the dividing line being drawn between liberty for the individual's self-expression and his licence to exploit the weakness of others.

The police's power of discretion will inevitably cause them to be involved in the administration of justice, but the study and treatment of crime have now become specialized sciences. A police officer in New York described the change in his function, which is similar to what has taken place in the UK: 'In the old days the cop on the beat kept the peace by handing out kerbstone justice. The only time he took anything to court was when he couldn't handle it with his night-stick.' At the same time as fulfilling their primary role of seeing that crime does not pay, the police could make a much greater contribution to the study of its cure. 'Crime', being a loose generic term for a wide variety of behaviour, elicits correspondingly wide responses.

But – as in medicine – before any successful treatment of criminals can be achieved, it is first necessary to diagnose the causes of criminal behaviour: our punishments have lacked success in the past because of our ignorance about what we are trying to cure or deter. If trained to be able to analyse their experience, all police officers could provide valuable field reports. In their work they accumulate first-hand knowledge of the social causes of crime which the simplistic slogans of some of their leaders do not always reflect. The present trend in penal policy towards probation and parole makes such studies of criminals in the setting of the community of greater value than research about them in the artificial environment of closed institutions. Police officers' experience could be combined with the findings of academic researchers and others at, for example, Bramshill to formulate reforms in criminal law, criminology and other social problems. In the past policemen have tended to be suspicious of progress in penal reform: but a greater contribution by the police to socio-psychiatric research into crime would constitute in fact the modern form of the preventive role which they have always had. Its development should in turn bring benefits to them by helping to decrease the crime problem with which they are faced. If more money was spent by the government on constructive penal treatment, the work of the police would also be lightened: but such policies invariably have low priority among the promises made by all parties at election time.

How far the police should develop as active social workers, as distinct from making a passive contribution to the study of criminology, is a more open question. Some police officers and probation officers at present misunderstand each other's role: other policemen are developing formally or instinctively into case-workers hardly distinguishable from probation officers. It is difficult to deny the illogicality of training a man as a police officer and then employing him full-time in a juvenile liaison project. But just as prison officers have recently realized, it would enormously improve the morale and standing of the police (as well as the quality of their recruiting) if they were trained to deal with people as skilfully as they are taught to protect property. Police thinking would profit if it more often came out of its shell and concerned itself with wider questions about the role of the police and human relations. Since police life is unable to attract enough recruits from universities, serving policemen should instead become graduates: many more officers should be seconded to universities for courses and degrees. Abroad, the University of Pennsylvania, for example, has provided several hundred scholarships for police officers to study administration and human relations.

Improvements in the police's skills and technical resources will require money, at a time when national resources are limited. (One argument for the public ownership of insurance is the justice of this helping to pay the cost of the police and fire services, whose greater efficiency contributes to insurance profits.) Ideally most people would like a police service which is both efficient and humane. But as its tasks have increased in number and difficulty, it has not been supplied with the equivalent advances in training or equipment to accomplish them. When people do not adequately help or support the police, the result is that some officers develop their own less desirable methods against criminals. Sentimentality – from which the police themselves are not free, as their 'Black Museum' at Scotland Yard, with its bloodstained floorboards and rope-nooses, shows – has for too long caused maudlin writers to describe criminal behaviour in terms such as 'the art of murder'. Now that crime has for many years been increasing at a faster rate than our population, it is time to recognize the human harm it causes and to approach the whole subject scientifically. Having decided which measures are necessary for its prevention, while being at the same time compatible with liberty and the protection of the innocent, the gaps should be closed between theory and practice: at present the public square their consciences by playing a criminal with 'sporting' rules, and then making policemen the scapegoats if he is not caught or the rules are broken. One of the principal reasons for the excessive solidarity among policemen which is acting to the public detriment today is their consciousness that they need to employ quasi-legal (and sometimes illegal) means in order to trap criminals.

Much will depend on the leadership of the police service in the future. Sir David McNee can be counted on to pursue the restoration of integrity in the Metropolitan force as firmly as his predecessor. He is a quiet, strongly religious man, and even though many of the problems of his previous post and birthplace of Glasgow are different from those of London, he places great emphasis on the strengthening of community relations at the local level which he developed in Strathclyde: 'Frankly there is no more important man in the police service than the beat constable ... He is the first person to meet the public, usually in a moment of crisis, and upon his action rests the member of the public's impression of the whole police service.' Whereas Sir Robert Mark did a brilliant external job for the police which left him little time for his constituency, McNee is likely to be the converse. Mark was not the stereotyped liberal his critics imagined – though it was especially important to have such a civilized man as police Commissioner at the potentially hysterical time of the terrorist bombings – but was cogent and original in his views as well as courageous in expressing them. He was the first political – in a non-party sense – leader that the traditionally silent police have had in Britain; he believed in speaking directly to the public in an attempt to generate the reforms he believed were needed. This also had an intended effect on police morale: 'Before he came,' said one colleague, 'we had this Victorian attitude to our proper place in society.'

But once the police are given adequate powers we must then see that they keep to them. In law-enforcement ends never justify even slightly dubious means: official violence or threats undermine a society more surely than the crime they are intended to prevent. A society which resorts to them finishes by being the victim of them. It is a tragedy when the admirable bulk of the police service becomes linked with the image of a few bullies: it is vital for the police themselves that such men should be identified and expelled at the earliest possible moment. Their senior officers should remember that even though the prosecution and dismissal of these men is painful, the police will always be judged by the highest standards, because a single policeman has power to do great harm to other people as well as to the reputation of the force.

The maintenance of police morale depends, not on whitewash, but on a satisfying conception of the policeman's place in society. Most judges, for example, have high standards not because they are intrinsically different men from the people they have to judge but because of their concept of the job. The same self-respect is the key to excellence in the police force. An even greater degree of independence in inquiries than at present is essential: the police of a country whose justice depends on the jury cannot afford to lack the confidence of the public. Every means should be employed to develop this rapport. In the same way as CID officers at present have too little time to cultivate their vital contacts, so the uniformed Dogberry is growing increasingly distant from the public. His presence on the ground is scarcest where he is most needed – in the large conurbations. Urban migration and the break-up of old communities have exacerbated policing problems: no constable can patrol a tower-block of flats as he used to do a terraced street. To help diminish the isolation caused partly by an era of technology, the police's radio network should be linked to portable radios which should be provided, for example, to doctors and the drivers of buses, taxis and trains. Now that more than 80 per cent of Britain's population are living in towns – a pattern that, it is forecast, will be followed in other developed countries – it has become important that urban police areas should be split up into localized communities; the police as well as town-planners can encourage a sense of belonging in a neighbourhood. The growth of professionalism can insulate the police from the public's needs and feelings as well as from undesirable corrupt or political pressures: new ways must therefore be found to integrate the police in the community. It is in the interests of everybody to stop the development of a separate police culture, and to minimize the suspicion and antagonism which can become mutual between the police and the public. For their part, the police should attempt to increase their contacts and exchanges with the public – and particularly young people – on friendly and helpful occasions; work such as the crime prevention lectures and driving instruction they are giving in some areas should be extended throughout the country. Community relations should be a priority for all police officers and not just for a liaison department; and policemen should be encouraged to live in the community they work in. Ways must be found to reduce the enormous amount of police time still spent in court on traffic cases, so that more men can spend more time on the beat. The national inspectorate and local police committees should concern themselves not just with complaints, but with all aspects of relations between the public and the police, and promote the exchange of good ideas from different neighbourhoods. Atlanta has recently introduced a successful policy of making the officers on the beat responsible for following a case through, instead of turning it over to a detective: local officers have thereby been forced to develop neighbourhood contacts who could supply the required knowledge.

Professor Gutteridge of Aston University recently stated: 'The survival of democratic freedom in Britain will depend more on the quality, quantity and demeanour of the police than on any other single factor.' The crux is to improve the police's and the public's sense of identity with each other. But the gap must be closed from both sides. Policemen have a saying that people 'only remember God and the police when they are in trouble'. The main need is for the public to develop a greater awareness of social responsibility in peace-time. Such efforts should start early in families and schools (at present, inspector Jane Folan of the Metropolitan police believes, a growing number of young children commit offences in full view of a policeman on patrol and tell him, 'You can't touch me, I'm only nine'. Some are taught to shoplift by their Fagin-like parents.) Civic training and first aid should be part of basic education: a more drastic remedy would be for everybody to contribute a compulsory short period in welfare or police work. Young people who spent a few months civic service in being trained and then accompanying policemen on the beat might not be of much practical use, but the police would make some life-long allies, and in turn would lose something of their introverted isolation by learning from a cross-section of society. A conscript police service, despite its problems, would be the most democratic as well as the most cohesive for society.

Full enforcement of our present laws is physically impossible; in Britain, the police already arrest more people annually than there were known crimes in 1950. Even so, in 1977 the number of serious crimes in London increased by a further 12 per cent and, despite 110,000 people being arrested for indictable offences, only 21 per cent of crimes were cleared up. More police making further arrests will lead to even greater burdens upon the courts, where there is already concern at delays. The police's discretion in prosecuting has consequently expanded with the number of offences and quantity of legislation. This discretion forms an area of great power, which has never been properly studied or discussed: the police have appropriated from the courts the judgement of many areas of mitigation. As John Alderson says, 'Too much is expected of our system of criminal justice, which at very best is capable of coping with only some of the worst excesses, though in the main it disposes of only incompetent offenders.' Public opinion about policemen is linked with the public's feeling about the law which the police are required to enforce. Citizens should be more active politically in getting legislation altered, instead of resenting its enforcement by the police. A legal code which was as simple as possible would benefit everybody. If people through their elected representatives radically reformed the law into a comprehensible shape which commanded general agreement and respect, a high conviction rate could then operate as a real deterrent from breaking it.

What, to end where we began, do we want the police for? Only by resolving the conflict in values between liberty and law enforcement can we determine the paradox of the police's position in the future. A police officer occupies a key – if unenviable – position between the *status quo* and its challengers: as the most readily accessible personification of authority, he acts as a lightning-conductor for resentment against many aberrations of society for which he is not responsible. It is time to think clearly and to give our police a role in which we can help and not obstruct them. At present we offer them inadequate training, a virtually impossible task, and minimal support; while requiring them to demonstrate almost para-human skills and wisdom. In one sense, the present freedom of our society is largely due to the haphazard lack of efficiency in our authorities; yet too much amateurishness might cost us that same freedom. On responsive policing depends much of our ability to manage and resolve our social conflicts. It is the state of society rather than the state of the police which crime figures reflect: crime and the failure or otherwise to cope with it are indices less of police shortcomings than of social health or disintegration. A knee-jerk attitude towards the police – either pro- or anti- – may throw light on the personality of an individual, but does not illuminate the task or performance of the police. Blanket stereotyping by the police and the public about each other is no longer enough. Each nation's police force is a mirror of its inhabitants' values. If we today ignore the police and their problems, we cannot complain if we end by getting the police we did not want.

APPENDIX A:

The Judges' Rules

These Rules do not affect the principles

(*a*) That citizens have a duty to help a police officer to discover and apprehend offenders;

(*b*) That police officers, otherwise than by arrest, cannot compel any person against his will to come to or remain in any police station;

(*c*) That every person at any stage of an investigation should be able to communicate and to consult privately with a solicitor. This is so even if he is in custody provided that in such a case no unreasonable delay or hindrance is caused to the processes of investigation or the administration of justice by his doing so;

(*d*) That when a police officer who is making inquiries of any person about an offence has enough evidence to prefer a charge against that person for the offence, he should without delay cause that person to be charged or informed that he may be prosecuted for the offence;

(*e*) That it is a fundamental condition of the admissibility in evidence against any person, equally of any oral answer given by that person to a question put by a police officer and of any statement made by that person, that it shall have been voluntary, in the sense that it has not been obtained from him by fear of prejudice or hope of advantage, exercised or held out by a person in authority, or by oppression.

The principle set out in paragraph (*e*) above is overriding and applicable in all cases. Within that principle the following Rules are put forward as a guide to police officers conducting investigations. Non-conformity with these Rules may render answers and statements liable to be excluded from evidence in subsequent criminal proceedings.

RULES

I. When a police officer is trying to discover whether, or by whom, an offence has been committed he is entitled to question any person, whether suspected or not, from whom he thinks that useful information may be obtained. This is so whether or not the person in question has been taken into custody so long as he has not been charged with the offence or informed that he may be prosecuted for it.

II. As soon as a police officer has evidence which would afford reasonable grounds for suspecting that a person has committed an offence, he shall caution that person or cause him to be cautioned before putting to him any questions, or further questions, relating to that offence.

The caution shall be in the following terms:—

> 'You are not obliged to say anything unless you wish to do so but what you say may be put into writing and given in evidence.'

When after being cautioned a person is being questioned, or elects to make a statement, a record shall be kept of the time and place at which any such questioning or statement began and ended and of the persons present.

III—(*a*) Where a person is charged with or informed that he may be prosecuted for an offence he shall be cautioned in the following terms:—

> 'Do you wish to say anything? You are not obliged to say anything unless you wish to do so but whatever you say will be taken down in writing and may be given in evidence.'

(*b*) It is only in exceptional cases that questions relating to the offence should be put to the accused person after he has been charged or informed that he may be prosecuted. Such questions may be put where they are necessary for the purpose of preventing or minimizing harm or loss to some other person or to the public or for clearing up an ambiguity in a previous answer or statement.

Before any such questions are put the accused should be cautioned in these terms:—

> 'I wish to put some questions to you about the offence with which you have been charged (*or* about the offence for which you may be prosecuted). You are not obliged to answer any of these questions, but if you do the questions and answers will be taken down in writing and may be given in evidence.'

Any questions put and answers given relating to the offence must be contemporaneously recorded in full and the record signed by that person or if he refuses by the interrogating officer.

(*c*) When such a person is being questioned, or elects to make a statement, a record shall be kept of the time and place at which any questioning or statement began and ended and of the persons present.

IV. All written statements made after caution shall be taken in the following manner:

(*a*) If a person says that he wants to make a statement he shall be told that it is intended to make a written record of what he says. He shall always be asked whether he wishes to write down himself what he wants to say; if he says that he cannot write or that he would like someone to write it for him, a police officer may offer to write the statement for him. If he accepts the offer the police officer shall, before starting, ask the person making the statement to sign, or make his mark to, the following:

> 'I, ..., wish to make a statement. I want someone to write down what I say. I have been told that I need not say anything unless I wish to do so and that whatever I say may be given in evidence.'

(*b*) Any person writing his own statement shall be allowed to do so without any prompting as distinct from indicating to him what matters are material.

(*c*) The person making the statement, if he is going to write it himself, shall be asked to write out and sign before writing what he wants to say, the following:

> 'I make this statement of my own free will. I have been told that I need not say anything unless I wish to do so and that whatever I say may be given in evidence.'

(*d*) Whenever a police officer writes the statement, he shall take down the exact words spoken by the person making the statement, without putting any questions other than such as may be needed to make the statement coherent, intelligible and relevant to the material matters: he shall not prompt him.

(*e*) When the writing of a statement by a police officer is finished the person making it shall be asked to read it and to make any corrections, alterations or additions he wishes. When he has finished reading it he shall be asked to write and sign or make his mark on the following Certificate at the end of the statement:

> 'I have read the above statement and I have been told that I can correct, alter or add anything I wish. This statement is true. I have made it of my own free will.'

(*f*) If the person who has made a statement refuses to read it or to write the above mentioned Certificate at the end of it or to sign it, the senior police officer present shall record on the statement itself and in the presence of the person making it, what has happened. If the person making the statement cannot read, or refuses to read it, the officer who has taken it down shall read it over to him and ask him whether he would like to correct, alter or add anything and to put his signature or make his mark at the end. The police officer shall then certify on the statement itself what he has done.

V. If at any time after a person has been charged with, or has been informed that he may be prosecuted for an offence a police officer wishes to bring to the notice of that person any written statement made by another person who in respect of the same offence has also been charged or informed that he may be prosecuted, he shall hand to that person a true copy of such written statement, but nothing shall be said or done to invite any reply or comment. If that person says that he would like to make a statement in reply, or starts to say something, he shall at once be cautioned or further cautioned as prescribed by Rule III(*a*).

VI. Persons other than police officers charged with the duty of investigating offences or charging offenders shall, so far as may be practicable, comply with these Rules.

ADMINISTRATIVE DIRECTIONS ON INTERROGATION AND THE TAKING OF STATEMENTS

1. *Procedure generally*

(*a*) When possible statements of persons under caution should be written on the forms provided for the purpose. Police officers' notebooks should be used for taking statements only when no forms are available.

(*b*) When a person is being questioned or elects to make a statement, a record should be kept of the time or times at which during the questioning or making of a statement there were intervals or refreshment was taken. The nature of the refreshment should be noted. In no circumstances should alcoholic drink be given.

(*c*) In writing down a statement, the words used should not be translated into 'official' vocabulary; this may give a misleading impression of the genuineness of the statement.

(*d*) Care should be taken to avoid any suggestion that the person's answers can only be used in evidence against him, as this may prevent an innocent person making a statement which might help to clear him of the charge.

2. *Record of interrogation*

Rule II and Rule III(*c*) demand that a record should be kept of the following matters:

(*a*) when, after being cautioned in accordance with Rule II, the person is being questioned or elects to make a statement – of the time and place at which any such questioning began and ended and of the persons present:
(*b*) when, after being cautioned in accordance with Rule III(*a*) or (*b*) a person is being questioned or elects to make a statement – of the time and place at which any questioning and statement began and ended and of the persons present.

In addition to the records required by these Rules full records of the following matters should additionally be kept:

(*a*) of the time or times at which cautions were taken, and
(*b*) of the time when a charge was made and/or the person was arrested, and
(*c*) of the matters referred to in paragraph 1(*b*) above.

If two or more police officers are present when the questions are being put or the statement made, the records made should be countersigned by the other officers present.

3. *Comfort and refreshment*

Reasonable arrangements should be made for the comfort and refreshment of persons being questioned. Whenever practicable both the person being questioned or making a statement and the officers asking the questions or taking the statement should be seated.

4. *Interrogation of children and young persons*

As far as practicable children (whether suspected of crime or not) should only be interviewed in the presence of a parent or guardian, or, in their absence, some person who is not a police officer and is of the same sex as the child. A child or young person should not be arrested, nor even interviewed, at school if such action can possibly be avoided. Where it is found essential to conduct the interview at school, this should be done only with the consent, and in the presence, of the head teacher, or his nominee.

5. *Interrogation of foreigners*

In the case of a foreigner making a statement in his native language:

(*a*) The interpreter should take down the statement in the language in which it is made.
(*b*) An official English translation should be made in due course and be proved as an exhibit with the original statement.
(*c*) The foreigner should sign the statement at (*a*).

Apart from the question of apparent unfairness, to obtain the signature of a suspect to an English translation of what he said in a foreign language can have little or no value as evidence if the suspect disputes the accuracy of this record of his statement.

6. *Supply to accused persons of written statement of charges*

(*a*) The following procedure should be adopted whenever a charge is preferred against a person arrested without warrant for any offence:

> As soon as a charge has been accepted by the appropriate police officer the accused person should be given a written notice containing a copy of the entry in the charge sheet or book giving particulars of the offence with which he is charged. So far as possible the particulars of the charge should be stated in simple language so that the accused person may understand it, but they should also show clearly the precise offence in law with which he is charged. Where the offence charged is a statutory one, it should be sufficient for the latter purpose to quote the section of the statute which created the offence.
>
> The written notice should include some statement on the lines of the caution given orally to the accused person in accordance with the Judges' Rules after a charge has been preferred. It is suggested that the form of notice should begin with the following words:

> 'You are charged with the offence(s) shown below. You are not obliged to say anything unless you wish to do so, but whatever you say will be taken down in writing and may be given in evidence.'

(*b*) Once the accused person has appeared before the court it is not necessary to serve him with a written notice of any further charges which may be preferred. If, however, the police decide, before he has appeared before the court, to modify the charge or to prefer further charges, it is desirable that the person concerned should be formally charged with the further offence and given a written copy of the charge as soon as it is possible to do so having regard to the particular circumstances of the case. If the accused person has then been released on bail, it may not always be practicable or reasonable to prefer the new charge at once, and in cases where he is due to surrender to his bail within forty-eight hours or in other cases of difficulty it will be sufficient for him to be formally charged with the further offence and served with a written notice of the charge after he has surrendered to his bail and before he appears before the court.

7. *Facilities for defence*

(*a*) A person in custody should be allowed to speak on the telephone to his solicitor or to his friends provided that no hindrance is reasonably likely to be caused to the processes of investigation, or the administration of justice by his doing so.

He should be supplied on request with writing materials and his letters should be sent by post or otherwise with the least possible delay. Additionally, telegrams should be sent at once, at his own expense.

(*b*) Persons in custody should not only be informed orally of the rights and facilities available to them, but in addition notices describing them should be displayed at convenient and conspicuous places at police stations and the attention of persons in custody should be drawn to these notices.

APPENDIX B:

The New System for Complaints

This is the text of a leaflet issued by the Home Office, which explains the procedure for members of the public who consider they have grounds for complaint against the conduct of a member of a police force in England and Wales. It also explains the way in which complaints are investigated and what action may be taken on them.*

The procedure described in this leaflet applies only to complaints about incidents occurring after 31 May 1977.

The handling of complaints

The law requires the chief officer of each police force to see that complaints against members of his force are promptly recorded, and are investigated. The deputy chief constable of a force outside London, or a senior officer in the Metropolitan or City of London Police, is responsible for considering what action to take as a result of each investigation. There is also an independent element in the procedure. This is provided by the Director of Public Prosecutions where a complaint suggests that a police officer may have broken the criminal law, and by

* *The relevant statutory provisions in England and Wales are sections 49 and 50 of the Police Act 1964, the Police Act 1976, the Police (Discipline) Regulations 1977, the Police (Complaints) (General) Regulations 1977, the Police (Copies of Complaints) Regulations 1977 and the Police (Withdrawn, Anonymous etc. Complaints) Regulations 1977. Under these provisions the chief officer can delegate his responsibilities for investigating and considering a complaint to his deputy or, in the Metropolitan or City of London Police, to another senior officer.*

the Police Complaints Board where there may have been an offence aganst police discipline. The records of complaints are regularly inspected by HM Inspectors of Constabulary and police authorities are required by law to keep themselves informed about the manner in which complaints are dealt with.

Making a complaint

Any complaint about the conduct of a police officer should be made in writing to the chief officer of the police force concerned (who is the Chief Constable of a force outside London and in London the Commissioner of Police of the Metropolis or of the City of London Police), or by calling at any police station. Only the police have the authority to investigate complaints against police officers. If a complainant writes to the Police Complaints Board, or to anyone other than the appropriate chief officer, his complaint has to be sent on to that chief officer; otherwise it cannot be investigated.

The investigation of a complaint

The investigation of a complaint against a police officer is carried out by a senior officer who may come from a different police force. It will normally start at once. If, however, the complaint is closely associated with criminal proceedings against the complainant or someone else and those charges are to be heard in court, the investigation will not as a rule begin until after the court proceedings are completed. The complainant will be asked to make a full statement, and the police will also seek information from anyone else who can help to establish the facts. The police officer who is complained about will also have an opportunity to make a statement. At the end of the investigation, a report will be sent to the deputy chief constable.

Criminal proceedings

Police officers, like everyone else, are subject to the law of the land. When a deputy chief constable receives the report of an investigation into a complaint he must first send it to the Director of Public Prosecutions unless he is satisfied that no criminal offence has been committed. The Director will consider whether or not criminal proceedings should be brought and he will inform both the deputy chief constable and the complainant whether or not he proposed to prosecute. If there is a prosecution, the complainant can be called upon to give evidence before the court.

Disciplinary proceedings

Police officers are also subject to a strict discipline code. The deputy chief constable will therefore consider (after any reference has been made to the Director of Public Prosecutions) whether as a result of the investigation of a complaint the evidence is such as to justify bringing a disciplinary charge. If the deputy chief constable decides that a disciplinary charge would not be justified he must send a report to the Police Complaints Board. If the Board accept that no disciplinary charges should be brought, they will inform the deputy chief constable and the complainant. If, however, the Board disagree with the deputy chief constable, they may recommend, and in the absence of agreement direct, that disciplinary charges should be brought. Where charges are to be brought the police will inform the complainant. (Even if a complaint proves to have some substance, it may not be necessary to deal with it by formal disciplinary charges; for example, advice to the officer concerned may be more appropriate.)

Hearing of disciplinary charges

Where disciplinary charges are brought against a police officer, there is a formal hearing. This will normally be before the chief officer alone but, in exceptional circumstances, the Police Complaints Board may direct that the charges should be heard by a tribunal consisting of the chief officer and two members of the Board. The hearing is in private, but, unless the accused officer has admitted the charges, the complainant has a right to attend and will normally be expected to give evidence.

Civil proceedings

A complainant may have a remedy at civil law. The police cannot give advice as to whether there is cause for a civil action: this is a matter for a solicitor. A Citizens Advice Bureau will be able to provide a list of solicitors practising in the area who can advise on this matter and give information about legal aid and advice schemes. If a complainant wishes to bring a civil action, the investigation of the complaint may sometimes be deferred until the civil action has been completed.

The rights of the officer

A police officer against whom a complaint has been made will normally receive a copy of the original complaint or of an account of it if the complaint was not made in writing. He is given a copy automatically if he is charged with any disciplinary offence as a result of the complaint; if he is not charged he can ask for a copy when the case is closed. A false and malicious complaint against a police officer may lead to his bringing legal proceedings for defamation.

Reminder

This leaflet explains what happens if you make a complaint about the conduct of a police officer. Inquiries into complaints are thorough and take a lot of police time. Before you complain please think carefully whether your complaint is against the police; it might, for example, be against some part of the law that the police have to enforce.

Remember that the police do a difficult and dangerous job on behalf of us all.

TERMS OF THE TRADE:

some police and criminal slang

accomplice = stickman
arrest = collar, feel the collar of, nick, bust, knock off, nib, finger, pinch, tickle, pull
bad cheque = kite
beat or area = patch, manor
bed = knife
bribe = dropsy, bung, sweetener, drink, slush, straightener
to bribe = put in the bung, give a drink to
to take a bribe = to cop a drop
cell = flowery, bin, peter
to charge = put on the sheet, do
on a charge = on a fizzer, on the fizz
confess = cough
to convict = put away
courage = bottle
crime = trick, tickle
a criminal = villain, chummy
criminal record = form
detective = busy, jack, nose, odd, split, dick, bogie, the filth
dishonest = bent
drug addict = arctic explorer
drug dealer = candyman
frame = fit up, stitch up
free meal for a policeman = mumping, mooching, on the arm (US)
fingerprints = dabs
flying squad = sweeney

gang = firm
girlfriend = mystery, fluff, talent
gloves = turtles
gun = shooter, rod, barker, piece, tool
handcuffs = nippers
heroin = smack, horse
house or flat = drum
housebreaker = screwsman
inform on = finger, grass, nark, nose, scream, shop, snide, come copper, snitch, snout, squeak, bubble, fink
investigate = snout around
jewelry = tomfoolery, tom
keys = twirls
lamp or torch = glim
a lawyer = a brief
lining up a victim = banged up
long sentence = a lagging
a month = a moon
murder = snuff, ice (US)
pickpocket = dip, whiz, dropstick, sticksing, reef
pickpocket team = cannon mob
planting of drugs on suspects = agriculture
the police = Bill or old Bill, blue, plume, Toby, bull, coppers, cops, fuzz, flatties or flatfoot, rozzers, bogies, jacks, bobbies, bluebottles, kipper-feet, filth, woollies, wooden-tops, Babylon (to blacks), swedes (city policemen's name for country officers), crushers, Esclop, Miltonians (nineteenth-century), John Laws, Charlies, peelers
police car = danny
police internal investigators = rubber heels
police station = booby-hatch, hutch, factory, nick, bill-shop, cop-shop
prison = slammer, stir, lumber, jug, nick
prison sentence = rap, porridge, bird, dose
three months prison = carpet
twenty-one months prison = a pontoon
ten years prison = cock and hen
prostitute = judy, lush, nancy, tail, broad, brass, lag, tom
protection money = the pad (US)
a punch = a bunch of fives

put on trial = sent up the steps
putting damaging words into defendant's mouth = verballing
reconnoitre = case
remand in custody = laydown
rob = clip, rip
safe = peter
search = toss, turn over, spin, shake down
sentence = weigh off
sex while on duty = cooping (US)
shoplifting = boosting, dragging, hoisting, hooking, palming
signature = monicker
sleeping with = going case
snatch = blag
Special Constables = hobby-bobbies
spouse = china
steal = vamp, rip off, reef
stolen property = poke
a summons = a blister
suspected person = suss, chummy
thief = gun, hook, tea-leaf, wire
wallet = wad, a leather
a watch = a kettle

Select Bibliography and Suggestions for Further Reading

ACKROYD, C. et al, *The Technology of Political Control* (Penguin, 1977).

ADAMS, T. F., *Law Enforcement* (Prentice-Hall, 1968).

ADORNO, T. W. et al, *The Authoritarian Personality* (Harper and Bros, 1950).

ADVISORY COMMITTEE ON POLICE IN NORTHERN IRELAND (Hunt Committee), *Report* (Cmnd. 535) (HMSO Belfast, 1969).

ALDERSON, J. C. and STEAD, P. J., *The Police We Deserve* (Wolfe, 1973).

ALLEN, SIR C. K., *The Queen's Peace* (Stevens, 1953).

AMERICAN CIVIL LIBERTIES UNION, *Secret Detention by the Chicago Police* (Free Press, 1950).

ANCEL, M., *Social Defence* (Routledge, 1965).

BANTON, M., *Police-Community Relations* (Collins, 1973).

BANTON, M. 'Policing a Divided Society', *Police Journal*, October 1974.

BANTON, M., *The Policeman in the Community* (Tavistock, 1964).

BARKER, T. and ROEBUCK, J., *An Empirical Typology of Police Corruption* (Charles C. Thomas, 1973).

BAYLEY, D. and MENDELSOHN, H., *Minorities and the Police* (Free Press, New York, 1969).

BAYLEY, D. H., *Forces of Order* (University of California, 1977).

BELSON, W. A., *The Public and the Police* (Harper and Row, 1975).

BENEWICK, R. and SMITH, T., eds, *Direct Action and Democratic Politics* (Allen and Unwin, 1973).

BENTHAM, J., *An Introduction to the Principles of Morals and*

Legislation (Blackwell, 1948).

BERKELEY, G., *The Democratic Policeman* (Beacon Press, 1969).

BLACK, A. D., *The People and the Police* (McGraw-Hill, 1969).

BOPP, W. J., *The Police Rebellion* (C. C. Thomas, 1971).

BORDUA, D. J. ed., *The Police: Six Sociological Essays* (Wiley, 1967).

BOTTOMLEY, A. K., *Decisions in the Penal Process* (Martin Robertson, 1973).

BOWDEN, T., *Beyond the Limits of the Law* (Penguin, 1978).

BOWES, S., *The Police and Civil Liberties* (Lawrence and Wishart, 1966).

BOX, S., *Deviance, Reality and Society* (Holt, Rinehart and Winston, 1971).

BRANDON, R. and DAVIES, C., *Wrongful Imprisonment* (Allen and Unwin, 1973).

BROWN, J., *A Theory of Police–Immigrant relations* (Cranfield Institute of Technology, 1974).

BROWN, J., and HOWES, G., *The Police and the Community* (Saxon House, 1975).

BROWNLIE, I., *The Law Relating to Public Order* (Butterworth, 1968).

BUNYAN, T., *The Political Police in Britain* (Julian Friedmann, 1976).

BURROWS, W., *Vigilante* (Harcourt, Brace, 1976).

CAIN, M., *Society and the Policeman's Role* (Routledge and Kegan Paul, 1973).

CASAMAYOR, *La Police* (Gallimard, 1974).

CHAPMAN, B., *Police State* (Pall Mall, 1970).

CHATTERTON, M. R., 'The Social Contexts of Violence' in *Violence in the Family*, ed. M. Borland (Manchester University Press, 1976).

CHEVIGNY, P., *Police Power* (Pantheon, 1968).

CHIBNALL, S., *Law and Order News* (Tavistock, 1977).

CHURCHES' BOARD FOR SOCIAL RESPONSIBILITY, *Police: a social study* (Church Information Office (London), 1967).

CLARK, R., *Crime in America* (Simon and Schuster, 1970).

CLARK, S. C., COOK, F. G., ROBERTS, K. and SEMEONOFF, E., *Crime and the Public: Criminal Victimization and Societal Reactions* (Dept. of Sociology, Liverpool University, 1975 (unpublished)).

CLIFFORD, B., 'Police as eyewitnesses', *New Society*, 22nd April 1976.

COATMAN, J., *Police* (Oxford University Press, 1958).

COHEN, S. ed., *Images of Deviance* (Penguin, 1973).

COLE, P. and PRINGLE, P., *Can You Positively Identify This Man?* (Andre Deutsch, 1974).

COLQUHOUN, P., *A Treatise on the Police of the Metropolis* (London, 1797).

COLQUHOUN, P., *A Treatise on the Commerce and Police of the River Thames* (London, 1800).

COMMITTEE OF INQUIRY (Edmund Davies), *Report* (Cmnd. 7283) (HMSO, 1978).

COOTE, A. and GRANT, L., *Civil Liberty: the NCCL Guide* (Penguin, 1973).

COX, B., *Civil Liberties in Britain* (Penguin, 1975).

COX, B., SHIRLEY, J. and SHORT, M., *The Fall of Scotland Yard* (Penguin, 1977).

CRAMER, J., *The World's Police* (Cassell, 1975).

CRIMINAL LAW REVISION COMMITTEE, *11th Report: Evidence* (Cmnd. 4991) (HMSO, 1972).

CRITCHLEY, T. A., *A History of Police in England and Wales 900–1966* (Constable, 1967).

CRITCHLEY, T. A., *The Conquest of Violence* (Constable, 1970).

CUMMINGS, E. et al, 'Policemen as Philosopher, Guide and Friend', *Social Problems*, Volume 12, 1964.

DAVIES, C., *The West Side, Shipton: Crime and Vandalism in a Problem Area* (Ch. 7., The Police and the Courts), (Dept. of Sociology, Liverpool University, 1975 (unpublished)).

DAVIES, C., 'Crime, Police and Courts', *New Society*, 23 February 1978.

DESBOROUGH COMMITTEE, *Reports* (HMSO, 1920).

DEVLIN, LORD, *The Criminal Prosecution in England* (Oxford University Press, 1960).

DICEY, A. V., *Lectures on the Relation between Law and Opinion in England during the nineteenth century* (1905).

DITCHFIELD, J. A., *Police Cautioning in England and Wales* (UK Home Office Research Study, 1975).

DITTON, J., *Part-Time Crime* (Macmillan 1977).

DRAPER, H., *Private Police* (Penguin, 1978).

DWORKIN, R., *Taking Rights Seriously* (Duckworth, 1977).

ENDELMAN, S. ed., *Violence in the Streets* (Duckworth, 1969).
EVANS, P., *The Police Revolution* (Allen and Unwin, 1974).
FISHER, SIR H., *Report of Inquiry into Confait Case* (HMSO, 1977).
FOSDICK, R., *American Police Systems* (Century, New York, 1920).
FOSDICK, R., *European Police Systems* (Century, New York, 1922).
FRIEDLANDER, C. and MITCHELL, E., *The Police: Servants or Masters* (Hart-Davis, 1974).
FRIEDMANN, W., *Law in a Changing Society* (Penguin, 1964).
GAMMAGE, A. Z. and SACHS, S. L., *Police Unions* (Charles C. Thomas, 1973).
GODWIN, W., *Enquiry Concerning Political Justice* (First Published 1798, Penguin, 1976).
GOLDSTEIN, H., *Police Corruption* (Police Foundation (Washington DC), 1975).
GORER, G., *Exploring English Character* (Cresset Press, 1955).
GREENWOOD, C., *Firearms Control* (Routledge and Kegan Paul, 1972).
GRIGG, M., *The Challenor Case* (Penguin, 1965).
GROSS, H., *Criminal Investigation* (Sweet and Maxwell, 1962).
HAHN, H., *Police in Urban Society* (Sage, 1971).
HART, H. L. A., *The Concept of Law* (Oxford University Press, 1961).
HART, H. L. A., *Law, Liberty and Morality* (Oxford University Press, 1963).
HART, J., *The British Police* (Allen and Unwin, 1951).
HEARN, C. V., *A Duty to the Public* (Muller, 1965).
HEWITT, P., *Privacy: The Information Gatherers* (NCCL, 1977).
HEWITT, W. H., *British Police Administration* (Charles Thomas (Springfield, USA), 1965).
HOLDAWAY, S., 'Changes in Urban Policing', *British Journal of Sociology*, June 1977.
HOME OFFICE, *Consolidated Circular to the Police on Crime and Kindred Matters* (HMSO, 1969 etc.).
HOME OFFICE, *Feasibility of an Experiment in Tape-recording of Police Interrogations* (Cmnd. 6630) (HMSO, 1976).
HOME OFFICE, *Police Manpower, Equipment and Efficiency*

(HMSO, 1967).

HOME OFFICE, *Police Recruitment and Wastage* (Cmnd. 6061) (HMSO, 1975).

HOME OFFICE ADVISORY COMMITTEE ON DRUG DEPENDENCE, *Powers of Arrest and Search in Relation to Drugs Offences* (HMSO, 1970).

HONEYCOMBE, G., *Adam's Tale* (Hutchinson, 1974).

HOOD, R. ed., *Crime, Criminology and Public Policy* (Heinemann, 1974).

HOPKINS, E. J., *Our Lawless Police* (Viking, 1931).

HORAN, J. D., *The Pinkertons* (Robert Hale, 1970).

HORNE, P., *Women in Law Enforcement* (Charles Thomas, 1975).

HOUSE OF COMMONS ESTIMATES COMMITTEE, *Police* (HMSO, 1966).

HOUSE OF COMMONS SELECT COMMITTEE ON RACE RELATIONS, *Report on Police–Immigrant Relations* (HMSO, 1972).

HUMPHRY, D., *Police Power and Black People* (Panther, 1974).

HUMPHRY, D., *The Cricket Conspiracy* (NCCL, 1975).

JACK, J., *Lady Policeman* (Michael Joseph, 1967).

JACKSON, R. M., *Enforcing the Law* (Penguin, 1972).

JAMES, A. E., *Report of Inquiry into Sgt. Challenor's case* (Cmnd. 2735) (HMSO, 1965).

JENKINS, RAY, *The Lawbreakers* (Penguin, 1969).

JONES, H., *Crime and the Penal System* (University Tutorial Press, 1965).

JONES, H., *Crime in a Changing Society* (Penguin, 1965).

JONES, H., 'Policemen as Social Workers', *New Society*, 14 November 1963.

JONES, M., *The Police and Citizen* (NCCL, 1969).

JONES, M., *Privacy* (David and Charles, 1974).

JUDGE, A., *A Man Apart* (Arthur Barker, 1972).

JUDGE, A., *The First Fifty Years* (UK Police Federation, 1968).

'JUSTICE', *The Prosecution Process in England and Wales* (Justice Trust (London), 1970).

KENNEDY, D. and B., *Applied Sociology for the Police* (C. C. Thomas, 1973).

KING, J., *Control Without Custody* (Cambridge Inst. of Criminology, 1976).

KING, M. ed., *Guilty Until Proved Innocent* (Release, 1973).

KNAPP COMMISSION, *Report on Allegations of Police Corruption* (New York City, 1972).

KROES, W. H., *Society's Victim – the Policeman* (Charles C. Thomas, 1976).

KROES, W. H. ed., *Job Stress and the Police Officer* (US Department of H.E.W., 1975).

LAFAVE, W., *Arrest: the Decision to Take a Suspect into Custody* (Little Brown, 1965).

LAMBERT, J. R., *Crime, Police and Race Relations* (Oxford University Press, 1970).

LANGLOIS, D., *Les Dossiers Noirs de la Police Francaise* (Editions du Seuil, 1971).

LAURIE, P., *Scotland Yard* (Bodley Head, 1970).

LEE, C. D., *The Instrumental Detection of Deception* (Charles Thomas, 1953).

LEE, W. M., *A History of Police in England* (Methuen, 1901).

LEIGH, L. H., *Police Powers in England and Wales* (Butterworth, 1975).

LEWIS, D. and HUGHMAN, P., *Just How Just?* (Secker and Warburg, 1975).

LEWIS, R., *A Force for the Future* (Temple Smith, 1976).

LIANG, H., *The Berlin Police Force in the Weimar Republic* (University of California Press, 1970).

LIPSET, S. M., 'The Politics of the Police', *New Society*, 6 March 1969.

LLOYD, D., *The Idea of Law* (Penguin, 1964).

MAAS, P., *Serpico* (Collins, 1973).

MACDONALD, I., 'The Creation of the British Police', *Race Today* (5), 1973.

MACK, J. A., *The Crime Industry* (Saxon House, 1975).

MAITLAND, F. W., *Justice and Police* (Macmillan, 1885).

MANNING, P. K., *Police Work* (MIT Press, 1977).

MARK, SIR, R., *Policing a Perplexed Society* (Allen and Unwin, 1977).

MARSDEN, G., 'What About the Workers?', *Police*, January 1976

MARSHALL, G., *Police and Government* (Methuen, 1965).

MARTIN, J. P. and WILSON, G., *The Police: a Study in Manpower* (Cambridge Institute of Criminology, 1969).

MCCABE, S. and PURVES, R., *The Jury at Work* (Blackwell, 1972).

MEEK, V., *Private Enquiries* (Duckworth, 1967).

MILL, J. S., *On Liberty* (first published, 1859, Penguin, 1974).

MILLEN, E., *Specialist in Crime* (Harrap, 1972).

MILLER, W. R., *Cops and Bobbies* (University of Chicago, 1977).

MILLER, W. R., *Cops and Bobbies* (University of Chicago, 1977).

MORRIS, N. and HAWKINS, G., *The Honest Politician's Guide to Crime Control* (University of Chicago Press, 1970).

MORRIS, T., *Deviance and Control* (Hutchinson, 1976).

MOSSE, G. L. ed., *Police Forces in History* (Sage, 1975).

MURPHY, P. V., *Commissioner* (Simon & Schuster, 1978).

NEW COMMUNITY, Volume III, Number 3, *Community Relations Commission* (London, 1974).

NIEDERHOFFER, H., *Behind the Shield* (Doubleday, 1976).

NORRIS, D. F., *Police-Community Relations* (Lexington, 1973).

OLIVER, Ch. Insp. I. T., 'The Metropolitan Police Juvenile Bureau Scheme', *Criminal Law Review*, p. 499, 1973.

PACKER, H. L., 'The Courts, the Police and the Rest of Us', *Journal of Criminal Law, Criminology and Police Science*, Vol. 57 No. 3, September 1966.

PACKER, H. L., *The Limits of Criminal Sanction* (Stanford University Press, 1968).

POLICE COUNCIL FOR UK, *Report of Working Party on Police Pay* (1975).

Police Manpower, Equipment and Efficiency, Report of 3 Working-parties (HMSO, 1967).

POPE, C., *Community Relations – The Police Response* (Runnymede Trust, 1976).

POWIS, D., *The Signs of Crime* (McGraw-Hill, 1977).

PRESIDENT'S COMMISSION ON LAW ENFORCEMENT, *The Challenge of Crime in a Free Society* (US G.P.O., 1967).

PRICE, C. and CAPLAN, K., *The Confait Confessions* (Boyars, 1977).

PUNCH, M. and NAYLOR, T., 'The Police: a Social Service', *New Society*, 17 May 1973.

PURCELL, W., *British Police in a Changing Society* (Mowbrays, 1974).

RADZINOWICZ, L. and KING, J., *The Growth of Crime* (Hamish Hamilton, 1977).

REINER, R., 'Reds in Blue?', *New Society*, 7 October 1976.

REISS, A., *The Police and the Public* (Yale University Press, 1971).

REITH, C., *A Short History of the British Police* (Oxford University Press, 1948).

REITH, C., *British Police and the Democratic Ideal* (Oxford University Press, 1943).

REITH, C., *Police Principles and the Problem of War* (Oxford University Press, 1940).

REYNOLDS, G. W. and JUDGE, A., *The Night the Police Went on Strike* (Weidenfeld, 1968).

RITCHIE, M. and MACK, J. A., *Police Warnings* (Glasgow University Bookshop, 1974).

ROBERTSON, G., *Reluctant Judas* (Temple Smith, 1976).

ROCK, P., *Deviant Behaviour* (Hutchinson, 1973).

ROLPH, C. H., *Living Twice* (Gollancz, 1974).

ROLPH, C. H. ed., *The Police and the Public* (Heinemann, 1962).

ROSENTHAL, A. M., *Thirty-Eight Witnesses* (McGraw-Hill, 1964).

ROYAL COMMISSION ON POLICE POWERS AND PROCEDURE, *Report* (HMSO, 1929).

ROYAL COMMISSION ON THE POLICE, *Report*, (Cmnd. 1728) (HMSO, 1960 and 1962).

RUBENSTEIN, J., *City Police* (Ballantine, 1973).

RUCHELMAN, L., *Police Politics* (John Wiley, 1974).

RULE, J. B., *Private Lives and Public Surveiliance* (Allen and Unwin, 1949).

RUSSELL, B., *Authority and the Individual* (Allen and Unwin, 1949.

SANDFORD, J., *Smiling David* (Calder & Boyars, 1974).

SARGANT, W., *Battle for the Mind* (Heinemann, 1957).

SCHUR, E., *Crime Without Victims* (Prentice-Hall, 1965).

SCHUR, E., *Radical Non-Intervention* (Prentice-Hall, 1973).

SELLIN, T. and WOLFGANG, M. E., *The Measurement of Delinquency* (Wiley, 1964).

SETH, R., *The Specials* (Gollancz, 1961).

Sheffield Police Appeal Inquiry (Cmnd. 2176) (HMSO, 1963).

SKOLNICK, J. H., *Justice Without Trial* (John Wiley, 1967).

SMITH, B., *Police Systems in the United States* (Harper and Bros., 1960).

SMYTHE, T. ed., *Civil Liberties and the Judges' Rules* (National

Council for Civil Liberties, 1972).

SPARKS, R. F., GENN, H. R. and DODD, D. J., *Surveying Victims* (John Wiley, 1978).

STEER, D. *Police Cautions* (Blackwell, 1970).

STREET, H., *Freedom, the Individual and the Law* (Penguin, 1963).

SUTHERLAND, E. H., *White Collar Crime* (Holt, Rinehart, 1949).

SUTHERLAND, E. H. and CRESSEY, D., *Principles of Criminology* (Lippincott, 1966).

TAYLOR, L., *Deviance and Society* (Michael Joseph, 1971).

TAYLOR, M., *Study of Juvenile Liaison Scheme in West Ham 1961–65* (HMSO, 1971).

THOMPSON, E. P., *The Making of the English Working Classes* (Penguin, 1968).

THOMSON COMMITTEE, *Criminal Procedure in Scotland* (Cmnd. 6218) (HMSO, 1975).

TOBIAS, J. J., 'The Future Challenge of Police Manpower', *Police Journal,* July 1971.

TREGER, H., *The Police–Social Work Team* (Charles Thomas, 1975).

TURNER, W., *The Police Establishment* (Putnam, 1968).

TYLER, L. G., *Police and Community* (Church Information Office, 1969).

UNION INTERNATIONALE DES SYNDICATS DE POLICE, *Panorama* (Druckerei (Koblenz), 1970).

U.S. PRESIDENT'S COMMISSION ON LAW ENFORCEMENT, *Task Force Report* (U.S. Government Printing Office, 1967).

VOLLMER, A., *The Police and Modern Society* (University of California Press, 1936).

WALKER, D., *Rights in Conflict* (Dutton, 1968).

WALKER, N., *Crime and Punishment in Britain* (Edinburgh University Press, 1965).

WALKER, N., *Crimes, Courts and Figures* (Penguin, 1971).

WALLS, H. J., *Forensic Science* (Sweet and Maxwell, 1976).

WARNER, M. and STONE, M., *The Data Bank Society* (Allen and Unwin, 1970).

WEGG-PROSSER, C., *The Police and the Law* (Oyez, 1973).

WESTLEY, W. A., 'Secrecy and the Police', *Social Forces,* Volume 34, 1956.

WESTLEY, W. A., *Violence and the Police* (MIT Press, 1970).

WHITAKER, B., *Crime and Society* (Blond Educational, 1967).
WHYTE, W., *Street Corner Society* (University of Chicago Press, 1943).
WILCOX, A. F., *The Decision to Prosecute* (Butterworth, 1972).
WILLETT, T. C., *Criminal on the Road* (Tavistock, 1974).
WILLIAMS, D., *Keeping the Peace* (Hutchinson, 1967).
WILLIAMS, G., *The Proof of Guilt* (Stevens, 1963).
WILLIAMS, W. J. ed., *Moriarty's Police Law* (Butterworth, 1974).
WILSON, J. Q., 'The Police and their Problems: a Theory', *Public Policy*, Volume XII, 1963.
WILSON, J. Q., *Thinking About Crime* (Basic Books, 1975).
WILSON, J. Q., *Varieties of Police Behaviour* (Harvard University Press, 1968).
WILSON, O., *Police Administration* (McGraw-Hill, 1963).
WISE, D., *The American Police State* (Random House, 1976).
WOLFLE, J. and HEAPHY, J. eds., *Readings on Productivity in Policing* (Police Foundation (Washington DC), 1975).
WOOTTON, B., *Crime and the Criminal Law* (Stevens, 1963).
WRIGHT, S. F., *Police and Public* (Fowler Wright, 1929).
ZANDER, M., 'The Criminal Process – a Subject ripe for a Major Inquiry', *Criminal Law Review*, 1977.

INDEX